Texts in developmental psychology

Series Editor:

Peter Smith
Goldsmiths College, University of London

ALSO IN THE *TEXTS IN DEVELOPMENTAL PSYCHOLOGY* SERIES:

FRIENDS AND ENEMIES
Barry H Schneider

ATTACHMENT AND DEVELOPMENT
Susan Goldberg

Forthcoming:

AGEING AND DEVELOPMENT
Peter Coleman

The Child at School

Interactions with Peers and Teachers

Anthony D Pellegrini
Professor of Educational Psychology,
University of Minnesota, USA

Peter Blatchford
Professor of Psychology and Education, Institute of Education,
University of London

A member of the Hodder Headline Group
LONDON
Co-published in the United States of America by
Oxford University Press Inc., New York

First published in Great Britain in 2000 by
Arnold, a member of the Hodder Headline Group,
338 Euston Road, London NW1 3BH

http://www.arnoldpublishers.com

Co-published in the United States of America by
Oxford University Press Inc.,
198 Madison Avenue, New York, NY10016

British Library Cataloguing in Publication Data
A catalogue record for this book is available from the British Library

Library of Congress Cataloging-in-Publication Data
A catalog record for this book is available from the Library of Congress

ISBN 0 340 73181 8 (hb)
ISBN 0 340 73182 6 (pb)

1 2 3 4 5 6 7 8 9 10

Production Editor: Anke Ueberberg
Production Controller: Fiona Byrne
Cover Design: Terry Griffiths

Typeset in 10pt Plantin by J&L Composition Ltd, Filey, North Yorkshire
Printed and bound in Great Britain by MPG Books Ltd, Bodmin, Cornwall

What do you think about this book? Or any other Arnold title?
Please send your comments to feedback.arnold@hodder.co.uk

For Antonio, with kindest memories
(A.P.)

To the memory of Harry McGurk
(P.B.)

Contents

1 An introduction to *The Child at School*

A personal introduction

The idea for this book began almost 10 years ago when one of us (AP) was spending the year at Sheffield University conducting research on children's behaviour on the school playground. Each of us had been invited to participate in a symposium on bullying and aggression on the playground. After that day, and the subsequent evening in the pub, we each recognized the fact that children's social lives in schools were both very important and very understudied.

Since that time we have collaborated on a number of projects. Most centrally, our work has been concerned with that place in the school day where much of children's social interaction takes place: the playground at breaktime. Over the past number of years we have participated in a number of symposia on both sides of the Atlantic addressing the role of breaktime in the lives of children at school. In the course of this interaction, our focus has broadened to include social interactions among peers and teachers in the classroom. This book is a result of those efforts.

Our orientation

Our orientation to the study of children in schools is psychological, drawing extensively from the sub-fields of developmental, social and educational psychology. It seems to us that research in these different traditions has tended to be conducted separately, and not always with knowledge of research in other areas. One of our aims in this book is to seek a more unified approach.

We stress a developmental perspective on children in schools because children are qualitatively different from adults and developmental psychology captures this distinction most directly. Below, we make a number of points about the way the term 'development' is understood and used, and what we believe are still some widely held misconceptions. First though, we identify some other main themes in the book.

As the subtitle of the book states, another important theme of the book is a focus on interactions. We feel that interactions in school have tended to be considered by researchers in a fragmented way; for example, interactions between teachers and pupils have tended to be considered quite separately from research on relations between children. Often the two types of interaction have been studied from very different theoretical perspectives, and even disciplines. While peer interactions have been studied extensively by developmental psychologists, this is not true of teacher–pupil interactions. It is our aim in this book to offer a unifying perspective on interactions that draws on developmental, but also educational and social psychology, in order to inform both types of interaction. Although we take a developmental perspective, in this book we do not seek to cover areas such as cognitive and emotional development and learning – rather the focus is on the interactive and social nature of school life, involving peers and adults. The book also differs from others which have focused on interactions in school contexts, because our approach is concerned with the psychological dimensions of these interactions (in contrast, for example, with Delamont, 1983, which is informed more by sociology and ethnography).

In our view, children's interactions with peers and adults are complementary, and of equal importance. It seems to us that peer interactions in schools have tended to be underestimated by educationalists, and one aim of this book is to give equal weight to peer and teacher–child interactions. In this book we seek to point out ways in which these two types of relationship affect children in different ways. So, for example, adults may be effective at helping a child plan the shopping trip, but peers are much better at affording opportunities for children to use diverse functions of language. So, for example, when pre-schoolers are playing, they use a variety of functions. By contrast, when children are interacting with the teacher over lessons, they typically are in the role of responder and reciter.

As part of this discussion of interaction, we also explore in great detail those venues or contexts within school where children interact with peers and teachers. School environments are often considered purely in terms of settings for academic development. Of course, the classroom is a prime place for interaction, at least between children and teachers, and these interactions have a specific role in children's academic development. As we show in Chapter 7, interactions between teachers and pupils have been considered in much research as if existing in a vacuum; in contrast we consider some of the particular ways in which the classroom context can affect the nature of interactions between teachers and children. But we also believe that other contexts in schools are important. In particular we have both spent much time researching children's behaviour on school playgrounds, and consider this a neglected but important area. Indeed, we consider the school playground, and school breaktime, as one of the best places to study children's social behaviour. Additionally, we also show how breaktime, and social behaviour on the playground, can be important to children's academic and social skills. Children can also be seen to interact with 'context' as well as with people. In this book we discuss ways in which contexts affect children; for example, when children are given doctor props with which to play, they typically engage in play which has a medical theme.

On a more global level, children are embedded in classrooms and schools which have different levels of structure. In less structured, 'open field' situations, children may be free to choose their activities and partners. In this sort of context, children are likely to choose a friend with whom to interact and their interaction is likely to be cooperative, rather than disruptive. Additionally, interactions with friends, compared to other classmates, around academic tasks are likely to be sophisticated and result in high performance. In more structured, 'closed field' situations, children do not have such a choice, and their interactions are less cooperative and in many cases less productive (Hartup, 1996).

We also recognize that children affect contexts. By this we mean that children choose contexts which are consistent with their personality; for example, aggressive children choose other aggressive youngsters to play with, while shy children choose other shy children. As children continue to interact with each other they tend to re-enforce this similarity.

As well as developments with age in interactions, and a concern with contextual factors, in this book we will be interested in the effects of, or consequences of, interactions in schools, for example in terms of the consequences of having/not having friends in school, of being rejected by their peers, of receiving different kinds and quantities of interactions from their teachers, and of teachers having low expectations of children in their class. These effects can be seen in the short term and the long term; for example, difficulties in interactions with peers can be considered in terms of immediate effects, but can also be considered in relation to long term effects on personal adjustment (e.g., Parker and Asher, 1987).

This attention to the effects of interactions is consistent with our developmental approach, and is also connected to a concern with the role or function of interactions in different school contexts, e.g., friends in school, interactions on playgrounds, interactive teaching in classrooms, different interactions of boys and girls in classroom and playground. A broad approach to effects is useful because the value of interactions in some school contexts can be overlooked and underestimated, with sometimes unfortunate consequences. To take an example: many schools in the US and the UK are limiting or eliminating breaktime, because there is a belief that it can interfere with achievement in school subjects (Blatchford, 1998). In fact, breaks during the school day may have an important social function (Blatchford, 1998), and may improve achievement (Pellegrini and Smith, 1998). Further, the social cognitive skills used in the playground have important implications for achievement.

We also stress the fact that different opportunities for interactions have different consequences. As noted above, when children interact with friends rather than acquaintances, their interactions result in higher levels of achievement. Relatedly, when children make the transition from pre-school to primary school with a friend in their classroom, they adjust to school more successfully than children without friends. These sorts of comparisons between different types of peers are particularly important because they are often the opposite of what gets done in schools; for example, teachers often separate friends because they think it will interfere with achievement.

Another theme of this book is a concern with differences between children. This will be evident in two main ways. In the first place we are interested in individual differences, for example, differences between children in their social relations in terms of rejected v. popular, key v. rejected players, friendless v. befriended, high v. low expectation etc. In the second place we will be interested throughout in group differences, mainly male v. female, and differences between ethnic groups. As we shall see in several chapters, it can also be important to examine interactions between gender and ethnicity.

It is our opinion that school policy and practice should be informed by current research findings. But it is important that these findings are firmly grounded, reliable and valid, and to that end it is important to examine in a critical way different research methods for studying children in schools. Most specifically, we concentrate on the use of direct observational methods for studying children in different school settings such as the playground or the classroom. Observational methods are important because they enable us to describe in a systematic and rich way the everyday interactions children have with their social and physical environments.

We also situate ourselves in the current debates, or 'wars', between different educational research traditions. The us v. them approach of the so-called paradigm wars is, we believe, both unproductive and artificial. For example, in our discussion of observation methods, we, like some ethnographers, stress the importance of inductive categories. Similarly, like some branches of ethnography, we talk about the transaction between children and their contexts. Yet we also, in contrast to many working from a qualitative or ethnographic framework, see value in quantifying our observations, when this is appropriate as a way of addressing research questions. In the tradition of ethological studies of children's development and children in school (McGrew, 1972a and b; Smith and Connolly, 1980), we too agree that children should be studied in their natural habitats to maximize our understanding. This is one reason why we were drawn to the school playground as a research site.

We also recognize the value of using experimental analogues of naturalistic settings. The field experiments of Smith and Connolly (1980) and Pellegrini and Huberty (1993) are examples of the ways in which experiments can be conducted in schools to understand more closely the nature of things. After all, teachers often 'experiment' with different techniques of teaching – this is no different.

But we also comment critically on the use of experimental methods, for example, as used to study teacher expectations and class size differences. Experimental methods are usually seen as the 'gold standard' for addressing causality, and we discuss studies that have used such designs. But there are also alternatives which may, for some purposes, be more valid, and we discuss these as well; for example, the use of longitudinal 'correlational' research on the effects of class size differences in school (see Chapter 7).

We also recognize and stress the role of longitudinal research. Indeed the only way in which development *per se* can be studied is longitudinal, for developmental research is concerned with the 'process' of change. Cross-sectional studies of different age groups do not meet that criterion. Neither do they, nor can they, examine the ways in which children address transitions in development, such as from pre-school to primary school or from primary to middle school. Longitudinal research embedded in a naturalistic design is a very powerful tool in understanding children in schools, and one that researchers of all stripes should aspire to.

What do we mean by 'development'?

The term 'developmental' is used in many different ways by those interested in children. Most basically, the term has its origins in biology (recall that Piaget was trained as a biologist) and addresses the process of change that living organisms undergo from conception until death. The construct 'Development' is also of interest to those of us interested in children in schools and educational psychology. Even at the level of public educational policy, the notion of 'development' is evoked: some states in America have 'Developmental Kindergartens'; 'development' in such cases is defined implicitly as a classroom for children not promoted to first grade from kindergarten.

Also in terms of applications to schooling, development is used in terms of curricula and evaluation procedures for children as being 'developmentally appropriate'. Here 'development' means that curriculum and evaluation procedures should be congruent with the children's level of competence. For example, in the area of evaluation, because pre-school and kindergarten children's motivation in assessment situations is highly variable (e.g., affected by the sex and/or race of the tester), more naturalistic approaches of evaluation (e.g., observation of behaviour) are developmentally appropriate for this period. Similarly, if peer relations are a hallmark of the pre-school and early school years (Waters and Sroufe, 1983), developmentally appropriate practice should therefore involve opportunities for children to interact with each other in a variety of settings.

Two views of development

It should be clear that the term 'developmental' has wide and disparate use. In this chapter we discuss the construct 'development' as it applies to children's development in the context of schools. We begin our discussion with two very different models of development. We also make connections to the related fields of social and educational psychology.

The first, and probably more familiar, model considers the child as an unfinished or incomplete adult. This view is represented in the theories of Piaget and Vygotsky (See Pellegrini and Smith, 1998). The second view, however, considers each developmental period valuable for that specific time. 'Childish' behaviours are not considered to be imperfect but as important responses to the niche of childhood. This view is represented in the theories of Bateson (1978) and Kagan (1971). Each of these views presents the child in very different lights in terms of their competence and what is expected of them. For these reasons, each of these views has very important implications for the ways in which we interact with children.

Development as a continuous process towards a finished adult

Probably the more common view of development is the view of theorists such as Vygotsky and Piaget. In each of these theories, development is considered to be a continuous path toward the outcome of adulthood. Most developmental theories under this heading assume the existence of an extended period of childhood in terms of training for adulthood (Bruner, 1972). Thus children's behaviour is understood in terms of adults' behaviour (e.g., preoperational thought is deficient relative to formal operational thought) and early behaviours are seen in terms of how they are 'transformed' into mature behaviours. In Piaget's terms, the end point is formal operational thought. The thought and behaviour of pre-school children is thus considered to be 'less developed' than formal operational thought or merely a means to the end of operational thought. It is the job of the developmentalist to chart the course from infancy and early childhood, through adolescence, to adulthood. Typically, and as exemplified by Piaget's model, one developmental pathway is specified. Piaget's discussion of egocentricism is a good example of this 'unfinished' orientation. The egocentric child, in this model, has neither the ability nor the desire to take another person's perspective. This limitation is 'overcome' through repeated clashes with the social world. In short, egocentricism is a liability to be overcome.

The educational implications of this view are that we present children with materials and activities at their 'developmentally appropriate' levels but the importance of these tasks is considered in terms of the ways in which they contribute to operational thought. Further, we often consider the specified pathways as the only ways in which children can reach desired outcomes. For example, we may think that all children must engage in symbolic play if they are to develop into competent adults. Alternative pathways to competence are not typically considered.

Related to the notion of continuous progress toward adulthood, is the stress on early experiences. If development is continuous, the argument goes, disturbances in the early processes should have important, and sometimes irreversible effects. It is these early experiences upon which subsequent development is based. Viewing infancy and early childhood as 'critical periods' (to be discussed below) is an example of this perspective.

Development in the niche of childhood

According to the second, alternative, view, developmental processes can be viewed as responses to the specific demands of specific niches in development, such as childhood. So, specific behaviours, such as egocentric responses and pretend play are not viewed as immature versions of adult behaviour but as adaptive responses to the special needs of the niche of childhood. Take the example of very young children's limited locomotor capabilities. These could be viewed in immature, unfinished terms or could be viewed as adaptive in that this limited mobility results in children staying closer to their care givers (Bjorklund and Green, 1992). Educationally, this stance also stresses the need for 'developmentally appropriate' practice, but stress is placed on the role of these activities for the specific needs of childhood, rather than as preparation for adulthood.

This view of development also has implications for our views on the continuity of developmental pathways. Accordingly, this view suggests that individual children may take many different pathways to developmental competence in different periods (Kagan, 1980). There is no one royal road to competence. The road taken is a result of children's individual differences and a result of different niches. We will discuss implications of this view for 'critical/sensitive periods' later. Suffice it to say for now that we have two views of development, one stressing the child as an incomplete version of adults, and the other viewing childhood as having its own integrity. Correspondingly, the behaviours and cognitions characteristic of childhood have value for that period. Because of the importance of our conceptions of development for children in schools, we will discuss below some crucial dimensions of development.

Current views of development

Hinde (1983) has documented the principles of development, with guidance from biology, psychology, and ethology. In this section, however, we will only be concerned with those principles which are most relevant to children in schools.

The first concept that we discuss is that of optimum stage or critical/ sensitive periods. This concept, in its strong form (i.e., critical period), holds that there are certain periods in development which are critical to development of specific behaviours; if this period is missed, the behaviour or concept will probably not develop. The weaker version, realized in the 'sensitive period' hypothesis, holds that some periods are more optimal than others for developing specific behaviours or concepts. If these periods are missed, there can be compensation later, but it will be more difficult.

A familiar example of the critical period hypothesis comes from the attachment literature. Early theory held that if infants did not securely attach to the mothers they would suffer from subsequent personality anomalies (see Bowlby, 1969 for a thorough review). The critical period hypothesis was based on Lorenz's (1935, cited in Hinde, 1983) imprinting experiments with birds wherein the young bird would learn to respond to a moving object as they would a parent within the first hours of life. This process was thought to be irreversible; thus, the notion of a *critical* stage.

Subsequent research has shown that adverse conditions encountered during those critical periods were indeed reversible; thus, the notion of a *sensitive*, rather than a critical period. For example, the effects of maternal deprivation in monkeys during a critical period can be remediated in later life through exposure to younger peers (Suomi and Harlow, 1972). The sensitive hypothesis can, and has, been applied to an important aspect of child study, infant day care. There is debate over the long term effects on children of day care while they are infants. The sensitive period hypothesis holds that a sensitive period for attachment exists; this attachment is hypothesized to be the basis for subsequent social competence.

Another example comes from language development. There seems to be an optimal period to learn language (Lenneberg, 1966) and biology seems to be implicated in this process, either through an innate Language Acquisition Device (Chomsky, 1965), which enables youngsters to learn language (i.e., syntax) with relative ease, or through natural selection (Dunbar, 1988), where syntax evolved so that humans could keep track of those with whom they interact. The evidence here shows that children and prepubescent youngsters learn language quite easily. Not only is language learning more difficult after this time, but the brain is less capable of using alternative structures in language learning after puberty (Lenneberg, 1966). Thus if language is to be learned it must be done during this time. Similarly, languages can be most effectively taught to children, beginning at a young age. It should follow that foreign languages should be taught in the earliest grades in school.

Relatedly, the notion that oral language has a strong biological component is also relevant to current debate around the ways in which early literacy is taught in school. No theory, to our knowledge, has a biological programme implicated in the learning of reading, as is the case for oral language. Further, much of the difficult work in learning language has been done by the time children are only just beginning to read; that is, there is little correspondence between optimal times for learning language and learning to read. This leads us to question the assumption of one group of literacy researchers who suggest that reading and oral language are learned in the same ways, and thus minimal formal instruction in skills is needed.

The second concept of development involves individual differences. This concept suggests individual variations exist within a species. Individual differences in children are often considered in terms of 'temperament', especially those differences in emotionality and mood (Campos *et al.*, 1983). For example, some boys may be physically active while others may be more sedentary. Individual differences are often thought to have biological components (e.g., they are related to certain hormones) and are stable across the life span (Campos *et al.*, 1983). For example, a child's level of activity may be affected by prenatal factors, such as mother's level of tobacco and alcohol consumption, and factors within the child, such as the nature of the individual child's limbic system (see Kagan, 1980). The expression of these differences, however, is mediated by the environments in which children are raised. Differences will be exacerbated if children are encouraged to be active (e.g., children reared in spacious and enriched environments) or limited if high levels of activity are not supported by the environment (e.g., children are reared under crowded and dangerous conditions). This argument has recently been applied to children diagnosed with Attention Deficit/Hyperactivity Disorder (Pellegrini and Horvat, 1995). For example, active children may not be viewed as a problem in a classroom with a more social regimen where youngsters are allowed to walk around the classroom and talk to each other.

The third concept, concerning the sequence of stages, suggests a regularity despite individual differences. Regularity relates to the specific sequence, or order, in which behaviours appear. This well known concept is best illustrated in Piaget's (1970) theory of cognitive development wherein children progress from sensori-motor, to preoperational, to operational levels of intelligence. Though the ages may vary for each stage, they appear in the specified order. This stage sequence concept further incorporates the idea that stages are qualitatively different from each other. That is, experiences and concepts at stage 1 are qualitatively different to similar phenomena at stage 2. For example, a preoperational child's concept of the number five is different from that of a formal operational child to the extent that for the former this array (1 1 1 1 1) may be greater than this array (11111); they would be equal for the older child.

The value assigned to these between-stage differences, as noted above, varies. Some see them as limitations to be overcome while others see them as strengths to be exploited. For example, it is well known that young children overestimate their own competence in academic work (e.g., Blatchford, 1997; Stipek and Daniels, 1988) and may well do in social groups. One could choose to correct this 'misperception' or one could allow children to continue with these views. With the latter strategy, children's self-efficacy and task persistence may improve.

The fourth developmental concept relates to functional considerations (Hinde, 1983); that is, the use of specific behaviour. Function can be considered at the level of reproductive fitness or in terms of beneficial consequences. Beneficial consequences are those outcomes of a specific behaviour which are positive. For example, a beneficial consequence of an infant's smile might be that an adult approaches him or her. Beneficial consequences of a behaviour can be either immediate to the developmental period during which it is observed or deferred to a later period. Take the example of locomotor play during childhood. Immediate benefits of this activity could be muscle and cardiovascular fitness for that period. Alternatively, deferred benefits of locomotor play could be considered in terms of later skeletal development (Fagen, 1981). The idea that a behaviour, such as play, has immediate, not deferred, benefits is consistent with the view of development as an adaptation to the specific demands of a niche, such as childhood. The important point to stress here is that behaviour may serve different functions at different periods of development. To use Hinde's (1983) simple, but cogent example, caterpillars are superb leaf eaters but poor at the skill required of butterflies. The lesson here is that we should not consider the function of a behaviour in childhood in terms of skills relevant to adulthood. The deferred benefits argument is consistent with the idea that childhood is a period of preparation for adulthood and those skills learned there will be useful for functioning as adults.

The final aspect of development to be discussed here relates to discontinuity/continuity in development. Like other developmental concepts discussed, this concept explores the extent to which behaviour, traits, or skills are continuous, or stable, or discontinuous, or unstable, across the life span; for example, is intelligence or temperament stable from infancy through childhood? This concept, in conjunction with the earlier concepts, is particularly important from an applied perspective to the extent that it informs us of the relative importance of specific behaviours/skills at specific periods. In this section, based on Kagan's (1971) discussion of the issue, we will address in detail this concept because of its importance to children in schools.

Continuity, or stability, in behaviour may be endogenous (i.e., an internal process), e.g., the stability in intelligence in a pre-school child is responsible for the stability of his/her verbal ability across the pre-school and primary school periods. Stability may also be exogenous, or external. For example, the above noted stability in verbal ability may be due primarily to a stable home environment rather than internal processes. Of course, as said above, we should keep in mind that such dichotomies between internal/external and Nature/Nurture are outmoded. The point to be made here, however, is that stability in development is affected by internal and external forces, probably working in conjunction with each other.

In some cases, continuity of very similar behaviours is observed across time; for example, a child may be very active during the infancy and pre-school years. This is a *homotypic continuity*, in which we have very similar response modes across time, i.e., locomotion. Heterotypic continuity is more difficult to gauge to the extent that it involves the inter-relation of different response modes across time. Though in different modes, heterotypic continuity can be established when the behaviours are theoretically related. For example, the ability to engage in make believe play at 3 years of age is related to word reading at 5 years of age (Galda *et al.* 1989). In this case, make believe play and word reading involve different response modes but are theoretically related to the extent that both involve the manipulation of symbolic representations.

Heterotypic continuity has rightfully been labelled cryptic by Kagan (1971). It is cryptic to the extent that discovering relations between dissimilar phenomena is akin to solving a puzzle or mystery. This is, however, the essence of 'being developmental' in that there are qualitative changes, via transformations, across the life span. Our job is to try and chart them. Our map in this journey must be good developmental theory. Only through such theory can we explain the relation between seemingly different sets of behaviours.

There are situations which provide clues to the solution of this mystery. Kagan (1971) lists principles which can be applied to detecting continuity/discontinuity. First, homotypic continuity is less common during the first 10 years of life than later. Specifically, there are two critical junctures during this period where heterotypic continuity is most likely to occur: 18 and 24 months of age and 5 to 7 years of age. During the first period, children's interactions with objects become dominated by their talking about them. In short, children move from concern with sensorimotor coordination to symbolic concern. The second period, 5 to 7 years of age, is marked by a qualitative change in children's cognitive functioning whereby children become more able to inhibit irrelevant acts and select appropriate ones, maintain a problem-solving set, and appreciate the requirements of a problem. In short, children become more reflective.

To conclude, in this section we have shown that a developmental approach involves conceptualizing of children as qualitatively different from each other at different periods. They are certainly different from adults. In the applied realm, this translates into identifying those behaviours/skills which are typical for a particular stage or period. Again, in making the choice we should be aware that the criteria for such a choice are that they should be relevant for that period, *not* adulthood. The next step in our applied endeavour involves making the theoretical connection of behaviours/skills from one stage or period to another.

This book

In this volume therefore, we view the child in school as a developmental being, interacting with his/her social and physical environments. From this view we can better understand those seemingly idiosyncratic behaviours of young children and help make schools more effective and happier places for children to live in. Importantly, we have pointed out how some common misconceptions about children, their social lives, and school achievement (e.g., regarding breaktime and friends) have resulted in ineffective school policy. We have identified some main themes in this book – its developmental perspective on interactions in schools, but also its concern with contextual factors and the effects of interactions, differences between children and research methods.

The book is divided into two halves. In the first we look at peer interactions. We draw on our own research experiences to cover what we consider to be key aspects of the social world of children and their peers at school. In Chapter 2, we examine children's social competence and peer relations. Social competence is considered broadly and developmentally. While there are different demands in different developmental periods, the ability to adjust and contribute to one's context is a hallmark of competence.

This is followed by a chapter on friendships in school (Chapter 3) which, in line with much research, summarizes how friendship relations develop with age, but concentrates on the significance of friendships in the school context. It also examines the school breaktime as a context for friendships. As said above, the authors have both championed research on children's play behaviour and experience on school playgrounds (e.g., Blatchford, 1998; Pellegrini, 1995b), and we devote two chapters (Chapters 4 and 5) to research on play and breaktime, respectively. In our discussion of play, we define play from a number of different dimensions, outline different forms of play that are observed during childhood, and then make inferences about the value of each form for children. We examine the pro v. anti recess/breaktime debate, describe 'within-child' influences of gender, temperament and age on playground behaviour, and the influence of the timing of recess, and end with an examination of the cognitive and social implications of recess/breaktime.

In Chapter 6 we discuss a dark side of peer interaction in school – aggression. An aspect of peer aggression in schools, studied recently, is bullying. For this reason our discussion will concentrate on problems of bullying and victimization. Bullying is defined as persistent negative behaviour directed at a specific child or group of children. Victims are typically weaker and more submissive than bullies, so there is also a power differential between bullies and victims.

In the second half of the book we turn to teacher–pupil interactions and influences on children's school performance. In Chapter 7, we examine research and conceptualizations of the classroom environment. The chapter is structured in two parts: first, ways of conceiving contexts at the class level, in terms of the physical layout of classrooms, the number of pupils, the psychological environment, classroom task and reward structures, participation structures, and, second, in terms of within-class contexts such as behavioural segments, tasks, activities, and within-class groupings. The point is made that classroom contexts can be influential in affecting teachers and pupils and the educational interactions between them. We also look at the way that contexts can be 'nested' within each other, in a way recognized in Bronfenbrenner's (1979) ecological model. We examine the connections between class size and the size and number of within-class groupings.

Given Gage's conclusion in the mid 1980s: 'Teaching is the central process of education' (Gage, 1985), it is appropriate to devote a chapter to research on teacher–pupil interactions. It is probably true to say that developmental psychologists are not as familiar as they might be with research on classroom interactions, but in turn educational psychologists tend not to be familiar with developmental research, for example, on parent–child interactions and peer interactions. In Chapter 8 our coverage is necessarily selective; we look at teacher–pupil interactions in two main ways: first, descriptive research on the nature of interactions in classrooms, and, second, the effects of these interactions on educational outcomes. In line with much debate in this area, the chapter looks critically at competing paradigms of research on teaching.

In Chapters 9 and 10 we examine specific learning contexts – literacy and mathematics learning, respectively. Our treatment of the topic reflects our developmental and social orientations towards schools. From this view, literacy is viewed, as a form of explicit oral language which is written and read. We discuss the ways in which different social configurations maximize the uses of this form of oral language.

In Chapter 10 school mathematics is discussed. Similar to literacy, we discuss the social context in which children learn mathematics. Using the construct of the developmental niche, we compare the social configurations, materials and belief surrounding mathematical activities at home and at school.

In Chapter 11 and Chapter 12, we concentrate on two specific topics, involving teacher–pupil interactions, that have been the subject of much debate and research and which can be helpfully informed by psychological perspectives. In Chapter 11 we show how the notion of low expectations has a wide currency in explanations of pupil underachievement, but look critically at research on teachers' expectations and, in particular, the possible effects they have on pupils' educational progress, and processes through which expectations might be mediated.

In Chapter 12, we argue that better understanding of influences on the relative performance of boys and girls is a main challenge for educational research, with important theoretical and practical implications. In line with the overall concern of this book with interactions in school, the chapter focuses on the role of teaching and classroom interactions, but we also look at ways in which other within-child factors such as self perceptions, self concept and motivational processes help inform gender differences in interaction and achievement.

In conclusion, our aim in this book is to stress the importance of research on interactions for educational as well as social policy. Perhaps the best example of the importance of this perspective comes from our research on breaktime. Breaktime is a period during the school day which is currently being re-evaluated. Unfortunately, this policy is not being guided by research. As a result of ignoring what research tells us is effective, the lives of teachers, children, parents, and rate payers may be adversely affected. School policy and practice, like other aspects of social policy, should be based on our best available knowledge. In this book, we have provided what we see as the best knowledge on children's social lives in school. Further, in anticipation of unanswered and unasked questions, we provide a thorough exposition on methods for studying social processes in school.

2 Children's social competence and peer relations

Introduction

In order to begin to understand children fully we must study the inter-relations among the social, cognitive, and affective aspects of their behaviour and development. For example, if we were interested in studying what is typically considered a dimension of cognition, reading, we should be concerned with cognitive linguistic processes (such as knowledge of letter–sound correspondence), social processes (such as the ways in which children's knowledge of the social conventions governing classroom discourse), and affect (such as achievement motivation). Similarly, in studying children's social behaviour, such as cooperation with peers, we must consider cognitive processes, such as the ability to take another person's perspective. The reason for the examination of social, affective, and cognitive processes is simple: they affect each other.

While it is very clear that much of social competence involves peers interacting with each other, we will discuss specific aspects of peer relations (popularity and friendship) in a separate chapter. There is simply too much research in these areas to incorporate into a general chapter on social competence.

In this chapter we will be examining children's social competence, generally. Social competence is a measure of children's adaptive or functional behaviours in their environments (Waters and Sroufe, 1983). Extending this to a developmental framework, there are different social competencies at different ages, so there are different hallmarks for children at different ages. By implication, the hallmarks for toddlers should not be considered as unfinished, or incomplete versions of adult behaviour; they represent adaptations to that specific developmental niche.

We will also examine children's social competence in different contexts. We will look at the ways in which children interact with peers and show how these processes affect children's subsequent social competence. The impact of children's social competence on subsequent development is very important as maladaptive patterns in childhood are predictive of subsequent problems with peers and adults and in school as well as society at large (Parker and Asher, 1987).

What is social competence?

The term social competence has been used extensively in the fields of education and psychology. Social competence has been defined differently by a number of scholars (e.g., Anderson and Messick, 1974; Dodge *et al.*, 1986; Zigler and Trickett, 1978). As noted above, social competence involves cognitive, affective and social processes. Social competence is defined in terms of children's functioning, but the type of functioning and the contexts in which they are expected to function will vary with the age of the child. For example, competence in a kindergarten classroom, would involve effective communication with peers and teachers, attending to class work, cooperating with peers, washing hands after going to the toilet, and attending school regularly, to name but a few examples.

A general definition of competence refers to 'an ability to generate and coordinate flexible adaptive responses to demands and to generate and capitalize on opportunities in the environment' (Waters and Sroufe, 1983, p. 80). This definition, is neither age, nor situation, nor skill specific. Above, however, we stressed a developmental approach to social competence such that there are hallmarks of social competence for different periods. This approach is consistent with the view of development which stressed the integrity of individual developmental periods. For example, crying may be effective for an infant to secure food. It should not be considered an inferior variant of more mature behaviour.

Scholars have attempted to measure social competence for a number of years, using tests for children (e.g., Circus, 1975), questionnaires completed by teachers (Fantuzzo *et al.*, 1995) or children (Pellegrini *et al.*, 1987), and by direct observations of children in natural situations (White and Watts, 1973). Despite the data source, it is important to define the construct of social competence such that it reflects the integrity of children in different developmental periods.

Waters and Sroufe (1983) have provided such a model. Generally, they consider competence 'as an integrated concept which refers broadly to an ability to generate and coordinate flexible, adaptive responses to demands and to generate and capitalize on opportunities in the environment (Waters and Sroufe, 1983, p. 80). Waters and Sroufe further specify their definition of social competence by listing some of its subcomponents for the pre-school period. First, individuals must contribute to situations. Responding to others (e.g., answering questions) or making one's own contributions (e.g., asking questions) to conversations are ways of contributing. Second, children must recognize the opportunity or demand to respond. For example, in conversation children are obligated by the rules of social discourse to respond to questions. Third, children should possess a repertoire of response alternatives. For example, children should have an array of responses to others' discourse; they can ask for questions to be clarified, change the topic, or answer the question. Fourth, they should be able to choose alternatives that are appropriate to specific situations. For example, if a child does not understand another's questions he/she should either repeat the question or ask for clarification of the question. Fifth, children should be motivated to respond. That is, children should want to engage in social discourse or interact with materials. As such, children should want to interact with different forms of stimuli; they should be active not passive. Sixth, children should persist at their interactions and change their responses to meet situational demands. For example, children's play with their peers should be sustained. Individual children may have to alter their social responses (e.g., sharing toys) in order for the interaction to be sustained. Last, children's responses should be fine tuned. That is, children should be able to decide quickly when to use certain types of behaviour. In addition, they should be adept at using them in different areas.

This approach to social competence suggests that children should, initially, seek out different physical and social stimuli. Further, they should develop repertoires of behaviours within each context that are adaptive. That is, in each context they should act in such a way that their interaction is sustained.

How do these individual processes relate to specific developmental hallmarks? Waters and Sroufe (1983) have listed social competence hallmarks through childhood, and they are displayed in Table 2.1.

The issues presented in this table are meant to highlight those specific competence that are appropriate for each age level. After mastery of one set of competencies, the child moves on to the next set of skills, each solving the problems germane to that specific period.

Table 2.1 Salient issues in early development*

Age	Issue
0–3 months	Physiological regulation
3–6 months	Tension management
6–12 months	Establishing effective attachment relationship
12–18 months	Exploration and mastery
18–30 months	Autonomy
30–54 months	Impulse management, sex role identification, peer relations
Middle childhood	Forming loyal friendships Sustaining relationships Functioning in stable groups Coordinating friendships and groups
Adolescence	Forming intimate relationships Commitment in relationships Functioning in relationships network Coordinating multiple relationships

*Based on Waters and Sroufe (1983, p. 85)

During middle childhood and adolescence, youngsters' social competence becomes concerned with investment in the peer worlds and integrating self and peer relationships, respectively. Specific to middle childhood, children are becoming more concerned with sustaining their relationships with peers at both the friend and group levels. With friends they are beginning to form loyal friendships. Part of this process involves negotiating conflicts, tolerating a range of emotional experiences, while at the same time using relationships to enhance self. At the group level, individuals in middle childhood are learning to adhere to group norms and maintaining gender boundaries. In the end, of course, children must coordinate their friendships and group functioning.

In adolescence, relationships become more intimate as well as more varied. During this period, youngsters are just beginning to form intimate relationships in same- and cross-gender relationships. By way of exhibiting commitment in these relationships, they must learn to negotiate self-relevant conflicts. Successful relationships at this level of intimacy require management of one's emotional vulnerability, self-disclosure practices and self-identity. Adding to the complexity, this management must be accomplished across different relationships, both same- and cross-gender.

In the next section we discuss social competence in a specific setting, school.

Social competence in the school

One way in which to consider children's social competence in school is to use theory derived from studies of children in other institutions, such as the family. In this chapter, we consider one such theory, derived from Baumrind's (1971) model of family socialization, and more recent adaptations by Steinberg and colleagues (1992). Parents and teachers alike use different socialization strategies in the service of teaching children. Baumrind's model, expanded by Maccoby and Martin (1983), can be represented as a four-fold scheme. This scheme, then, is a socialization model which impacts directly on children's social competence.

Table 2.2 Fourfold scheme of socialization patterns*

	Accepting Responsive Child-centered	Rejecting Unresponsive Adult-centered
Demanding Controlling	(1) Authoritative–reciprocal, high in bi-directional	(2) Authoritarian, power assertive
Undemanding Low in control	(3) Indulgent	(4) Neglecting, ignoring, indifferent, uninvolved

*From Maccoby and Martin (1983, p. 39).

The rejecting–demanding parent (number 2 in the table), is characterized by adults making demands on their children but not accepting their children's demands. This type of adult restricts children's expression of needs. This is the classic case of 'Children should be seen but not heard'. Adults' demands are neither questioned by children nor subject to discussion; children must obey the demands. Children are typically punished, often severely, when they do not comply with adult demands.

Children from such authoritarian families tend not to interact frequently with peers but when they do they are dominated by their peers. These children, though obedient, lack spontaneity and affection. Additionally, they tend to perform poorly in school. In short, they do not seem to be socially competent. Pre-school children from authoritarian families are dependent, socially withdrawn and unhappy (Baumrind, 1967, 1971, cited by Maccoby and Martin, 1983). When this type of child was examined in elementary school the girls did not show signs of social responsibility (e.g., altruism, cooperative interaction and social imitation) and cognitive competence. In high school, these children achieve at low levels (Steinberg *et al.*, 1992).

Indulgent–undemanding adults (number 3 in the table), are contrasted with the rejecting–demanding group. They are characterized as being permissive with their children. They take a tolerant and accepting attitude towards children's impulses. They make few demands and do not impose restrictions on children. Children are allowed to regulate their own lives. These adults can be either a warm, caring group, or cool and uninvolved. Baumrind (1967, 1971, cited in Maccoby and Martin, 1983) found that children of permissive parents tended to lack impulse control, self-reliance, independence and social responsibility.

The demanding child–centered orientation (number 1 in Table 2) is characterized by adults having clear expectations of mature child behaviour, firmly enforcing rules, encouraging child independence, and recognizing rights of both children and adults. Based on Baumrind's research (1967, 1971, cited in Maccoby and Martin, 1983), children experiencing this form of parenting tend to be the most competent. Generally, children tend to be socially responsible and independent. Steinberg and colleagues suggest, specifically, that parental warmth and acceptance when paired with democracy (or considering children's points of view), and supervision of children are responsible for the positive outcomes.

Unresponsive–undemanding (number 4 in Table 2), is the last socialization style to be discussed, and probably least represented among teachers. Generally, these adults minimize the time and effort spent with their children (Maccoby and Martin, 1983). Parents in this group want to keep their children at a distance. As such, the behaviours related to children's long-range developmental status (e.g., establishing rules for doing homework) are not attended to by these parents. Parents attend only to those behaviours necessary for children's immediate survival (e.g., feeding).

However, these parents sometimes even neglect these basic survival responsibilities. It has been reported that unresponsive–undemanding parents often abuse and neglect their children (Egeland and Sroufe, 1981, cited in Maccoby and Martin, 1983). In short, these parents are not interested in their children. What are the consequences of this type of parent for children? For pre-schoolers, parent non-involvement was a good predictor of children's aggression and disobedience (Maccoby and Martin, 1983).

The role of adults and peers in eliciting and supporting social competence

It is important to recognize that children's exhibition of social competence varies according to the context in which they are observed. At a more micro-level with schools, we find that peers and adults, differentially, elicit and support social competence. If we conceptualize competence as one's ability to take from one's environment, then, those environments which differentiate between those who are capable/incapable from doing so are important. Generally, environments that are highly structured by adults elicit lower levels of competence from children than do less structured environments. Simply, when children and adults are together, adults often do most of the work that initiates and maintains social interaction. It may be for this reason, that children with low levels of social competence choose to spend time with a teacher on the playground during recess than with peers: teachers probably initiate a conversation and keep it going whereas peers are probably less likely to do so.

This has been confirmed in a number of studies. For example, in an observational study of pre-school children, Wright (1980) attempted to identify positive indicators of children's social competence. Her general definition of social competence, like others, was children's socially adaptive behaviour. She identified a number of naturally occurring behaviours which were related to various measures of social adaptability. More specifically, she first examined child–child and child–adult interactions. She then examined how these behaviours related to children's test scores; test scores were used as a measure of adaptability in pre-school. She found, first, that the child–adult behaviours tend *not* to be related to measures of adaptability. Three types of peer interactions were, however, related to social adaptability: the successful and positive seeking of peers' attention; successfully using peers as instrumental resources; and successfully leading peers. Children must exhibit higher levels of competence to secure resources around peers than around adults. Adults, it seems, do much of children's work for them.

Similar results have been obtained in a study of elementary school children on the playground at recess. Generally, children who were adult, rather than peer, oriented were less competent. These results seem to support Waters and Sroufe's (1983) notion that social competence involves children seeking out social stimuli and having an effect on those stimuli.

These results are also important in terms of schools providing contexts which provide opportunities for children to learn and exhibit socially competent behaviours. To our knowledge the playground at recess is the context *par excellence* which does this. It is one of the very few places in school, where there is minimal adult direction, where children can interact with each other on their own terms. We should note that minimal adult supervision does not mean neglect. Adults should be available to discourage aggression and help children in need, not to form and direct children's play groups. It is these peer contexts in which children learn so much about the consequences of their behaviours.

Peer relations

The term 'peer' refers to individuals of equal status. We typically use the term 'peer' to refer to same-age children. Children of the same age are often equal in status in a number of ways.

The study of peer relations in the fields of education and psychology has recently experienced a re-birth. Until recently psychologists, educators and others interested in children have been more concerned with the cognitive aspects of children's behaviour than with the social aspects. Piaget, as noted earlier in this book, was concerned with peer interaction. Indeed, he stated that peer interactions were the best context for spurring children's cognitive and social development. In peer contexts children experience views discrepant from their own and often compromise their views. This accommodation of one's own point of view to another's is said to result in conceptual growth. As a result, different peer configurations have potent effects on children's behaviour. To understand children's social competence we must understand their peer configurations because of this potent effect.

Children's ability to interact with peers, however, undergoes significant developmental change across the early childhood period. Piaget's (1970) popular notion of the egocentric pre-schooler was a dominant concept until recently. He noted that sensorimotor and preoperational children were socially egocentric to the extent that they were neither willing nor able to consider the point of view of others.

Psychological research, however, has challenged Piaget's concept of egocentricism in young children (e.g., Blatchford, 1979; Garvey, 1977; Mueller, 1972; Mueller and Brenner, 1977; Mueller and Rich, 1976). Generally, this more recent body of research suggests that very young children (e.g., 6 months old) are very *willing* to interact with others but their ability to coordinate social interaction continues to improve through the early and middle childhood period. The pioneering work of Parten (1932) began a tradition of documenting the social interactive behaviours of young children.

Social participation

Parten suggested that young children's social participation with their peers progressed in a three stage sequence, from solitary to parallel play to co-operative interaction. Briefly, solitary interaction has a solitary child involved with a prop, not a social partner. Parallel interaction has two children next to each other interacting with similar props, but not with each other. Cooperative interaction is sustained reciprocal interaction. Subsequent research suggests that these patterns of social participation were not stages *per se*, but strategies used by children in different situations. For example, parallel interaction is often used by young children to enter a group. Once they have gained access, they engage in cooperative interaction. If they were unsuccessful in gaining access, they may use parallel interaction again. For these reasons, children who spend a significant portion of the time in parallel interaction may lack the social skills necessary for sustained peer interaction.

The effects of props on social participation

Work with pre-school-age children has examined the effect of toys on social participation. An early study by Johnson (1935, cited in Hartup, 1983) found that when the availability of toys was decreased children experienced both more positive and more negative interactions. The specific types of toys with which children interact also affect their social behaviour. A number of naturalistic and experimental studies have shown that when children interact with art materials they engage in non-social play (i.e., parallel and solitary) (Pellegrini, 1984 a and b; Pellegrini and Perlmutter, 1989a). When these same children interact with dramatic props (e.g., dressing-up clothes) or blocks they more frequently exhibit social, or cooperative, interaction.

The effect of toys on children's behaviour is not a direct one, however. The ways in which children play with toys depends in part, on their age, gender, the gender of their playmates, and the level of sex role stereotype of the toys. For example, when 3-year-old girls play together with a male-preferred toy, such as with large wooden blocks, their play behaviour is *more* sophisticated than the play of 5-year-old girls with the same toys (Pellegrini and Perlmutter, 1989a). Girls seem to learn at a young age that they should not exhibit competence with male-preferred toys. The lesson, here, is that toys do not have an effect, independent of personal variables, on children's behaviour.

Research on the effects of toys on older children's behaviour is, generally, not available (Hartup, 1983). By the time children enter elementary school they are not expected to interact with toys during class time.

The effects of peers and adults on children's social participation

The number and type of people, both adults and children, in an area also affects children's behaviour. These results, like those discussed under social competence above, suggest that adults often *inhibit* pre-school children's social interaction with peers (Field, 1979; Pellegrini, 1984a and b; Rubenstein and Howes, 1976). Hartup (1983) suggests that adults inhibit children's peer interaction because children interact with them, not with peers. Pellegrini (1984a and b) found that as the number of adults increased within activity centres in a pre-school classroom, children's social interaction, generally, decreased. In classroom settings adult presence may facilitate children's attention to physical activities and tasks, not social interaction.

Peer presence, on the other hand, facilitates children's social interaction. In the same study (Pellegrini, 1984a and b) it was found that as numbers of children in activity centres increased so too did children's social interaction. The comparisons of adult presence and child presence on children's social interaction seems to support the Piagetian hypothesis that peer presence may facilitate development (i.e., eliciting more advanced forms of behaviour) while adult presence may inhibit development (i.e., it inhibits advanced forms of behaviour). Further, playmates' gender, as noted above, also affects behaviour.

The influence of peers on children's social behaviour can be interpreted from a social cognitive theory as well as a Piagetian perspective. Peers serve as models and reinforcers for each other. Peers reinforce each other by giving positive attention and approval, affection and personal acceptance, and by submitting to each other's wishes. Peers also serve as models for each other. However, both positive and negative behaviours are modelled and subsequently learned from peers. Children tend to imitate those peers most similar to themselves (Hartup and Coates, 1967, cited in Hetherington and Parke, 1979). Further, children are more likely to imitate those peers who are warm, rewarding and powerful (Hetherington and Parke, 1979). The notion of peer similarity and mutual reinforcement seems to be a powerful determinant of children's behaviour. In the next chapter, on friendship, we will see how these dimensions also influence children's friendship choices and the stability of those friendships.

Again, if we want to maximize the sorts of behaviours associated with social competence, then it is important to provide opportunities which maximize peers interacting with each other, with minimal adult direction. Free play contexts in classrooms and recess/breaktime on the playground are two of the more obvious and powerful examples.

Conclusion

In this chapter we have examined children's social competence and peer relations. We chose to examine social competence because the construct represents the processes children must use in order to be a functioning member of society. Further, the notion of social competence includes both social and cognitive behavioural measures.

The construct 'social competence' is enormously important for educators to consider. As Zigler and Trickett (1978) noted a generation ago, educational programmes for children should consider the whole child, not just cognitive dimensions such as IQ and achievement. Broadly defined, social competence for primary school children certainly does include cognitive dimensions, such as achievement. It also includes other behaviours which are important in children's functioning in those institutions (school, families, and neighborhoods) in which they live. To that extent, it is also important for us to consider children's interactions with peers and adults in their lives. Children who exhibit maladaptive behaviour with peers and adults also have problems with achievement in school (Coie and Dodge, 1998). This constellation of behaviour leads to problems, such as juvenile delinquency, and substance abuse, in later life. Thus educators must pay more attention to social competence. In the next chapters we discuss, more specifically, the importance of two dimensions of peer relations: friendship and popularity.

3 Pupil friendships in school

One of the most taken-for-granted aspects of life is the everyday contacts we have with friends. We probably all value our friends, and our most enjoyable moments are in their company. Although we invest much in our friendships, and can be upset if we fall out, we usually do not examine them analytically. Yet the everyday encounters we have with friends depend on, and reveal, a bewildering and sophisticated set of skills and understandings. These are developed over the course of childhood. Making and maintaining friendships are major aspects of a child's life, and, as we shall see, friendship relations during childhood may be important for later social development and personal adjustment.

One of the main settings within which children get a chance to meet friends is the school. In a longitudinal study of pupil perspectives on school (Blatchford, 1996), it was found from interviews with the same pupils at 7, 11 and 16 years that they were affected by two main things: work in school and friends. Throughout school, pupils valued the opportunity to socialize with their friends. In this chapter we examine friendships at school. We will not seek to provide a comprehensive review of research on friendships (see Bukowski *et al.*, 1996; Hartup, 1996); rather our aim will be to draw out particular features of friendships in school settings, show their positive as well as possible negative aspects, and discuss the implications of research findings for schools and what teachers can do. A main feature of this chapter will be to examine the significance of friendships at school.

In this chapter there are three main sections:

1. developmental trends in children's friendships
2. school contexts for friendships: breaktime in school
3. the significance of children's friendships

Developmental trends in children's friendships

A lot of research and comment on children's friendships has been concerned with charting main developmental trends in friendship relations (see Parker and Gottman, 1989). An early developmental account was provided by Sullivan (1953). There are four main stages. In the first stage (around 2–5 years) children are not seen to maintain peer relations without adult help and children are seen to play with whoever happens to be at hand. In the second stage (4–8 years) children are seen to have playmates, independent of adult help, but these relations are transitory, without commitment, and continued only in so far as they serve immediate needs. In the third stage (around 7 to 12 years) friendships become more intense, as intimacy and reciprocity appear, and efforts are made to please friends and reinforce the relationship. This is the stage of 'pre-adolescent chumship' and is followed, at adolescence, by a fourth stage where the challenge is to translate some of the characteristics of chumship (loyalty, mutual support, commitment, etc.) to heterosexual relationships. Friendships also develop in terms of a more sophisticated sensitivity to the feelings of friends and loyalty and self disclosure. A central theme of Sullivan's approach is the value of close peer relationships in the development of the ability to empathize and sympathize with others. Friendship relations are therefore seen as important for later social development.

The well known developmental model of Selman (1980) has a number of similarities, but is largely based on Piagetian stages and links friendship relations to cognitive development. Other models have also been advanced. Maxwell (1990) has reviewed these and argues that there is a good deal of consensus about the main stages of progression:

1. At pre-school and early infant/elementary school, thinking about friends is egocentric, with superficial awareness of the friend as a person and low commitment to the relationship.
2. In the middle primary years, there is greater awareness of personal characteristics and views of others; the child is more committed to friendships and more selective.
3. From the later primary school years on, there is more intensity, sense of loyalty and commitment, more self-disclosure, intimacy and integrating of views, opinions and values.

(from Maxwell 1990, p. 179)

There is, then, some agreement about general developmental progression in friendship relations, though there are some differences in views about underlying processes. Selman's view is consistent with the notion, which owes much to Piagetian thought, that developments in friendship relations reflect more general structural transformations in the child's understanding of the social and physical world. A somewhat different view is seen in the work of Youniss (1980), who sees friendships as developing through the elaboration of a single construct – social reciprocity. A third view sees friendship relations developing more on the basis of the accumulation of separate experiences such as common interests, intimacy, and commitment.

Much of the empirical work supporting these early developmental models of friendship has tended to involve children's descriptions of friendship relations in the context of interviews or structured tasks. A general point to make (which applies to other areas of developmental psychology) is that there has been a gradual revision of what were previously seen as limitations on young children. So, in line with Piagetian thought, it was thought that children younger than around 6 or 7 had very limited abilities to relate to each other and friendships were consequently fleeting and transitory, depending on proximity above all. But one theme of more recent research has been to question this view, and this has to a large extent come about because of observation and study of children in real life situations. Asking children about friendships can be informative about a number of things, but it may seriously underestimate their experience of it. As Dunn (1993) argues, even when children are articulate, it is not easy to describe what friendship means and there may not be much correspondence between reports of intimacy, self disclosure and expectations of prosocial behaviour on the one hand and actual friendship behaviour on the other.

Around the time of writing this chapter, one of the authors spent some time overhearing his 5-year-old son playing with his friend (who lives two houses away). The two boys would move from house to house as the fancy took them. It was summer and the boys spent much time outside playing football, making camps, or playing with objects from the garden. Often the friend's older brother would also appear, and another boy from around the corner. In the event of rain or boredom they would move indoors to play with lego, action men, or create mayhem with cushions in the sitting room. An interesting feature of their play was its specific nature, that is, the way it would be specific to the individuals concerned. So when the two boys were alone the nature of play was very different. Obviously they did fall out on occasions, but it was noticeable that they would make a series of adjustments and conciliatory gestures in order that play proceed. (Reconciliation during play with peers, in order to maintain interaction, has been clearly documented in children as young as 3 years.) There was also a recognition, albeit in embryonic form, of personality differences and allowances made in order to keep the contact smooth and enjoyable. This was different to relations with the other children. Perhaps most noticeable, but easily overlooked, was the huge amount of enjoyment it provided both boys, which no doubt lay behind the constant requests to go and play with each other. They clearly valued the relationship, especially within the context of an activity with minimal adult supervision.

In line with this anecdotal observation, a number of studies have shown that even young children can show in their day to day behaviour some of the friendship qualities and social skills previously expected only of older children. As long ago as the 1970s, one of the authors found on the basis of an observational study of dyads that there was a developmental progression of contacts over the first two years, and a surprising degree of reciprocity and interest in each other (Blatchford, 1979; see also Mueller and Lucas, 1975).

Even young children can show understanding of, and sensitivity toward, others, and can maintain at least a degree of intimacy in friendships. Friendships from a young age can also show a degree of stability over time. Howes (1987, cited in Dunn, 1993) found that pre-school children tended to maintain friendships over a two year period and sometimes much longer. Another study, cited by Dunn (1993), found that more than two thirds of pre-school children had reciprocated friendships (Gershman and Hayes, 1989). Dunn (1993) found that the average time that 4-year-old children had been close friends was two years. Of course, these friendships between such young children will depend on living close or having ready access to each other but, as Dunn reminds us, and as parents know, this does not always guarantee that children will be friends.

Dunn (1993) gives an example of the specific nature of children's friendships.

> (5-year-old in Pennsylvania)
> *I*: How about if your sister took a toy from you – would that be ok or not ok?
> *C*: Not ok! I would be pissed off, and I would kick her!
> *I*: Why?
> *C*: Because she'd be taking something from me. Because she'd be stealing it. A CRIME!
> *I*: What about if Jeff took something from you?
> *C*: That would be ok . . . because I wouldn't mind.
> *I*: How about if you took a toy from Jeff?
> *C*: I would never do it. Because he's my friend. My best, best, best, best friend!
> *I*: What about if you took a toy from your sister? Would that be ok or not ok?
> *C*: Ok . . . because she's my sister and I hate her guts . . . . Well I don't actually hate her, but . . .
>
> (Dunn, 1993)

In line with the observations above concerning one of our sons, the specific nature of friendship is significant here, and different to that with his sister! It may be the case, as noted by Hartup (1996), that friends, unlike siblings, operate in an 'open field', that is, they have an opportunity to leave the interaction at any time. This option maximizes children's need to compromise if they want to maintain the interaction.

School contexts for friendships: breaktime in school

Research on children's friendships has tended to be non-specific about contexts within which friendship relations occur, and little is known about friendship relations in different contexts. Broadly speaking there are three main settings in children's lives:

1. classroom
2. playground/recess
3. out of school (this could be further sub-divided, for example, into home and street/outside, though the latter is becoming less common for primary-aged children).

There may be very little overlap, between settings, in a child's friendship network. Children may have a school friendship network which is quite separate from their out of school network. It may be difficult for children to meet their school friends out of school. At secondary level children may as a matter of course travel some distance to school – usually in a car – and are unlikely to meet school friends, unless visits are arranged by parents. Children who attend private schools may also be driven long distances to get there. This situation may be becoming more common for those in the maintained sector where the encouragement of parental choice of schools can result in long journeys to the desired school, rather than the automatic choice of the nearest, local school.

Within classrooms there are also likely to be contextual influences on friendship relations. Maxwell (1990) refers to research by Hallinan (1981) who compared peer relations in traditionally organized classrooms and those of a more 'open' type, with children organized in groups and where more interaction was encouraged. It was found that in the traditional classes friendship choices were more polarized, with more very popular and very isolated children, while in the open classrooms they were more evenly spread, and there were more stable, reciprocated friendship choices. Ramsey (1991) reports results from Bossert (1979) who compared social patterns in classrooms structured around ability grouping and academic competence, and those in which children worked in interest groups and at several tasks at once. In the former, friendships tended to be between children of similar ability, while in the latter friendships developed out of a shared interest. Interestingly, friendship patterns changed when children changed settings, so that when, in the following year, children in the multitask setting changed to a competitive one, they abandoned previous friends and interacted with same-ability peers. The reverse pattern occurred in the case of children moving from a competitive to a multitask classroom.

However, in general there appears to be very little knowledge about how the social organization of schools and the dynamics of classrooms affect friendship formation and collaboration between friends (Zajac and Hartup, 1997). It might be thought, for example, that in more individualistic, and more competitive classrooms, friendship relations may be affected and collaboration between friends in class may not be so effective, but there has been little research on this.

Friendships and the breaktime context

A particular setting within school, where children meet their friends, is breaktime or recess (see Chapter 5). For some children, it may be just about the only setting within which friendships can form and develop. The important characteristic of breaktime is that it is the main 'open' setting in school, that is, a time when they are relatively freed from adults and where the rules of engagement are more their own. Friendship networks in school and breaktime contexts may not overlap exactly. It may be, for example, that in the classroom children will tend to be seated with children of similar ability and this may affect who they are friends with. However, breaktime friendship relations may have a different basis; for example, they may play with, and make friends with, children who enjoy similar games and activities. In Britain, a main playground activity – at least at primary level – is soccer, and this can draw boys together, and sometimes seal friendships, though the boys may be academically at very different levels. Breaktime is implicated in the development of friendships in school because it is the main setting within which pupils, possibly not in the same class, have the opportunity to meet.

Changes with age in breaktime friendship relations

On the basis of pupil accounts, Blatchford (1998) found that breaktime had a role in the development of friendships in school, but the nature of this role changed with age. Friendships between primary-aged children were often manifested in, and supported by, active breaktime activities and playground games (see below). But during secondary school (11 to 16 years) friendships were furthered in the context of – in a sense – an absence of activity. It is relatively easy for adults to underestimate the value of 'hanging around' to pupils' social relations.

Brown (1990) has observed that adolescent peer groups differ from primary-aged peer groups in being more based in school buildings and needing independence from adult attention and supervision. Pupils at this age are more likely to make deliberate efforts to escape from adults, and keep interactions private. So in the school context there may be a special role for breaktime at secondary level, because it is the main school setting within which a degree of privacy and freedom from adults is possible.

Nature of friendship groups: size and networks

The well known research of Berndt (Berndt *et al.*, 1986), like many others (e.g., Furman, 1989), has set in place the assumption that childhood friendships are mainly dyadic in nature. Bukowski and Hoza (1989) in fact define friendships as 'the experience of having a close, mutual, dyadic relation'. Blatchford (1998), in a small scale study, used children's own accounts as the basis for conclusions about friendship group size, and concluded it would be wrong to see the development of friendships as only or principally occurring in dyads. The 8-year-old girls had formed unisex 'cliques' of between 4–5 friends. It has been said (Selman, 1980 in Furman, 1989) that it is not until adolescence that peer groups share common interests and a consensus of norms. Blatchford's study, though, suggests that the friendship groups shared a common interest, purpose and identity, and this was particularly revealed at breaktime. Though exact comparisons are not possible, it appeared that friendship groups in the older pupils studied by Blatchford (16 years) were larger and there was little difference between boys and girls in the size of friendship groups. Girls, though, were more likely to say they had best friends and to meet friends out of school.

Examination of pupil accounts also showed that categorization of friendship distinctions even in terms of best friend, friends, and non-friends would not be fine enough (Blatchford, 1998). Again the breaktime context was an important arena for friendship relations. Some children described a hierarchy of friendships, with one or perhaps two children at the apex and groups of varying size at lower levels. Some did not have or want to have best friends, preferring to be in a larger group of friends. Furthermore, changes over time in friendship groups could involve shifts in friendship status within groups, as well as movement between groups.

As with the younger children, analysis of 16-year-old pupils' descriptions showed that accounts of friendship networks simply in terms of numbers of friends failed to capture their complexities. Some pupils had a few friends or one best friend, some had hierarchical networks, as with the younger children, with perhaps a few or one best friend in the context of a larger group, and some preferred to maintain a more equal degree of friendship with a number of people.

Influences on friendship choices at breaktime

Research has identified relatively 'surface' factors such as age and proximity, as factors which affect friendship choice, and also the degree of similarity between friends (Epstein, 1989; Erwin, 1993). There is some agreement that 'deeper' factors such as personal characteristics of pupils become more important in adolescence, though it is possible (as above) to underestimate the extent to which friendship choices in younger children can also be based on personal characteristics. In Blatchford's (1998) study of friendships at breaktime it was possible to identify a number of factors that, from the pupils' point of view, explained why they became friends. These were: age, length of acquaintance, contact made at a previous school, shared interests, and personal characteristics like giving help, sharing a sense of humour, not being bossy, and working together. Many of these explanations involve variations of 'similarities' (see Epstein, 1989). Some show the important role of environmental factors, such as neighbourhood influences. Some factors, like age, are the 'surface of selection' (Epstein,

1989). Others, showing more 'depth of selection', involving appreciation of and grounds for friendship in qualities such as not being bossy, having a sense of humour and, most commonly, giving help. It seems likely that out of school and previous school factors play a part in and help support early friendships, but within-school and 'deeper' characteristics then become the dominant factors.

Gender and friendship relations at breaktime

There is evidence that boys' and girls' friendships differ, with boys being more extensive and less exclusive (Eder and Hallinan, 1978, in Hartup, 1989). There is also evidence that friendships in schools predominantly involve pupils of the same sex (Hartup, 1992). Friends tend to be similar on important dimensions (Hartup, 1996). Breaktime provides an important context for friendships between the sexes. Girls and boys can form separate groups but also be drawn together. The context provided appears to change with age of child (Blatchford, 1998). At primary level, preference for different activities can serve to separate the sexes, with, for example, boys preferring football. By 16 years football, active pursuits and games are less common, and 'hanging around' can now be the context within which boys and girls meet (at least in mixed sex schools).

The significance of friendships

What defines friendships?

We look first at the definition of friendships. We need to distinguish popularity from friendship. Though popular children may have a lot of friends and, conversely, rejected children may have few friends, they are still different aspects of social functioning. A child may not be popular and may be isolated or neglected by others but may have a meaningful friendship. To know that a child is more or less popular does *not* necessarily tell us much about the closeness or strength of their friendship. So social popularity is not a sufficient condition for success in social relations. Rubin (1980) in Maxwell (1990) warns against uncritical promotion of popularity on the grounds that it may lead to an emphasis on superficial relationships.

A good deal of research has shown that behaviour between friends differs from that between non-friends. Dunn (1993) in reviewing this work has said that children spend more time interacting with friends, that behaviour when in conflict with friends differs from that with non-friends (for example, they are more likely to attempt reconciliation, though the overall amount of quarrelling may be no different) and they may be more forgiving of friends. Newcomb and Bagwell (1996) show that research has tended to stress two main factors – mutuality and stability – in defining friends. Hartup (1992) has drawn up a list of defining characteristics of friendships. They involve reciprocity (equality) and commitment; are affiliative rather than attachment based (as with parents); involve common interests; and are egalitarian. Friendships between children are therefore symmetrically and horizontally organized, as opposed to adult–child relations which are asymmetrical and vertically organized.

However, showing that the behaviour of friends differs from that between non-friends does not in itself indicate the importance of friendships.

We now turn to the main topic of this chapter: how important are friendships in development and at school? This may appear to be a straightforward question – of course friends are good for you! Actually, there are as many dangers in a generalized view about the positive effects of friendships, as there are in overlooking the significance of friendships in development. Views on this vary on a continuum starting with little or no importance, through to useful but not essential, to a view (as Sullivan) that friendships are essential in development. But a main problem is that it is very difficult empirically to establish the developmental importance of friendship relations. Newcomb and Bagwell (1996) make the point that when assessing the developmental significance of friendships they overlap with, but are not necessarily the same as, peer relations and much less is known about the developmental significance of friendships specifically – a point also made by Hartup (1996).

So what can we say about the importance of children's friendships? Hartup, who is perhaps the most widely respected researcher and author on peer relations, has concluded on the basis of his review of evidence that:

> Correlational studies show that children with friends are more socially competent than children who do not have friends, and that troubled children have difficulty in friendship relations. Causal models, tested with longitudinal data, suggest that friendship experience forecasts developmental outcome in conjunction with personal attributes and other experiences. Making friends, keeping them, and making new ones are all relevant. The current evidence suggests, however, that we can better argue that friendships are developmental *advantages* than argue that these relationships are developmental *necessities*.
>
> (1992, pp. 200–201, our emphasis)

This opinion appears to qualify the importance of friendship, though in practice there may be a very fine line between 'advantage' and 'necessity'. Newcomb and Bagwell (1996) are equally careful in their choice of words, though rather more optimistic about the importance of children's friendships: 'the jury remains out . . . relations are not singularly viewed as a necessity, an advantage, or a hindrance. Instead, high-quality friendships can at times have negative consequences and low-quality friendships may provide some positive outcomes.' After stressing the need for research that can establish the causal significance of friendships, they conclude: 'Logically, if peer relations are significant to developmental outcome, then the more intense affective ties afforded by friendships could only be that much more potent.' (p. 294). But: 'we are left with little more than our conviction that the friendships of children and adolescents have a special place in development' (1996, p. 318).

A starting point for a consideration of the importance of children's friendships is the well-established view that peer relations have particular value for social and even cognitive development. In an influential book, Youniss (1980) adapted the theories of Piaget and Sullivan to show how peer relations were qualitatively different to adult–child relations. In contrast to adult–child relations, peer relations are characterized by equality, cooperation, reciprocity and mutuality – all of which make a contribution to social development. Youniss did not argue that adult–child and peer relations were better or worse than each other; rather that they served different functions and had different effects. Piaget's theory – not usually seen as stressing the social context of development – has been reevaluated in order to highlight the role of peers in cognitive development (DeVries, 1997). Indeed, Piaget did not note anything but the positive aspects of peer relations.

Friendships can be seen to have a general role in children's self image. The idea here is that children develop a notion of themselves through interaction with significant others, and this will include friends. So a child can construct a self image on the basis of feedback from those with whom they identify. So the peer group and friends can provide information on which a child's view of herself is based.

In line with Hartup (1992) the following main headings will be used to structure a discussion of the importance of friendships:

1. Context for acquisition of social skills
2. Information source
3. Emotional resource
4. Help adjustment to school
5. Aid subsequent relationships

Some of these headings are more obviously relevant to school experiences, and this will be highlighted below.

Context for acquisition of social skills

In a rather inelegant but useful phrase, friendships have been described as 'cooperative socialization contexts' (Hartup, 1989). Overall, friendships support cooperation, reciprocity, effective conflict management, intimacy and commitment, and these begin early in life and extend into adolescence.

Later, as we have seen, say between 11–17 years, self disclosure and intimacy become important, as do giving and sharing, exclusiveness and intimacy and commitment. All of these are important aspects of social relations and social skills, and all can have their roots in friendship relations.

Evidence for the important connection between friendship and social skills comes from studies which have compared the behaviour of children who differ in terms of whether they have friends or not. Newcomb and Bagwell (1996) conclude that:

> Taken together, the research literature comparing school-aged children with and without friends reveals a distinct pattern of characteristics related to being friendless. Friendless children display less adaptive social competencies and social skills when interacting with peers. They are less likely to show altruism and trust toward peers, their play with peers is less coordinated and positive, and they have less mature conceptions of friendship relations. The social reputations of friendless children amongst their peers are further characterized by greater negativity including less sociability and greater isolation and disruption. Children without a peer are less well adjusted and more negatively perceived by themselves and others than are children who experience the affective bond of friendship.
>
> (p. 313–4)

Approaching this in a slightly different way, Howes (1989) found that in young children social behaviour between stable friends was more competent, children were more successful in group entry, more complementary and reciprocal in their social play, more cooperative, and more likely to engage in pretend play (Howes, 1989 in Hartup, 1992). Maxwell (1990) describes friendships in terms of a socialization function – for example, through learning to control aggressive impulses in socially acceptable ways. He concludes: 'The peer group provides arguably the most efficient and highly motivating context for the learning and development of social skills which will ultimately enable children to live effectively as a member of adult society' (p. 171).

The authors have been studying the connections between friendships and playground games in primary-aged children, and this is revealing a number of ways in which social skills, friendships and breaktime activities are linked. Games and meeting friends are the two main playground 'performances' (Sutton-Smith, 1990), and are likely to be related. Games appear to serve different functions in friendship relations during different stages in the school year (Blatchford, 1999). In the early stages after entry, games appear to support or scaffold new social contacts – entry to and suggestion of games could be seen as opening gambits in emerging social relationships.

Shared knowledge of games may minimize the importance (at least initially) of other social knowledge skills necessary for competent interaction. Davies (1982) has also commented on the connections between play and friendships, and has argued that much of the building of shared understandings that lies at the heart of friendships develops through play. She describes how the compulsive dynamic of a game can draw children in, aiding friendship formation, and providing access to a shared children's culture.

One social process affecting development in games seems to be the formation and stability of friendship groups and social networks (Blatchford, 1998). With the development of more stable and defined friendship groups, the social function of games can change from a role in the formation of friendship groups to one of supporting and maintaining friendship groups. Games played by friends can, in part at least, define them as a group, different to others. But one consequence of this increasing stability in friendship groups can be reduced opportunities to try new games. Games and friendships can also be connected in the case of falling out with friends. The playing of a particular game can be a marker of reconciliation, and games can play a part in the management of conflict. In Blatchford's study (1998) evidence was found of more play over the year involving boys and girls (Thorne, 1993). Through such games children appear to be checking boundaries of what is permissable with the opposite sex. A kind of creativity in games can reflect developments in social relations between boys and girls. We have, by now, moved well beyond the game as scaffold; the game is now an aid in social exploration. Thorne (1993) has used the term 'borderwork' to describe cross-gender playground chasing games, in which girls often create safety zones, for example, toilets adjoining the playground, to which they can retreat.

There also appears to be a link between friendship status and games. Children, even as young as 8 years, can show considerable skill in creating, and then managing complex social networks, and gradations of friendship status. Different games could be played with best friends, friends and non-friends (Blatchford, 1998).

Information source
One obvious way in which friends can be a source of information was provided by one of the author's daughters: she said that friends help you with your homework!

A general context here is the role of peer interaction in cognitive development. A main influence is Piaget, and the notion that conflict produced by interacting with others at a similar cognitive level, and therefore equally egocentric, can provide the impetus for the process of decentring – which, according to Piaget, can affect the structure of cognitive development.

The role of peers in academic progress has been looked at recently in terms of peer tutoring, cooperative group work and peer collaboration. But as Hartup (1996) has said there is little evidence for the importance of these three in relation to friendships; for example, in terms of whether friends working in cooperative groups do better than non-friends.

There are strongly held professional views about whether friends should be seated together. Some teachers believe that children will work less effectively when with a friend because they will distract each other. On the other hand, it might be expected that friends would work better, because they know each other well and their collaboration would be more effective. Zajac and Hartup (1997) have recently reviewed evidence on the role of friends as co-workers. They review studies involving problem-solving, creative activity and communication (not play and other social situations). They looked at 13 studies which they have concluded are the 'entire literature dealing with the relations between friendship interaction and cognitive performance'. They argue, first, that friends can cooperate more effectively, for example, there is more positive emotion ('affect') expressed than between non-friends, more attention to equity rules, more task orientation, and friends are more likely to remember the task later. One study involved foursomes. Three had to work cooperatively in order to simultaneously operate mechanisms so that a fourth child could see cartoons through a small window. Foursomes who were friends cooperated more efficiently, took turns more readily, and achieved higher viewing times per child.

Second, they argue that friends can solve school-type academic problems more effectively. Chauvet and Blatchford (1993) examined whether the composition of groups affected the performance on end of Key Stage 1 (7-year-old) Standard Assessment Tasks in a London school. It was found that children in friendship groups had higher performance scores in maths tasks, and were more involved in the group, than did the same children when placed in ability groups or groups chosen at random. Recent studies, reviewed by Zajac and Hartup, have compared the dialogue of friends and non-friends working on problems involving the isolation of variables and deductive reasoning. Friends show more disagreement during collaborations, more elaboration of partner's proposals, and more frequent checking of progress. Importantly, disagreements between friends were not debilitating but facilitated correct deductions. Generalizing from this, Zajac and Hartup feel that disagreements between friends may have positive outcomes during collaborative performances – friends can use their disagreements to good effect, while non-friends may well not. Pellegrini and colleagues (Pellegrini et al., 1998) found that with friends, conflicts were likely to be resolved (more so than with acquaintances) and that resolutions in turn lead to children reflecting on linguistic and cognitive processes which were the source of their disagreement.

So far, this looks as if teachers might be advised to put friends together to work on tasks. However, things may not be so simple. There is some evidence that friends work better together on difficult than easy tasks. Zajac and Hartup interpret this in Vygotskian terms, that is, in terms of the zone of proximal development. The knowledge friends have of each other can mean that when problems are difficult (but not too difficult) collaboration can be productive for both, while on easy tasks, friends may not be motivated to talk.

Third, and relatedly, friends may perform better on written narratives, specifically creative writing. This might be seen as a kind of complex problem-solving task. In a study by Hartup and colleagues (Daiute *et al.*, 1993, in Zajac and Hartup, 1997), children, after a classroom topic on tropical rain forests, were asked to write a story based on a rain forest adventure. The amount of talk did not differ between friends and non-friends but friends' talk was more orientated to one another, there were more agreements, more repetitions of their own and the other's utterances, and friends spent twice as much time discussing the story content and writing mechanics as non-friends. Friends also spent less time 'off task' in comparison to non-friends – a surprising result for some teachers, perhaps. There were advantages with regard to quality of writing as well – friends' stories were rated of higher quality. Similar results were obtained by Jones and Pellegrini (1996) who found that friends (5- and 6-year-olds) used more sophisticated oral and written language in a computerized writing task than acquaintances. They argued that the emotional support provided by friendships may have been particularly important when they encountered the relatively new task of writing with a computer (compared to paper and pencil writing).

There is some experimental evidence that when friends (6-year-olds), compared to acquaintances in the same classroom, work on literacy tasks, such as writing and talking about books, friends' interaction is more 'academic' (Pellegrini *et al.*, 1998). By that we mean that friends tend to use language which indicates that they are reflecting on cognitive and linguistic processes constitutive of literacy; for example, in talk about language (e.g., 'How do you write "trick"?') and thought processes (e.g., 'Try to put this one first.'). These findings suggest advantages in grouping friends together in academic tasks, rather than separating them, as is commonly done (Blatchford *et al.*, 1999b).

Zajac and Hartup (1997) refer to another study which they say supports their conclusions. In this study, meta analysis was used to review the literature on differences between friends and non-friends, for example, on cognitive tasks. Newcomb and Bagwell (1995) reviewed 82 studies in which 524 variables were examined in relation to friendship status. According to Zajac and Hartup, there were four main advantages in favour of friends. First, there was more positive engagement between friends (talking, smiling and cooperation), second, better conflict management (resolving conflicts constructively), third, more task activity (staying on task, communicating about performance), and fourth, relationship properties were better (concern with equality and loyalty, less dominance and submission).

Why are friends better co-learners? There are several possibilities. First, they know each other better and it is likely that, for example, suggestions may be more appropriate; second, there is more commitment to each other, and more reciprocity; third, children are more secure with friends, which may help problem-solving tasks, and novel tasks; and fourth, friends can manage and resolve conflicts more effectively, so conflicts do not interfere so much in tasks. Indeed, conflicts and their resolution seem to support social cognitive growth among friends.

One limitation of much research on friends as co-learners is that they are often set in rather artificial situations, which do not necessarily reflect, and may not generalize to, the situation in actual classrooms. For example, friends tested in small groups may not behave in the same way in busy classrooms with 25–30 other children. We do not seem to know so much about the possible value of friendships in normal classroom life.

Emotional resource

Friends can help in solving everyday problems, buffer stress and provide security when experiencing new things and meeting new people. In a classic and poignant study, Freud and Dann (1951) studied six children who had spent their early years during the Second World War in close contact with each other but without stable care or attention from adults. The children had been passed from hand to hand during their first year, lived with each other in an age group in their second and third years, and were uprooted three times during their fourth year. On the basis of examination of the children after the end of the war, it was concluded that they were hypersensitive, restless, aggressive and difficult to handle. However, they were not seen to be deficient, delinquent or psychotic. It appeared that continual contact with each other had ameliorated the effects of a terrible early life, including lack of contact with their parents or other adults. Interestingly, this study also reinforced the point, made above, that friendship relations need not just be dyadic.

In early, disturbing research by Harlow (1969) and Harlow and Harlow (1965), monkeys were reared in a variety of different environments. It was found that social contact between young peer monkeys was of paramount importance in the development of social and sexual relations later on in life. In one experiment, the long term social adjustment of infant monkeys deprived of mother contact was very bleak, but, when reared with contact with other infant monkeys, they were surprisingly unaffected. Interestingly, infant monkeys deprived of contact with other monkeys from the age of 4 to 8 months, but who experienced normal mothering, were found to be less affectionate with peers and more aggressive.

These two famous studies are indicative of the possible value of early peer relations and friendships as a resource in times of stress and difficulty. Schools can also be places where children experience stress and it would be expected that having friends would help. This may be particularly true soon after entry to a new school.

Adjustment to school
The importance of friendship as a support in adjusting to school has been the subject of recent research, particularly in the US (Ladd *et al.*, 1996; Savin-Williams and Berndt, 1990). There appears to be some consensus that friendships can provide support for people faced with stressful events, and can improve children's social and academic adjustment to school. More supportive friendships can help children have more positive perceptions of school and help them behave better (Berndt and Keefe, 1992). Berndt and Keefe make the point that the success of friends in helping adjustment to school will depend very much on the quality of friendships involved. If based on mutual respect and collaboration, and if viewed positively, then they will help involvement in school, but if friendships are viewed more negatively then behaviour may become more disruptive.

Berndt (1989) makes the point that friendships do not appear to be equally supportive at all ages. They may be more significant later in the school years. With adolescence, friendships are likely to involve more intimacy, as we have seen, and friends will show more sensitivity to each other, and be able to offer more support.

Berndt (1996) found that the stability of children's friendships across school transitions was related to school adjustment (he studied the transition to junior high school). Children who had more stable friendships were more popular and more sociable, though this could just mean that better adjusted students are better able to maintain friendships. Better evidence comes from the finding that children with more supportive friendships at the beginning of seventh grade (the equivalent of Year 7 in the UK) showed increased popularity by the next Spring. This is consistent with the view that children who have close friendships on entry to school will often get to know friends of friends and so develop a positive set of relationships in the class as a whole.

However, the mere fact of forming new friendships after starting at a new school is not necessarily a sign of good adjustment. Children who quickly form new friendships may not be able to maintain old friendships. Ladd *et al.* (1996) studied younger children on entry to school. Their findings are not clear cut. They found that two features of friendship quality – validation and aid – predicted gains in perceptions of classroom peer support, and also children's perception of their own affect in school. Also, children who thought their friendships offered higher levels of aid tended to like school better as the school year progressed. So having friends who are seen to offer higher levels of personal support or aid, for example, by helping with difficult social situations, may enhance children's feelings of competence and security in school. Ladd *et al.* also noted some complications; for example, talk with friends about negative affect was associated with gains in loneliness over the school year. Higher levels of perceived exclusivity were negatively related to children's school readiness and progress (perhaps because they were more intense and possessive, and this distracted them from school work?). Further research is required on the role of friendships in school transitions. This research may be particularly important in the UK where children enter school at an early age – in England as young as just 4 years.

In this section we have concentrated on the role of friends as an emotional resource in times of stress. It might be noted that perhaps the main attraction of friendships is that they are a source of enjoyment. We enjoy being with our friends. Most pupils like breaktime more than any other part of school, and one of the main reasons they like breaktime is because they are able to meet their friends (Blatchford, 1998).

Help subsequent relationships

According to Sullivan, friendship relations between children can lay down the basis for future relationships; later relationships are generalized from earlier ones. So although new relationships are never exact copies of old ones, formative friendships can in a sense be 'templates' used in constructing future relationships (Hartup, 1992). Main features of 'chumship' in adolescence (e.g., loyalty, mutual support etc.) become translated into later relationships which involve sexual dynamics.

What do we know about the developmental significance of friendships and peer relations, and long term effects on later relationships? Parker and Asher (1987) in a widely cited review, have identified the long term consequences of peer difficulties (in terms of peer acceptance, aggressiveness, and shyness/withdrawal) on later personal adjustment (in terms of dropping out of school, criminality and psychopathology). Strongest support was for a link between peer adjustment, in terms of aggressiveness and peer acceptance, and later adjustment in terms of dropping out of school and criminality.

There are two basic models recognized in many papers on friendships, and specifically by Parker and Asher, and, with regard to friendships, by Newcomb and Bagwell (1996). In the first model, social difficulties and poor peer relations and friendship relations play a direct role in the development of maladjustment. This might be because children who are aggressive or withdrawn are disadvantaged in social situations and this leads to poor developmental outcomes. Conversely, good social experiences will reinforce social skill and friendship networks and lead to good developmental outcomes. However, a second model does not assume that peer relations directly affect developmental outcomes. Rather, underlying individual differences and behavioural/social difficulties lead to poor peer and friendship relations and hence poor developmental outcomes. So, according to this model, poor peer relations do not cause maladjustment, but are a reflection of it. Returning to Hartup's distinction between developmental 'advantages' and 'necessities', friendship relations, according to the first model are the former, and according to the second, more the latter.

Bagwell *et al.* (1994, see Newcomb and Bagwell, 1996) provide the first study to examine the relationship of friendship status and peer preference in early adolescence and later adjustment. The links they found were indirect and complex with some suggestion that existing differences reflected a propensity to maladjustment which continued through to adulthood.

To conclude this section, friendship relations may have a positive role at school. However, as Hartup (1996) has said, good evidence to support the developmental importance of friendships during childhood is not strong. Much evidence is correlational, that is, some features are related to friendships, but not necessarily causal.

Can friends be bad for you?

We end this section by considering the possible negative side to friendships. A realization that friendships may have a more negative side is related to several very high profile crimes in both the US and UK involving young friends. Hartup discusses one of these cases in his 1996 paper. Two friends opened fire on classmates in their school playground. In the UK there was the troubling case of the murder of a 2-year-old (James Bulger) by two 10-year-old friends. The combination of the young age of the culprits and the fact they were friends created a sense of unease about the reasons why it is that young people can engage in such behaviour, but also how friendships can be a driving force in deviant behaviour.

There has been recognition more recently (Hartup 1996, Newcomb and Bagwell, 1996) that one cannot consider the developmental significance of friendships without first distinguishing at least two factors: the identity of a child's friends (e.g., their personality characteristics), and the quality of friendships (Hartup, 1996).

Identity of one's friends

Friends tend to be similar to each other, and may become more similar over time (Newcomb and Bagwell, 1996). Friends may then be caring, intimate and supportive. There is some evidence that friends' influence can work positively, in that students with high-scoring friends in turn received higher scores later in the school year, even controlling for initial scores (Epstein, 1983 in Newcomb and Bagwell, 1996). But children who associate with friends whose behaviour is antisocial, antischool or delinquent may be influenced to behave in these ways.

Friendship quality

There is much recognition now that any consideration of the effect of friendships needs to consider the quality of their relations. This would be a main consideration in trying to explain how friends could commit the awful crimes cited above. A large effort by researchers has gone into devising methods for assessing friendship qualities, for example the Friendship Qualities Scale (FQS) has five dimensions: companionship, conflict, help, security and closeness (see Hartup, 1996). There is growing evidence that friendship quality is implicated in psychological adjustment, e.g., loneliness, and complex models have been evolved to show the place of friendship quality in this connection (e.g., Newcomb and Bagwell, 1996).

Ladd *et al.* (1996) found that young children were more satisfied with friendships when relationships were seen to offer higher levels of validation and exclusivity and lower levels of conflict. Also friendships characterized as high on validation and low on conflict tend to be maintained over a longer time. Berndt and Keefe (1992) argue that negative friendship relations not based on mutual respect will have negative outcomes.

There are less dramatic ways in which friendship groups may be a negative influence. Savin-Williams and Berndt (1990) point to the way that friendship groups can support rejection of children, and stereotyping, and how they can lead to insecurity, jealousy and resentment. Friendship groups can separate on the basis of gender and ethnic group (Blatchford, 1998), and this can reinforce stereotypical views on different groups.

Conclusions

We finish by examining some implications of research on friendships for schools and classroom organization. Although there are differences of opinion, it does seem clear that friendships in school are important to children and probably do play an important role in their social development. It is important for teachers to consider friendships between pupils. Indeed, it is probably the case that teachers cannot avoid affecting children's friendships, in that their style of teaching and classroom management will affect the context for relationships between children.

But this chapter makes it clear that there are no simple answers to questions about friendships in school. It is likely that decisions about seating friends together in classrooms will need to be informed by a number of factors. It is likely, for example, that friends may be good for some tasks and situations but not others. As we have seen, friends may be better on more difficult tasks. So teachers would need to consider the nature of the task and situation, and use friendship groups accordingly. We have also seen that friends tend to be similar to each other and that there may therefore be problems when friends are antisocial – they may be more aggressive and less stable. It may not therefore be advisable to put such children together, or they would need to be monitored closely by the teacher. An allied point concerns friendship quality. We have seen that friendships can differ on dimensions such as closeness, support, intimacy and constructiveness. The quality of friendships may be as important to consider as whether children are friends or not.

There has been debate over the appropriate degree of intervention in social relations between pupils. Maxwell (1990) appears to adopt a more interventionalist view: 'planning class activities based on friendship pairings or grouping' (p. 184). But some teachers deliberately set out not to do this, that is, they will seek to separate friends. At very least it would seem advisable for teachers to have as full an understanding as possible of the social relations and friendships in their class, and research suggests that adults would do well to supplement their own impressions with children's own accounts. They might even find some kind of sociometric analysis helpful.

A specific direction of work has concerned ways of helping children who have difficulties with friendship relations. One main approach has involved efforts to help individuals develop more effective social skills. The evidence that less popular children have less competence in general social skills, suggests that rejected children could be helped by programmes of social skill training. One famous approach was developed by Spivak and Shure in the 1970s (Spivak and Shure, 1974), and aimed to help children become more effective in social problem-solving, by analysing causes and generating solutions to social problems. However, it is probably over simplistic to think that difficulties faced by some children are just to do with inadequacies in their social skills repertoire. It may have much to do with the more general aims and attitudes of children toward others. As a result of social skills training, children may be able to behave appropriately, but their underlying social orientation toward others may be unaltered, for example, they may still want to dominate others, or always want others to show that they like them.

We have seen that friendships can be affected by the classroom environment. The way a teacher organizes her classroom can affect the nature of peer relationships and friendship relations. It would help for teachers to be aware of the two developmental pathways identified by Berndt and Keefe (1992); that is, those resulting from negative and positive friendship relations. It is likely that the possible negative influences are more salient to teachers and affect their decisions about classroom organization. Teachers may therefore assume that more troublesome students will adversely affect their friends if seated together. Berndt and Keefe (1992) cite Epstein

(1983): 'Many school policies are based on the suppression of peer relations in classrooms.' This strategy may avoid unnecessary trouble but is largely reactive. It may therefore weaken existing friendships and will not help children make new friends. It may also, by default, leave friendless children isolated. Berndt and Keefe's results suggest this may lead to further deterioration in friendship relations and hence a less positive view of school. This suggests the benefits of a more active involvement on the teacher's part in enhancing friendship relations in classrooms, though it is less clear what this involvement might be. Berndt and Keefe discuss the benefits of cooperative learning programmes and groups, though these are less common in Britain.

Berndt and Keefe (1992) feel that a combination of individual skills-based programmes and more general programmes directed at cooperation are likely to maximize the positive effect of friends. But even this view may not be sufficient. It may be that interventions based in classrooms will always be at best partially successful, because, as we have seen in this book, the classroom is only one school context within which children meet. Of equal importance are breaktime experiences and informal peer cultures more generally (Blatchford, 1998). There is much work that can be done within schools to encourage social skills and skills in friendship building (see Roffey et al., 1994), but friends are most likely to meet at breaktime, when their interactions are most open and sustained, and freed from adult control. Changes in classroom relations, without reference to breaktime relations, may therefore be insufficient. This also raises questions about the extent to which adults can and should affect informal relations between children, which are taken up in Chapter 5 and in Blatchford (1998).

4   Children's play

Play in many ways is the quintessential developmental activity of childhood. Play is what young children do and in some ways play is the activity that defines children as different from later developmental periods. Indeed, play is often defined as behaviours in which juveniles engage: if juveniles do it, it must be play. Additionally, most theories of play assume that it is beneficial, though there is widespread debate on the magnitude of the benefits and when during development they occur. Despite these considerations on the magnitude and location of the benefits of play, it is assumed that it does indeed have benefits. Consequently, observations of children at play provide the investigator with insight into child competence in a number of areas (e.g., communication skills, role taking, cooperation, motor coordination). As noted in the first chapter, however, play can be viewed as an imperfect version of mature behaviours that must be learned. The notion that play is used in the assembly of skills and is disassembled when the skill is mastered has been labelled the 'scaffolding' view of play (Bateson, 1981) and is consistent with the theories of Piaget and Vygotsky. For example, the role of pretend play would be an aid to children's learning adult societal roles.

On the other hand, when play is considered to be important to the niche of childhood and not an imperfect version of adult behaviour it is considered 'metamorphic' (Bateson, 1981). For example, pretend play during childhood relates to a child's sense of potency and self efficacy during a period when he/she is often confronted with his inability to do things. This confidence motivates children to persevere at various tasks.

Second, play can be used as an instructional mode. Again, the distinction between scaffolding v. metamorphic views of play is crucial to maintain. Play is often used in the former sense as a way of teaching skills and concepts. For example, pretend play is often used as a way in which to teach reading and writing (Christie, 1991; Pellegrini and Galda, 1993). Alternatively, play can be encouraged in school as a way in which children gain confidence and skill with their bodies and their minds.

In this chapter children's play is examined in terms of the forms it takes in school.

What is play?

Play is most generally defined in terms of it serving no immediate purpose. For example, an activity is considered play if it is: not serious, an exaggerated version of its functional equivalent, or where means of an activity are stressed over the ends. In this section, we explore definitions of play suggested by Rubin *et al.* (1983). They define play along three dimensions: as psychological disposition, according to contexts that elicit playful behaviours, and as observable behaviour. These dimensions are summarized in Table 4.1.

Play as disposition

The six dispositional criteria are: intrinsic motivation, attention to means, the 'What can I do with this' disposition, non-literal behaviours, flexibility and active engagement. The intrinsic motivation criterion for play suggests that children play because they want to, not because of appetite drives, social demands, or rewards external to the play act *per se*. Vygotsky's theory provides some guidance as to what motivates children to play: the sense of mastery and potency in much of children's play, especially fantasy play, is a motivator.

It is difficult to observe intrinsic motivation, however, and this may be partially responsible for the fact that neither children nor adults use it as a criterion to differentiate play from non-play (Smith and Vollstedt, 1985).

Attention to means is related to intrinsic motivation to the extent that the play behaviours are self-imposed and free from external sanctions; children are more concerned with the playful acts themselves than with the outcomes of those acts. To use an adult-oriented example here, swimming

Table 4.1 Dimensions of play

1. Play as disposition
   a. intrinsic motivation
   b. attention to means
   c. 'What can I do with it?'
   d. non-literal
   e. flexibility
   f. active engagement

2. Play as context
   a. familiar
   b. free choice
   c. stress free

3. Play as observable behaviour
   a. functional
   b. symbolic
   c. games-with-rules

would be playful if the adult enjoyed the act of swimming. It would be less playful if it were done primarily to stay slim. The means over ends criterion, however, does present an interesting problem: how can play simultaneously serve important functions but not be concerned with ends, or function? It may be that play serves no immediate function but does serve a function, deferred until adulthood.

The 'What can I do with it?' disposition is prevalent. As such, play is person-directed, where exploration is stimulus-directed. Children must explore stimuli before they can play with them. That is, in order to play with something, we must first be familiar with the stimuli. Exploration serves this familiarization function. This path from exploration to play is evidenced both ontogenetically and microgenetically. Ontogenetically (or in terms of development across all human children), infants up to about 7½ months explore objects. After that time, play accounts for increasing proportions of time, until, at about 15 months, infants spend close to equal time in exploration and play. Thereafter, however, play displaces explorations (Belsky and Most, 1981).

Microgenetically (or in terms of development within a specific task), we find that when presented with a new or novel toy or tasks, children explore that stimulus before they play with it (Rubin *et al.*, 1983). From an assessment perspective this continuum is relevant: it is imperative that children are familiar with toys before we assess their ability to play with them (Rubin *et al.*, 1983). Very often the toys we use in assessment contexts are unfamiliar to certain groups of children. So as not to artificially suppress children's exhibition of competence we should take care to use familiar stimuli.

Non-literal behaviours suggest that children use an 'as if' disposition to simulate, or represent, other persons, activities, or objects in play. This criterion limits play to acts of pretence, or make believe. However, pretence play might be considered the paradigmatic example of play in that children and adults alike use it as a defining attribute of play (Smith and Vollstedt, 1985).

The flexibility criterion differentiates play from games with externally defined rules. Play is ruled governed but the rules are constructed within the play event by players and the rules are subject to change during play episodes. For example, in playing house children may have rules about the ways in which mothers and fathers behave. These rules, however, are defined by the children during play and are subject to change. Children often disagree about rules during play and renegotiate the rules. Games with rules, like checkers, on the other hand, have permanent, predetermined rules.

Play is characterized by children's active engagement with objects and other players. Players themselves choose the activities they participate in and then define the nature of their interaction in that activity. That is, they are not passive participants in activities to the extent that they redefine objects and roles. They do not play with these stimuli in ways specified by predetermined rules.

These play criteria should be used to categorize the degree to which children's activities are playful. Thus, behaviours meeting three criteria would be more playful than those meeting one or two (Krasnor and Pepler, 1980). As a result, play can be categorized as 'more or less play' not dichotomously as 'play or not play.' Behaviours meeting all criteria might be categorized as 'pure play,' whereas behaviours with fewer components are 'less purely play' (Krasnor and Pepler, 1980). Simply put, acts should not be categorized as 'play' or 'not play'; they should be rated along a continuum from 'pure play' to 'non-play.'

Play as context

Play can also be defined according to contexts that typically evoke playful behaviour (Rubin *et al.*, 1983). While this set of criteria confounds the situations in which play is observed with the behaviours themselves, context can be useful in determining if a behaviour is playful or not. For example, a behaviour observed on a playground is more likely to be play than one in a school study hall. Such 'relational' criteria in defining play (Martin and Bateson, 1988) are, however, limited. Obviously, not everything on the playground is play; it might be aggression, for example. Similarly, when young children are interacting with peers, compared to adults, it is often assumed that the interaction is play. While this may not always be the case, it frequently is.

Relation criteria can be useful in determining those dimensions of the contexts which support play. Familiar peers and play props that actively engage children are usually present in play-eliciting contexts. As was noted in the section on play as disposition, children must explore, or become familiar, with stimuli before they play with them. Further, children in play-eliciting contexts often are free to choose the activities in which they engage. Thus, adult intervention in play-eliciting contexts is minimal. If children are to engage actively with peers and materials they must be free from stress. Stress can be caused by hunger, fatigue, illness and the presence of unfriendly adults and/or peers.

In short, play occurs in safe, comfortable contexts. For this reason, the presence of play can be used as a gauge of the quality of an environment. For example, some guidelines for care of animals in laboratories stipulate the occurrence of play in the animals as an indicator of a quality environment. Quality environments are those where children exhibit playful behaviours. Low quality environments inhibit play.

Play as observable behaviour

The behaviours comprising this definition are based on Piaget's (1962) observations of children's play. The observable categories of play according to this model are practice or functional play, symbolic play and games-with-rules. Research has documented these play categories as hierarchic (Pellegrini, 1980; Rubin and Maioni, 1975). That is, they occur in this specified order. Indeed, these categories correspond to Piaget's sensori-motor, preoperational and concrete operational forms of intelligence, respectively.

In this model of play as observable behaviour, Piaget (1962) conceived of play primarily as assimilation; that is, in play, children incorporate stimuli into existent cognitive schema with minimal changes to those schema. Play behaviours are immature forms of their adult variants. Play helps children, through consolidation and practice, to move toward operational intelligence. As such, play, as conceptualized by Piaget, does not lead development because children are minimally accommodating to external stimuli during play; play serves a consolidating role.

In functional play, children detach motor behaviours from the contexts in which they were developed by way of combinations, repetitions and variations of these behaviours (e.g., reaching for and grasping of different objects). In symbolic play, children practice using representational media (e.g., gestures or words) to designate real events and/or persons. They are exercising their semiotic, or representational, skills in symbolic play. With games-with-rules, children practice obeying externally imposed rules. Such subordination to external rules assumes operational thought because children must subordinate their behaviour to abstract, externally imposed, rules.

Play across the period of childhood

In this section we analyze in more depth those forms of play which are most common during the period of childhood: symbolic play and physically vigorous play.

Symbolic play

Symbolic, or pretend, play is defined as non-literal play, where one thing represents something else. Pretend, as noted above, can be either social or solitary and it begins during the second year of life, often in the context of parent–child play. The play of securely, compared to insecurely, attached children with mother is more sophisticated. This basis in adult play may provide the base from which children play with peers. At around 3 years, children are capable of sustaining pretend play with peers (Garvey, 1977). Pretend peaks during the late pre-school period, and then declines. It accounts for about a third of children's free behaviour at 5 years of age, though girls engage in pretence, particularly play following domestic themes, more frequently and at more sophisticated levels than boys (Rubin *et al.*, 1983).

More specifically, in pretend play, children have one thing *represent* another thing. For example, a broom can represent a horse. These representations often are part of a larger play theme enactment. For example, using a broom to represent a horse might be part of enacting a cowboy episode.

The ways in which children represent objects in play can be classified along two dimensions: object and ideational transformations. These two dimensions indicate the extent to which children's symbolic play transformations are dependent on objects (object transformations) or independent of objects (ideational transformations). For example, an object transformation might involve a child holding a baby doll and singing to it. An ideational transformation, on the other hand, might involve a child cradling an invisible baby in her/his arms and singing to it; no object is present. By 3 years of age children are adept at using ideation transformations in their play. McLoyd's (1980) categorization of object and ideational transformations, provides some concrete examples of the dimensions of these categories.

Factors affecting symbolic play

As noted above, girls, compared to boys, are more competent at pretend play, as are securely attached, compared to insecurely attached, children. At a more macrosystem level, we find that factors such as the value placed on play by society and its institutions (e.g., school boards) has an obvious effect. Play is more frequent and more sophisticated in those settings where it is valued.

At the level of culture, we find few differences between the play of African American and European American children. Where differences do exist, they are often due to the unfamiliarity of the setting and/or props and when children are given opportunities to become familiar, differences are minimized (McLoyd, 1982). At a more micro-level, the props that children play with affect the extent to which they will use object/ideational transformations and the level of theme integration. Generally, children's play follows the themes suggested by the toys with which they are playing. However, with props which do not have a clear definition, or functionally ambiguous props, for example, pipe cleaners or Styrofoam shapes, pre-schoolers use more ideational than object transformation (Pellegrini, 1987a). The reason is straightforward. The props have no explicit function so children do not depend on them for their make-believe play. Functionally explicit props (e.g., dolls), on the other hand, tend to elicit more sustained fantasy themes (Pellegrini, 1987a). It may be that pre-schoolers' limited cognitive resources result in their inability to transfer an ambiguous prop (e.g., verbally re-define it) *and* weave that prop into a complex theme. With explicit props, the first step is done for them to the extent that the props do not need to be re-defined.

Outcomes of pretend play

Numerous benefits have been associated with pretend play. As noted above, many theories of play predict deferred, not immediate benefits; however, most of the studies have only examined benefits during childhood. Further, many of the positive benefits associated with pretend play, such as increased creativity and more creative solutions to problems were due to experimenter bias, not play (Smith, 1988). There is evidence, however, that pre-school children's use of abstract play transformations relates to their subsequent ability to write individual words (Pellegrini and Galda, 1993). Both individual word writing and symbolic representation are examples of first order symbolization (Vygotsky, 1978) where symbols represent concrete entities. Further, during social pretend play, children talk about cognitive and linguistic processes, e.g., 'Doctors can't say that'. This ability to talk about language and thought is evidence of children's metacognitive and metalinguistic abilities, which, in turn, are related to reading.

Physical activity play

As children move through primary school they are given fewer opportunities to play in classrooms. What opportunities they are given are typically in the form of recess on the playground (Pellegrini and Smith, 1998). Play opportunities beyond pre-school are limited, usually, because educators think that they interfere with the primary business of schooling, that is, learning the 3 Rs. As we noted earlier, this is a limited view of schooling in that even the current President of the USA is now stressing the role of social skills in schools. Because of the limited opportunities for play in classrooms, play at recess across the school years may provide some of the few opportunities youngsters have to interact with peers. These opportunities are very important in children's social competence, as discussed in Chapter 2.

In this section we will describe the forms of play that children exhibit on the playground during recess as well as examining factors which affect them. Finally, we will note some of the benefits associated with those forms of play.

While pre-school and kindergarten children's play can be captured rather well using the four-level scheme of functional, constructive, dramatic and games, it does not account for most of what elementary school children do when they play. Play for this group of children typically occurs outdoors at recess. A significant portion of that play, especially for boys, is physically vigorous and can take the form of chase, rough-and-tumble play (R&T), and games. We will suggest that R&T is the form of play that acts as a bridge between social pretend and games with rules.

Gross motor play is a basic form of physical activity and includes, chasing, running, jumping, swinging, etc. For children in the late pre-school and early primary school periods, this form of behaviour accounts for 15 to 20 per cent of their free play behaviour (McGrew, 1972a; Smith and Connolly, 1980).

Also, about this time, play is becoming much more social. R&T is that form of physical activity play which has social dimensions. The term R&T was first used in behavioural science by Harlow (1962; Harlow and Harlow, 1962) to describe the playful, quasi-antagonistic behaviours of rhesus monkeys. Since that time a group led by Blurton Jones (1972b, 1976) and P. K. Smith (Smith and Connolly, 1980) have provided extensive behaviour/structural descriptions of the category. R&T is characterized by the following behaviours: running, jumping, fleeing, wrestling, and open hand beating. Structurally, R&T involves children engaging in reciprocal role taking (Fagen, 1981; Humphreys and Smith, 1984). For example, in games of chase, children typically alternate between the chaser and chased and, in play fighting, aggressor and victim roles are alternated. Regarding the functional or consequential criterion, children remain together at the conclusion of R&T bouts (Humphreys and Smith, 1987), often engaging in other forms of social play like cooperative games (Pellegrini, 1988). Ecologically, R&T tends to occur out-of-doors, on soft, grassy surfaces (Humphreys and Smith, 1984; Pellegrini, 1989a). Importantly, R&T and aggression are distinct behaviours for most children; the exception being aggressive boys (Pellegrini, 1988).

Like other forms of play, with age R&T follows in inverted U-development function: accounting for 5 per cent of pre-school free play behaviour, increasing to around 10–13 per cent at 7 years of age and declining to about 5 per cent again for 11-year-olds (Humphreys and Smith, 1984). Boys engage in R&T more frequently than girls (e.g., Pellegrini, 1989a; Whiting and Edwards, 1973).

R&T is a controversial category because of its frequent confusion with aggression. Indeed, Brian Sutton-Smith (1988) has shown how adults, including child psychologists, educational psychologists and playground supervisors, often confuse the two categories. Close examination, however, illustrates clear distinctions between R&T and aggression. Behaviourally, aggression is composed of the following behaviours (which are independent of R&T in most children): fixating, frowning, hitting (with a closed hand), pushing, take-and-grabbing. These behaviours, unlike play, are stable through childhood (Olweus, 1979). Structurally, aggression is characterized by unilateral, not reciprocal roles: aggressors remain aggressors and victims, victims. Further, victims often try to separate themselves from aggressors after an aggressive behaviour. However, some work with non-human primates (de Waal, 1985) suggests that in many cases there is reconciliation after aggressive acts; that is, one participant (often the aggressor) approaches the victim after the aggressive act. It would be interesting to examine the degree to which aggressor or target initiate the reconciliation as well as the time lapse after the act.

Ecologically, aggression tends to occur in the context of property disputes, especially for pre-school children (Humphreys and Smith, 1984). Unlike R&T, no specific playground location seems to elicit aggression (Pellegrini, 1989a). Like R&T, boys, more than girls, tend to exhibit aggressive behaviours.

Another reason for the controversial nature of R&T lies in the different types of children who engage in it. Research suggests that sociometrically defined popular and rejected elementary school children engage in R&T that is qualitatively different and serves different functions for these two groups of children (Pellegrini, 1988, 1989b). Whereas for popular children R&T leads directly into games and continued cooperation, for rejected children it leads to aggression.

During the period of adolescence, frequency of R&T declines (Pellegrini, 1995a). Most boys spend their free time on the playground in more sedentary activities, often in groups which include both boys and girls. These adolescents, it seems, are becoming interested in heterosexual relationships. Those adolescent boys who still engage in R&T tend not to spend their time in groups which are integrated with boys and girls together. Boys who initiate R&T typically do it as a way in which to bully a weaker student and it typically ends with the tougher boys hurting the weaker boy. In short, R&T during adolescence, unlike childhood, is an aggressive category.

To conclude this section, we can state that R&T and aggression may be distinct categories *only* for popular children; they seem to be inter-related for rejected children and for adolescents. This finding, in addition to the confusion of R&T and aggression are probably responsible for R&T being considered an antisocial behaviour.

Factors affecting physical activity play

As we noted above, boys' play is more vigorous than girls'. Further, it tends to occur in spacious areas, like playgrounds and on soft surfaces, like grass. If we look at the influence of school schedules, we also find that children's play on the playground is more vigorous after they have been confined to sedentary work for longer, compared to shorter, periods of time (Pellegrini *et al.*, 1995a; Smith and Hagan, 1980).

Outcomes of physical activity play

We begin at the most general level. Regarding chase and gross motor forms of play, it is probably the case that these forms of activity are related to children's muscle and skeletal growth. The movements associated with these forms of exercise increase muscle strength and differentiation and bone density (Pellegrini and Smith, 1998).

Vigorous play breaks, or recesses, in the course of the school day also have implications for classroom learning. One of us found that breaks from school work, not physical play *per se*, increased children's attention to seat work (Pellegrini *et al.*, 1995a). This is consistent with work in Japanese schools, which has shown that students' performance in school work can be maximized if they are given frequent breaks (every 50–60 minutes) during the course of the school day.

The fact that specific groups of children assign different meaning to R&T behaviours has implications for possible functions of R&T. Functional examinations of play have generally been concerned with motor, cognitive, or social skills training (Martin and Caro, 1985). We will address only the possibility of R&T serving a social skills training function. We can examine the extent to which it serves an antisocial, aggressive function or a pro-social function by examining the probability of aggressive or cooperative acts, respectively, immediately following R&T bouts. For popular children, R&T moved into cooperative games at a greater than chance probability. For rejected children, on the other hand, it went to aggression in 1:4 (Pellegrini, 1988).

The relation between R&T and social problem-solving was also examined. In the play context, because of its safe, non-exploitative nature, children experiment with different social roles. Consequently, individual social routines and strategies get broken down, re-combined, and generalized. Research supports this claim, but only for popular, not rejected, children (Pellegrini, 1988, 1989a). The relation between R&T and social problem-solving for popular children may have been due to their exchanging R&T roles, such as offender/defender. Such exchange is one way of preventing playmates' boredom and thus ensures sustained play (Aldis, 1975). Further, role reversals provide children, usually those in submissive roles, with opportunities to rest during R&T. These rest periods may be another strategy to ensure sustained play. Using these varied strategies to sustain play is similar to what children were asked to do on the social problem-solving tasks: provide a variety of ways to initiate and sustain play.

It has also been suggested by Parke and colleagues (Parke *et al.*, 1992) that R&T serves the purpose of helping children to learn to encode and decode emotions. They argue that when children (especially boys) engage in rough play with a parent (usually father) they learn to read and encode facial signals denoting social intent, such as play. Children consequentially use these same skills, later, with their peers, contributing to their social competence.

The physical training benefits of physical play are clear-cut. By physical training we mean improvement in physical endurance and strength through cardiovascular functionings, muscle development, and bone reshaping. Through the period of childhood (and into adulthood) vigorous physical exercise has a physical training function. It is estimated that in order to significantly improve children's physical endurance and strength they should engage in vigorous activity for an hour a day, five days a week. This can be accomplished through organized physical education or by providing children with opportunities for free play in spacious areas. This level of exercise can be fulfilled for pre-school and primary school children, we suggest (see Pellegrini and Smith, 1998), by providing opportunities for play time in school and in the playground. After prolonged sedentary periods, children engage in higher levels of physical activity (Pellegrini *et al.*, 1995a).

Conclusion

In this chapter we suggested that children's play is an important part of childhood and one that is vital to their school experience. We recommend caution, however, about the role of play in development. Specifically, we must be cautious of the 'play ethos' (Smith, 1988); that is, the notion that play is all good. We know that play is related to something for some people. We should proceed with caution. Indeed, some of the problems in this area, particularly as they are applied to education, are the results of over simplifying complex problems, like the role of play in development and education.

This voice of caution should be applied to those areas where our knowledge base is still limited. In other areas, such as the role of breaktime, we have adequate knowledge to guide policy at a beginning level. That is, we know that breaktime improves children's attention to their classroom work. We now must expand our understanding of the ways in which other aspects of play generally, and breaktime more specifically, relate to children's social and educational outcomes. In the next chapter we address breaktime in more depth.

5 Breaktime in school

The school breaktime, or recess period, as it is known in Britain and North America respectively, is present in most primary schools in America and Britain and occupies an appreciable proportion of the time in the school day. Yet, surprisingly, with the exception of a few recent studies (Blatchford, 1998; Pellegrini, 1995b, Pellegrini and Smith, 1998), we know very little about it. We will argue that recess is an important part of children's experience in school, relating to traditional school outcome measures and, more broadly, to children's social experience and competence. First, we define what we mean by recess. Next, child-level and school-level variables that affect children's playground behaviour during recess will be discussed. Lastly, the educational and social developmental implications of recess will be considered.

What is recess?

School recess, playtime, or breaktime (the terms are interchangeable) is a recreational break period for children, typically outdoors and typically compulsory. Generally, children in schools from pre-school through the elementary or primary school stages have recess as a scheduled part of their day. Recess periods in North America tend not to exist in schools for adolescents, such as secondary schools. Organized sport and physical education is often used instead of recess (Miracle, 1987). In Britain, unusually, breaktime occurs right through infant school and secondary school stages.

The number and duration of recess periods vary greatly, especially in North America. Number and length of breaktimes in British schools are fairly consistent, though, as we shall see, presently undergoing change. In many British primary schools, children have two and sometimes three outdoor play periods per day. In North America, recess, too, is being scrutinized and the number of recess periods per day, the duration of the period(s), and supervisory policy for recess periods typically varies greatly from one school to another. In American elementary schools, the length of the period and its placement in the school day also varies by individual school. Additionally, the nature of supervision varies widely. In some schools teachers are expected to supervise during recess periods while in others, even schools within the same city/school district, this task is often relegated to para-professionals, or to other adults, with little or no training for the task. In England, supervision at primary level varies between morning and lunchtime breaks; in the former teachers usually supervise on a rota basis, while during the long lunchbreak supervision is now predominantly in the hands of supervisors, who, as in the US, are often untrained.

If breaktime takes up a sizeable part of the school day, the playground can also occupy a large part of the school grounds. School buildings can be dwarfed by surrounding asphalt and grass, though again there can be considerable (and seemingly arbitrary) variation in the size of school playgrounds (or, more properly, school grounds).

In short, recess is a main part of school life for most primary school children. Children's experiences at breaktime are likely to vary widely from school to school, yet we know very little, empirically, about it. Further, there do not appear to be explicit policies, at the school, local or national level, regarding recess. The closest thing that resembles such a policy might be school or local rules regarding aggression and bullying which may occur on the playground. Where policy is being made, as in the many cases of schools removing or limiting children's recess periods, decisions are being made independent of the data that do exist on the subject.

Given this diversity, an important first step, that still needs to be taken, is a description of the various configurations that recess takes. This could be accomplished using questionnaire methodology whereby schools would describe the number and duration of the recess periods, as well as any other policy, formal or informal, towards recess. In this way a classification system of recess configurations could be generated. Case studies of schools representative of specific recess configurations could provide information on the relations between recess configurations and children's classroom and playground behaviour.

This information, though important, is not collected nationally by government agencies. There have not been international studies that would enable us to compare the situation in different countries. We do have, though, some questionnaire data on recess configurations in both the USA and in England. In 1989, in America, the National Association of Elementary School Principals conducted a mail survey of state superintendents of education in all 50 states and the District of Columbia (see Pellegrini, 1995b for a summary of these data); 47 of the 51 responded. Results indicated that 90 per cent of the states had recess in some form. In 96 per cent of the cases, there were two recess periods daily and the period lasted between 15–20 minutes (in 75 per cent of the cases). About half had structured recess periods and the other half had unstructured periods. Children were supervised most frequently by their own teachers (50 per cent) and less frequently by teacher aids (36 per cent).

In the more recent and more exhaustive national survey of breaktimes in England, Blatchford and Sumpner (1998) chose a random sample of 1 in

10 of all primary and secondary schools in England. Altogether, question-naires were received back from just over 60 per cent – representing 6 per cent of all schools in the country (over 1500). It was found that the total average time at breaktime, that is, the total time at morning and afternoon breaks and lunchtime was 93 minutes at the infant stage (5–7 years), 83 minutes at the junior stage (7–11 years) and 77 minutes at the secondary stage (11–16 years). This amounts to around 24 per cent, 21 per cent and 18 per cent of the school day for the infant, junior and secondary stages respectively. The youngest children in school therefore have the longest breaktimes.

The role of recess in schools has, however, been recently questioned (Blatchford, 1998; Pellegrini, 1995b, Sutton-Smith, 1990). Embedded in the larger context of the 'effective education' debate teachers and parents have been questioning the role of recess in the school day (e.g., *New York Times*, 8 January 1989). Sides in a pro-recess and anti-recess debate have been drawn. Two main reasons are normally addressed by those opposed to recess (see also Blatchford, 1998 and Pellegrini and Smith, 1998). First, it is argued by the anti's that recess detracts from instructional time in an already crowded and long school day. Further, recess periods, often arbitrarily placed in the school schedule, could disrupt children's sustained work patterns. The second common anti-recess argument commonly advanced is that recess encourages aggression and antisocial behaviour on the playground. Connected to this, there is concern that the quality of outside play and traditional games are in decline (Blatchford, 1989).

Blatchford and Sumpner (1998), in their national survey, found that these concerns had led to signs of change in the duration and frequency of breaktimes. More than one half of the primary (56 per cent) and slightly less than half of the secondary schools (44 per cent) said there had been changes over the past five years (that is, from 1990/1 to 1995/6 school years). The main change was a reduction in the length of lunchbreak. Around a third of schools at junior and secondary level (38 per cent and 35 per cent) and a quarter at infant school level (26 per cent) had reduced the length of the lunchbreak. The other main change over the past five years was the tendency to have abolished the afternoon break. This was most apparent at the junior school stage where more than 1 in 4 schools (27 per cent) had done so; at infant and secondary level the figures were 12 per cent and 14 per cent respectively. These changes were despite an increase in the length of the school day over the same time period. The reasons given for changes were to increase teaching time and to help reduce problems of behaviour.

Both of these concerns are understandable, but it is important to examine them critically. As we shall argue below and in other chapters, there is concern that reductions in breaktime will also mean reductions in time spent in relatively 'open' settings, that may in turn be of value to children, for example, in terms of social, physical and cognitive criteria. There is still much that is unclear and contradictory. For instance, with regard to distraction from instructional time, some educators view recess as providing opportunity to vent 'excess energy', while others feel it will excite children to such high levels that subsequent attention to class work is difficult. While systematic data on this issue, as on most aspects of recess, are limited, what data do exist suggest that recess probably increases, rather than decreases, children's classroom performance. Blatchford (1989) provides anecdotal evidence from British teachers and head teachers which *both* supports and detracts from this argument. Some teachers suggest that providing recess gives children a much needed break from their work while others say it is disruptive; task oriented children are forced to leave their work and return distracted. Clearly, the variation in recess forms discussed above may be responsible for this state of confusion. Below, we will discuss specifically the role of recess in children's classroom attention.

Regarding aggression, suffice it to say that aggression on elementary (Pellegrini, 1988) and middle school (Pellegrini, 1992a) playgrounds is very uncommon, accounting for less than 2 per cent or 3 per cent of children's total behaviour. With this said, we should also note that aggression does occur on the playground but much of it is perpetrated by a very few number of children (i.e., bullies) and that with proper supervision occurrence of aggression drops dramatically (Olweus, 1993a and b).

The pro-recess arguments are almost mirror images of the anti's arguments. (See Sutton-Smith, 1987, 1990, for an alternative view.) Generally, reasons given for having recess are some folk variant of surplus energy theory whereby children need recess so as to 'blow off steam'; this reasoning is used by parents and educators in Australia (Evans, 1989; Evans and Pellegrini, 1997), Britain (Blatchford, 1989), and America (Parrott, 1975; Pellegrini, 1989a). Blatchford and Sumpner (1998) found in their survey that school staff named release of energy (or 'letting off steam'), and having a break from classroom activities, as two of the main values of breaktime for pupils. The argument goes something like this: as children sit for prolonged periods of time they accumulate surplus energy; physical activity in recess is necessary to 'blow off', or use up, the energy so that they can then concentrate on the more sedentary tasks of the classroom. The evidence given for this surplus energy theory, while scientifically questionable (Smith and Hagan, 1980, though see Burghardt, 1988 for a counter argument) typically involves examples of children fidgeting in their seats and, generally, showing lower levels of attention as a function of confinement time.

The empirical record for these issues is sparse indeed, especially in relation to the level of debate and the ubiquity of recess. In what follows, empirical research that bears on the role of recess in schools will be reviewed. First, we will review research which has examined variables that affect children's behaviour on the playground at recess; considering both child-level variables (i.e., gender and preference for outdoors, temperament and age) and then school level variables (i.e., recess timing). While recognizing that a dichotomy between the child-level and school-level variables is artificial, they are presented separately for reasons of clarity. An important school-level variable, playground design, will not be discussed because it has been reviewed elsewhere (Pellegrini, 1987a and b). Further, we will not discuss the content of children's playground behaviour *per se* in that this is a vast literature and clearly beyond the scope of one article or indeed any one book. The interested reader is referred to the works in this area by the Opies (Opie and Opie, 1959, 1969, 1985), Eifermann (1970, 1971, 1978, 1979), Sutton-Smith (1959, 1971, 1981, 1986), Block (1987), and King (1979, 1987). The omission of the content of playground behaviour should in no way be interpreted as our assuming that these behaviours are merely expressive and not formative. Indeed, a large and controversial literature exists on both the definition of playground/play behaviours (King, 1979, 1987; Miracle, 1987; Smith and Vollstedt, 1985; Smith *et al.*, 1985) and their possible functions (e.g., for reviews of this issue see: Blatchford, 1998; Block, 1987; Christie and Johnsen, 1983, 1987; Martin and Caro, 1985; Pellegrini, 1985; Pellegrini and Smith, 1998; Smith, 1982; Sutton-Smith, 1975, 1982). Like the vast majority of reviews in this area, limits are drawn for reasons of space.

Child variables affecting recess behaviour

Gender and indoor or outdoor preference

That boys are more physically active than girls is well documented (Eaton and Enns, 1986). This difference, often discussed in terms of temperament, is observed from infancy through childhood, though older children are noticeably less active (Eaton and Yu, 1989). Further, higher levels of physical activity are elicited in environments of low, compared to high, spatial density (Smith and Connolly, 1980). That is, children are more active in spacious, compared to restricted, environments. These two findings could be responsible for the fact that, given free choice, boys, more than girls, prefer to go outdoors for recess. Where free choice does not exist, girls, when asked, would rather stay in than go out; boys, on the other hand, prefer to go out (Finnan, 1982; Lever, 1976). Blatchford *et al.*, (1990) found that about twice as many girls as boys at 11 years would have preferred to stay in at recess. This gender related preference for outdoor play has been documented with behavioural observations in pre-schools (Harper and Sanders, 1975), in elementary school (Finnan, 1982), and in middle schools (Pellegrini, 1992a) and with interviews during the primary school years (Blatchford, 1989). Interestingly, Blatchford (1998) found that by

16 years the gender preference for going out at breaktime had disappeared, though girls still preferred to stay in to do work or something else (by 16 years going out at recess was not so likely to be compulsory).

Boys' preference for outdoor play is often explained in terms of their biological predisposition, or temperament, for high levels of activity (Harper and Sanders, 1975; Meaney et al., 1985). This line of reasoning would lead to the hypothesis that boys, more than girls, should be more active both on the playground and in the classroom. Boys' activity level, according to this hypothesis, should be of higher intensity and longer duration than the activity levels of girls. Behavioural observations of boys' playground behaviour are consistent with this hypothesis; for example, boys from the pre-school period through early adolescence engage in more vigorous physical activity, such as rough-and-tumble play and other forms of vigorous play, than do girls (Finnan, 1982; Humphreys and Smith, 1984; Maccoby and Jacklin, 1987; Pellegrini, 1989a, 1992a). There appear to be differences between boys and girls in physical activity in classrooms; boys are considered by their teachers as being more distractable and less attentive than girls (Serbin et al., 1990).

There are alternative, socialization, explanations for these gender-related differences (Birns and Sternglanz, 1983). For example, girls may prefer indoor to outdoor play space because they are less likely to be disturbed there. That is, when boys and girls are on the playground together, boys, because of their high levels of activity and their games, may intrude into girls' play space. Indeed, Maccoby and Jacklin (1987) proffer this as a reason for pre-schoolers' gender segregation. Anecdotal evidence presented by Blatchford (1989) suggests that girls and young children dislike outdoor play because boys, particularly older boys, invade their space with balls and charging bodies. An interesting test of this hypothesis would be to examine outdoor preference in an all girl school with age segregated recess periods, where such intrusions do not exist; it would be predicted that girls' choice of outdoor play would increase. Restrictions on boys' vigorous games, like football, should also have this effect. There are alternate explanations for gender differences in classroom behaviour: child gender differences are typically confounded by the gender of the teachers, who are often female. It is quite possible that female teachers react differently to active behaviour in boys and girls. Relatedly, we may also have cause for concern with gender-related bias of behavioural observers (Liss, 1983). That boys are typically considered to be more active than girls may bias observers in their ratings of activity. An obvious check on such bias would be through the use of mechanical activity recorders, like actometers (to be discussed later).

Thus, we have reasonably good data that boys, more than girls, prefer outdoor play because of their propensity for physical activity. Preference for physical activity often varies also as a function of children's temperament and age. Rather than dichotomizing gender differences in terms of biological *or* socialization origins, we, like Maccoby and Jacklin (1987), suggest that gender differences are the result of transactions between biology and socialization.

The role of temperament in children's recess behaviour

Temperament is a construct used to describe relatively stable individual differences in children that have an early origin and a biological component. Children's physical activity, as noted above, has often been treated as a dimension of temperament and can be measured behaviourally, using direct observations or mechanical recorders, or by parent and teacher completed checklists. Behavioural observations obviously are both expensive and time consuming. By way of remedy, Eaton and Yu (1989) have found that teachers' rank orderings of children in terms of their motoric activity correlates very well ($r = .69$) with motion recorder measures.

To our knowledge, no empirical research has been conducted on the relation between children's temperament and their recess behaviour, *per se*. Clearly such research is needed. For example, it may be that children who are temperamentally very active have a greater 'need' for recess than less active children. We do know that negative associations exist between children's activity level and self-direction in classrooms (See Martin, 1988, for a summary of temperament and classroom research). Further, and as will be discussed in depth below, we know that the longer children sit in classrooms the less attentive they become; these same inattentive children are also active on the playground at recess (Pellegrini and Huberty, 1993). It may be that making a provision for recess after specific periods of seat work would increase the attention of active children.

Age factors

Age is another, related, child-level moderator variable to the extent that physical activity seems to decline during the elementary school years (Eaton and Yu, 1989). Consequently, children's 'need' for outdoor recess may decline with age. The finding that children, as they move through adolescence, less frequently choose to play outdoors (Pellegrini, 1992a) supports this proposition. Further, gender and age seem to have interactive effects on physical activity observed on the playground at recess. Gender differences for British pre-school children's vigorous behaviour on the playground were not observed by Smith and Hagan (1980) whereas there were significant gender differences observed elsewhere in a sample of American 9-year-old school children. Multi-age studies, preferably longitudinal studies, where moderator variables, like temperament and gender, can be tracked across childhood will be necessary to address this age and gender interaction more thoroughly.

Changes with age in breaktime activities

As said above, in England children experience recess right through their school careers, that is, through primary and secondary stages, and the Institute of Education longitudinal study provided an opportunity to examine changes in breaktime activities over a longer time frame than is usual. Data came from individual interviews with the same pupils at 7, 11 and 16 years (see Blatchford, 1998, for discussion of the respective merits of observation and self report data on breaktime activities). Children were asked in detail about activities during their last lunch and morning breaks. Results here refer to the dinner time break (data on the morning breaktime gave a similar picture). Main analyses compared activities at 11 with those at 16 years. Results and methods are described in full in Blatchford (1996, 1998). Here we summarize main trends.

Pupils' first three answers at 11 years were coded and classified using a scheme based on the work of the Opies (1969) and adapted by Blatchford *et al.* (1990). Activities at 11 years were dominated by active games. The most popular were ball games and chasing games, and the most popular game of all was football (soccer); this was played by boys more than girls (84 per cent of boys, 36 per cent of girls). Other ball games such as netball, basketball, cricket were played by a third of children. Chasing games were defined in the same way as the Opies, that is, games in which a player tries to touch others who are running freely in a prescribed area. The most common chasing game by far was the basic game of 'it', 'had' or 'he' (46 per cent of children). Seeking games (17 per cent), catching games (16 per cent), racing games (12 per cent) and skipping games (9 per cent with a rope, 6 per cent with elastic) were also noted. In response to a separate question, concerning what else they did at breaktime, talking to friends (48 per cent), walking and hanging around (32 per cent) and just sitting down (28 per cent) were the most commonly cited activities.

At 16 years, different activities were described by the pupils and therefore different codes sometimes had to be used. The main change is that games apart from football have all but disappeared; football is now played by only 26 per cent of pupils, and only one pupil mentioned a chasing game. As we have seen, at 11 years other ball games were mentioned by a third of pupils; at 16 years, the proportion playing netball, basket ball, pat-ball etc. was down to 11 per cent. By 16 years, the most popular activity is talking to friends, hanging around and socializing (72 per cent of pupils). Another main change by 16 years is the extent of working at lunchtime (28 per cent of pupils). None of the children at 11 years reported this, and in any case they would have been much less likely to have been allowed into the school.

So the children's own accounts indicate that a main change with age in breaktime activities is from active games such as football, chasing and catching at the primary stage, to talking and socializing with friends by the end of the secondary stage. Pupils' own explanations for changes in breaktime activities between primary and secondary stages centred on a growing sense of maturity and self understanding, a greater value attached to choice about how to spend breaktime, the simple fact of not having to go out to the playground at breaktime, a greater sense of the importance of school work, and changes in the nature of social relations, in which the nature of talk is more central and not tied to games. Despite the seeming lack of activity at 16 years, pupils were still positive about breaktime, and one should be careful about concluding that it was of little value to them. With older children, activities and social concerns at breaktime are not so tied to location and activity, and in contrast to activities at primary school are not so visible to staff.

An important issue concerns the reasons for changes in breaktime activities; in particular, to what extent they are the result of developmental changes within the child or affected by outside factors. This longitudinal study could not provide an exact test, but the pressure of peers seemed to be a powerful force that had much to do with the development with age of an inhibition about playing games, and the development of a growing inactivity through the secondary years. The presence of playground games during the first years of secondary indicates the potential longevity of games as a feature of unsupervised activities. Some pupils who transferred from lower to upper secondary schools at 13 years reported a marked change in breaktime activities, indicating the likely influence of peer pressure and school culture once they enter the upper school. There appears, then, to be a transition stage during the early years of secondary when play activities from primary are at first carried over. It may be that games and play are useful in the early stages of secondary as a familiar medium through which to develop new friendships, but their decline is accelerated as other ways of mediating friendships develop. However, the possible role of playground activities and games after the transition to secondary school needs closer study.

Another possibility for future research could take advantage of the fact that in the English school system pupils can transfer to secondary education at 11 or at 12 years, depending on the arrangements in different LEAs. A comparison of breaktime activities of same age children, some of whom remain in middle schools (deemed primary), and some of whom transfer to secondary schools, would do much to separate effects of maturity from peer and school influences.

One feature of the research presented in this chapter was the opportunity to study sex differences in breaktime activities over a longer time period than previous research. There were differences between boys and girls at 11 years. Girls were more likely than boys to play seeking games, pretending games and skipping games. Daring games, guessing games, pretending games, games using playground markings, ring games, rhymes and clapping games and games using marbles or other materials were rarely or never mentioned, and only by girls. Boys seemed involved but less varied in their play than girls. Football dominated their playground activities. At 16 years there were still significant differences between boys and girls in reported breaktime activities. Boys were more likely to report playing football, other ball games, and cards and chess. Girls were more likely to talk to friends and socialize, do school work, and listen to music. In answer to a separate question, boys at 16 years were more likely than girls to say they played games (see Blatchford, 1996, 1998).

Consequences of changes in breaktime activities seemed different for boys and girls. Whilst both boys and girls became less active with age, boys' activities at primary level were dominated by football and active games, and there was therefore more continuity into the secondary years, where football still has a place. There was also a wider continuity into the world of adult male culture, where in Britain football has a dominant place. The change was more marked for girls, perhaps because there is less obvious continuity between games preferred at primary level and the predominantly social and non-active pursuits preferred at secondary. The sense of a lost or buried world of childhood, noted by commentators on children's culture, is therefore more noticeable in girls.

Other activities at breaktime were also studied. Teasing and name calling at breaktime also showed changes through the school years, seen not just in the prevalence and types of teasing, but in the role of teasing in peer relations (Blatchford, 1998). There is some evidence of a decline in teasing by the final years of secondary school, and this may have been partly because of the cohesiveness of social relations within groups. Fighting in school also changed with age. The intensity of physical activity during primary breaktimes could lead to fights, while secondary-aged children had come to learn the serious consequences of fights, which appeared to arise mainly as a reaction to threat or humiliation. Relationships with adults at breaktime also seemed to change, though this was not directly studied. At primary level, breaktime activities can be pursued with equal enthusiasm, whether or not adults are around, but by secondary level, pupils place more importance on independence from adults.

To conclude this section, children's behaviour on the playground at recess is moderated by a number of child-level variables. These child-level variables, however, interact with aspects of the larger social context, like school environment (Bronfenbrenner, 1979).

School-level variables affecting playground behaviour

Break timing

If a poll were conducted with a large sample of professional educators and parents asking them why breaktime should be included in the school curriculum, the most commonly voiced rationale would probably relate to some aspect of 'Surplus Energy Theory', such as children needing recess to 'blow off steam'. While the validity of Surplus Energy Theory as stated in this way is questionable (Smith and Hagan, 1980), being based on outmoded concepts linking energy and motivation, the idea that children may 'need' or benefit from periodic changes from sedentary class work is both reasonable and rooted in other, more current, psychological theory, such as deprivation theories of play (Fagen, 1981) and the novelty/arousal theory of Berlyne (1966). The effect of breaktime timing, or the amount of time that children are expected to work at their seats before going out to recess, on children's behaviour has been addressed in two experimental field studies. Both these studies assumed that children's physical activity would vary as a function of their previous confinement to a sedentary environment.

Smith and Hagan (1980) studied 3- and 4-year-olds in two English nursery classes. The children stayed in the classroom for shorter (45 mins) or longer (90 mins) periods before going outdoors for breaktime. Smith and Hagan based their hypotheses on the idea that the motivation for active physical play could increase as a function of deprivation. The indoor classrooms conditions were organized such that active play was almost entirely prevented. The hypotheses were supported; children were more active (level of intensity) for a longer period (duration) after the longer, compared to the shorter, confinement periods. Further, a decrement of activity on the playground was observed as a function of time spent outdoors. No gender differences were observed. The study suggested that confinement results in need for physical activity; physical activity, in turn, decreases with time spent exercising.

Extending this approach to older children, Pellegrini and Huberty (1993) examined the effects of confinement on 9-year-old boys' and girls' classroom *and* playground behaviour in an American elementary school. Like the Smith and Hagan study, children were confined for shorter and longer periods and the duration and intensity of their playground behaviour was observed. Pellegrini and Huberty also found the confinement increased the intensity of children's playground activity. They found significant gender effects at this older age: boys were more active on the playground than girls, particularly after the longer confinement period. Frequency and levels of active behaviour of the boys, further, decreased as a function of time on the playground. These results support the general model outlined above: boys are more active on the playground than are girls and their levels of activity can be increased by previously limiting their opportunity for vigorous physical activity. These findings were replicated with a larger group of children (Pellegrini *et al.*, 1995a).

This line of inquiry has important implications for subsequent research and educational policy. One pressing issue for school administrators concerns the optimal length for a recess period. We have very little information here. This information would be valuable in terms of theory (play deprivation theory and arousal theory would predict a decrement of activity in recess as a function of time) and certainly valuable for educational policy. The findings of Pellegrini and Huberty suggest that children's active play at breaktime does not last very long; there are marked decreases after the first 6 or 7 minutes. Future work should document the specific duration of active play and how it varies as a function of age and gender of children, previous confinement, and the length of the breaktime period. From a policy perspective, it seems important to answer these questions in order to design recess periods that maximize benefits, in terms of subsequent attention in class, and minimize children's boredom on the playground. The anecdotal evidence provided by Blatchford (1989), from both educators and children in Britain, suggests that dinner time play of over one hour is too long, to the extent that children become bored and sometimes aggressive towards the end of these periods.

However, duration of play periods and play bouts alone does not address the whole issue of possible benefits of physical activity exhibited at recess. It is probably the case that high intensity physical play bouts are characterized by short durations. Some of the literature on training of muscle strength and cardiac capacity suggests that short but intense periods are more effective than longer, less intensive periods (Pellegrini and Smith, 1998). It may be that children's attention can be maximized by encouraging short, but frequent, physically active bouts. This is clearly an area in which more work is needed.

The measurement of duration and intensity of physical activity has attracted much attention. Of course, behavioural observation of these aspects of activity is the most accurate, yet also the most time consuming method. While there are many objective measures of activity intensity, like actometers (Eaton *et al.*, 1987) and heart rate (Dauncey and James, 1979), they are both obtrusive and time consuming to use. Recently researchers have developed observational checklists that correlate highly with these more direct measures, and are more economical to use as well as yielding duration measures. These schemes, generally, code body posture, e.g., lying, sitting, or standing (Eaton *et al.*, 1987) or the part of body engaged in activity (upper or lower; Hovell *et al.*, 1978); intensity is then coded along three dimensions (high, medium and low). Maccoby and Jacklin (1987) used a 7–point scale to code intensity; the 3-point scale yields less information but may be more reliable for observers to use. Martin and Bateson (1988) suggest that agreement on intensity ratings, while difficult, can be maximized if ratings correspond to number of features present; for example, a low intensity rating would have two features and a high rating would have eight. Similar intensity ratings have been applied to children's level of fidgeting and concentration in classroom tasks (Pellegrini *et al.*, 1995c). Duration of activity is derived by multiplying these codes by the number of intervals in which they are observed. An inherent problem with both rating scales and behavioural observations is possible observer bias (Liss, 1983). Actometer and heart rate measures are less susceptible to such bias.

In short, there are reliable and valid measures of children's physical activity that can easily be applied to their recess behaviour. Their use should be expanded in our studies of recess in that children's activity level is certainly an important aspect of recess.

The educational implications of breaktime

Because recess is embedded in school, the question of its educational role is often voiced. Educational role typically refers to the cognitive implications of recess. We also include a broader definition of educational implications, involving issues of social competence, such as popularity with peers. To adapt successfully in schools, children must function in both social and cognitive spheres; indeed, the two are empirically inter-correlated and should not be considered separately (Block, 1987; Zigler and Trickett, 1978). We consider children's cognitive and social outcomes as appropriate measures for the educational impact of recess.

Cognitive outcomes

Researchers interested in relations between recess behaviour and traditional cognitive outcome measures, such as school achievement, can generally be put into two categories. The first category includes researchers, typically adherents of arousal/novelty theory, who suggest that the physical activity exhibited during recess has important cognitive consequences; for example, the physical activity of adults relates to immediate increase in attention (Tomporowski and Ellis, 1986). Further, exercise-related hormones have been implicated in adults' memory and attention (Sandman and Kastin, 1977). Research in the second category with school-age children, on the other hand, is not consistent with these adult results. Pellegrini *et al.* (1995c) found that vigorous play at recess was *negatively* related to attention to a post-recess achievement task while sedentary playground behaviour was positively correlated with attention, and negatively correlated with fidgeting. These results suggest that vigorous activity may actually interfere with the subsequent attention of some children. Adding further to the confusion, this relation between activity and attention was not replicated by Pellegrini *et al.* (1995c).

Clearly, much more research and replication is needed, but these results suggest that opportunities for vigorous play actually exacerbate active children's classroom inattention. It may be that these children need changes from seat work, but changes which are settling rather than exciting. Drawing on the adult findings and research with Israeli and British school children, it may also be the case that specific types of vigorous activity interact statistically with types of cognitive task and children's age and gender. For example, Eifermann's (1978) massive study of Israeli children's recess behaviour and Opie and Opie's (1969) study of British street and playground games clearly points to the dominant role of physical activity, not sophisticated cognitive strategies, while children are outdoors. This, according to Eifermann's (1970) data, changes as boys and girls get older. While games dominated by physical activity decrease and strategic games increase across the elementary school years for boys, the opposite is true for girls. In short, much more research is needed in this area because recess seems to do very different things for different children at different ages.

Possibly, physical activity *per se* at breaktime is not the most important variable relating to subsequent improved attention in the classroom. Following novelty theory (Berlyne, 1966), it may be that children habituate to stimuli, like school tasks and indeed recess time, as a function of familiarity; physical activity might then be just one of many ways in which children seek novelty. For example, sedentary social interaction provides a change from typical classroom regimens to the extent that children can choose a peer with whom to interact on their own terms. Recess provides opportunities for this form of behaviour. Pellegrini and Huberty (1993) found that non-social sedentary behaviour decreased as a function of recess time but social sedentary behaviour increased across time. Thus, optimal length of recess period may vary, depending on our desired behaviour. Shorter periods may be better for physical activity but longer periods may be necessary before children habituate to social sedentary activities.

Another interesting, and potentially important, aspect of this research relates to the type of tasks on which children are observed before and after breaktime. Classrooms vary in terms of requirements for concentration, social interaction, and sedentary activity; these factors may interact with corresponding dimensions of recess experience. Other task-specific measures, like motivation to work on particular activities, may also affect attention. For example, there may be reliable task attention differences as a function of gender preference for specific tasks. It may be that boys attend to and participate in male preferred tasks, like spatial tasks, while girls are more attentive in linguistic contexts (Pellegrini and Perlmutter, 1989a). Of course, these gender-related differences interact, in turn, with age as children's behaviour becomes more gender-role stereotyped. Future research investigating these interactive effects are clearly necessary. For example, experimental field studies, of the sort conducted by Smith and

Connolly (1980), that examine age × gender × task effects, in relation to recess variables, would help clarify the issues.

The cognitive implications of children's breaktime behaviour have also been studied from the point of view that children's cognition is facilitated by social interaction with peers. The theoretical orientations in this area can be traced to Humphrey's (1976) idea of the social origins of primate intelligence and to Piaget's (1970) equilibration theory whereby peer interaction facilitates cognitive conflict and subsequent re-equilibration. Following Piagetian theory, Pellegrini (1992a) examined the extent to which the social behaviour of kindergarten children on the school playground during recess predicted their achievement in first grade. Of specific interest was the relative roles of peer and adult interaction for children's cognitive development. The results were consistent with the Piagetian model in that a facilitative role of peers and an inhibitive role of adults were found. Specifically, interactions with adults and with peers were, respectively, negative and positive predictors of first grade achievement. These measures of kindergarten playground behaviour accounted for a significant amount of the variance in first grade achievement after kindergarten achievement was controlled. In short, what children do on the playground does have cognitive implications. Further, these behaviours seem to provide significantly more insight into children's functioning than do traditional measures of cognition. Relatedly, Polgar (1976), also following a Piagetian theoretical orientation, reported similar qualitative data for a group of sixth graders (equivalent to the British Year 6). She too found that interaction with teachers, compared to peer interaction, was restricted in terms of movement and speech, short (e.g., more time was spent in organization than in play activities), and disjunctive.

Paradoxically, then, reductions in recess or breaktime, in an effort to improve academic or cognitive outcomes, may be counter productive. However, while these results are consistent with theory, they should be interpreted cautiously as they are based on a few studies with limited sample sizes. Further, the measures of social interaction were rather gross. Pellegrini (1992a) coded children's social behaviour as peer-directed or adult-directed and whether children were talking or not talking. Clearly these variables are 'packaged' variables to the extent that they include numerous sub-variables which probably relate differentially to cognition. Polgar's study provided neither inferential statistics to test the extent to which her adult-peer contrasts differed from chance nor was observer bias considered (see Liss, 1983 and Smith, 1988). Future research should use specific theoretically relevant measures of social interaction as predictors of cognitive status. For example, Humphrey's (1976) theory suggests that diversity of social experience is important for intellectual growth; the variety of roles and behaviours that children exhibit with various partners could be used as predictors in future research. Further, does interaction with specific social configurations around specific types of tasks account for situation-specific cognitive effects? From a Piagetian perspective children's conflicts and resolutions should be considered. In short, the extant data tells us that social interaction has important cognitive implications. The time has come to test more specific theories of the ways in which this operates.

Social outcomes

The notion that recess behaviour is important for children's socialization has a long history (see Sutton-Smith, 1981, 1990 for summaries). While much of this work is on children on playgrounds, *not* in school settings specifically, a number of school playground studies do exist and they will be the focus of this section. The studies reviewed vary in terms of specificity of the outcome measures considered, from the global consideration of 'social skills necessary for adult life' (Sluckin, 1981, p. 2) and adult roles and occupational choice (Finnan, 1982; Lever, 1976), to specific measures of peer cooperation and popularity (Ladd, 1983; Pellegrini, 1988). We will begin with the global and move toward the specific.

Sluckin (1981) spent two years observing children in British (Oxford) first and middle schools. He concluded that there were similarities between the strategies and roles used and taken by children and adults. He noted that the facial gestures used by children to exhibit dominance are similar to those used by adults. Relatedly, Sluckin spent considerable effort explicating the ways in which children used ritual as a way in which to resolve conflict without violence. While adults do not face the likelihood of violence frequently, they too resort to ritual as a way in which to exhibit dominance. Sluckin, like Sutton-Smith (1971) before him, considers the social skills learned on the playground as important for later development. Indeed, they both argue, as did Suomi and Harlow (1972), that the context of interaction with peers is a unique one for learning social skills to the extent that the playful and non-serious tenor allows children to experiment with new and novel social strategies. Children also learn skills of presentation management (e.g., keeping status even after losing a game) and manipulation (e.g., ways of excluding unwanted children from a game). These social strategies are certainly not taught in most classrooms. Blatchford's (1998) more recent longitudinal study of children's experiences at breaktime at 7, 11 and 16 years is consistent with the view that breaktime is an important and productive context (at all ages) for developing skills in friendship relations and social networks, and conflict management.

The notion of recess play as preparation for adulthood is extended to the development of gender roles. Sluckin, for example, notes that the family oriented and competitive games that girls and boys played, respectively, may prepare them for the corresponding adult gender roles. Lever (1976) and Finann (1982), in observational studies of elementary school students on the playground at recess, both suggest that the play and games of children on the school playground contribute to traditional gender role divisions. Both Lever and Finnan found, like Harper and Sanders (1975) and Pellegrini (1992a) that boys, more than girls, preferred outdoor, public play; girls preferred indoor and more private play. Second, boys, more than girls, played in larger and more age-heterogeneous groups. This play often involved coordinating the different types of children around a competitive, team, theme. These games, Lever argued, prepare boys for adult leadership roles. Girls' play was more often cooperative than competitive and occurred in smaller, less diverse groups. When girls played with younger children, the older girls typically accommodated to the play of the younger child. Also, girls engaged in more close and intimate relationships in their small groups. Thus, it was argued, girls were learning to be nurturant in the playground; this, in turn, prepared them for later child-care duties.

In the work of Sluckin, Lever, and Finnan the socialization model is prevalent. That is, children's roles are the product of adult roles and children's play reflects these roles, generally, and as the role of women in American society changes, so too should the gender-role play of children. There is also support for the socialization model of playground behaviour in Eifermann's (1970) extensive observational study of Israeli school children. She found that the playground games of kibbutz children, compared to non-kibbutz children, was more group success oriented. This view of children's play as practice for adult life is consistent with numerous theories of play, most notably Groos (1901), Piaget (1932) and Vygotsky (1978) but not consistent with various conflict theories suggesting that play represents a revolt against adult values. While this practice notion seems reasonable, so too does the notion that children's play is not only imitative but also creative and, in turn, affects their later development. Indeed, a long-standing criticizm of socialization models is that the effect of society on children's social development is conceptualized as uni-directional; whereas individual differences in children, such as temperament and sociometric status, and resources available, actually mediate societal demands on children (Bronfenbrenner, 1979).

A study by Ladd (1983) of the recess behaviour of third and fourth grade boys and girls clearly illustrates these 'child effects'. It was noted above that boys' play groups are larger, or more extensive, than girls' groups. Ladd (1983) found that boys' and girls' social networks varied according to their sociometric status such that rejected children, regardless of gender, played in smaller groups than popular or average children; gender differences in the expected direction were observed for popular and average children. Further, the diversity of children played with at recess was affected by both gender and sociometric status; for example, while girls spent more time, compared to boys, interacting with same gender playmates, rejected boys, compared to other types of boys, spent a significant portion of their time playing with girls (Ladd, 1983). Thus, the way in which boys and girls interact on the playground is influenced by both gender and individual difference variables. That boys and girls merely reproduce dominant cultural values on the playground seems too simplistic; individual differences interact with broader societal norms to effect the ways in which they play at recess.

In the Sluckin, Lever, and Finnan studies, the social implications, or functions, of children's behaviour on the school playground was supported by an implicit argument from design features. That is, similarities between the behavioural and structural features of the playground and adult roles were described. While this is an interesting, and indeed a necessary first step, en route to establishing the functional significance of a behaviour, hypothesized associations between recess behaviour and social outcome measures must be tested more directly. Indeed, the Ladd (1983) study illustrated the ways in which such empirical study can add to our understanding of the meaning of children's recess behaviour. There are a few other studies of this kind, some of which also consider the ways in which individual differences in children mediate social development.

We will review studies using both contemporaneous and longitudinal correlation designs relevant to the implications of recess. Contemporaneous analyses, obviously, prohibit one from making functional, or causal, statements. Longitudinal correlational and experimental studies are necessary for getting at causation. Simple correlational studies are interesting, however, to the extent that they inform us that something important *may* be going on. That is, statistically significant correlation coefficients may suggest that one behaviour results in learning, or developing, another behaviour. More conservatively, it may also mean that one has already attained a certain skill and that the occurrence of a correlated behaviour indicates that one is practicing that skill. In either case, learning or practice, the correlation has educational meaning.

In separate studies Pellegrini (1988, 1989a and b) found that the recess behaviour of elementary school children related to their ability to solve hypothetical social problems and to their teachers' judgements regarding their antisocial personality. Again, these relations varied by both the gender and sociometric status of the children. Girls who engaged in physically vigorous behaviours, such as running and swinging, and rough play, like playfighting (Pellegrini, 1989a and b), were considered to be antisocial by their teachers; the same was not true for boys. It may be, following Lever, Sluckin, and Finnan, that teachers, too, considered the playground as a place for children to learn gender-role stereotyped behaviours. Those violating these norms were considered deviant. Relatedly, the rough play of rejected, but not popular, children (both boys and girls) related positively and significantly to their antisocial rating by teachers (Pellegrini, 1988). In this case, the correspondence between the two measures may reflect the fact that rejected children actually are antisocial (as evidenced by behavioural observations). Certainly, future studies should separate gender and sociometric effects.

Longitudinal work on rough play and antisocial personality ratings clarifies, to some degree, issues related to directionality, but gender and sociometric status are still confounded. Pellegrini (1995b) found that kindergarten children's aggression on the playground was a significant predictor of their being considered antisocial by their first grade teacher; children's kindergarten antisocial status was controlled so that the unique contribution of aggression, independent of a stable antisocial personality, could be assessed. This finding, while limited to the extent that children's gender and sociometric status were not considered, has implications to the extent that the playground at recess is used as a venue by some children to be aggressive and antisocial. This is consistent with work on bullying, which suggests that when bullying does occur, the most likely venue, especially in primary schools, is the school playground (Olweus, 1993b). This illustrates the darker side to recess. Some children do use recess as a place to be aggressive and bully their classmates, even though this may be infrequent in absolute terms. Further research on the role of various anti-bullying programmes in schools is needed (e.g., Smith and Thompson, 1991).

We have similar results and problems with the next set of findings for correlations between playground behaviour and social problem-solving ability. Significant and positive correlations between rough play and social problem-solving are reported for boys, not girls, and for popular, not rejected, children (Pellegrini, 1988). These sociometric status results were replicated in a longitudinal study whereby the rough play of popular, not rejected, elementary school students (mean age of 64 months) predicted social problem-solving one year later, while controlling for Year 1 social problem-solving status (Pellegrini, 1991).

To summarize, children's breaktime, or recess, does have educational implications. In both correlational and longitudinal research, children's recess behaviour is related, in theoretically predictable ways, to both cognitive and social outcome measures. Children's gender and sociometric status seem particularly important as mediators for recess effects. However, much more research, preferably longitudinal, needs to be carried out to clarify the causal relations and to put the findings obtained so far on a firm basis.

Conclusion

This chapter set out to address a very specific topic: the role of recess in schools. We made no attempt to exhaustively cover the field of all that occurs in school or even on the school playground. Further, we made no attempt to review the vast, but related, literature on children's play. As many others have noted (e.g., Fagen, 1981; Miracle, 1987; Rubin et al., 1983), students of play must make decisions which limit the scope of their work; the field is too vast to do otherwise. A vast number of review chapters and books in different fields attests to the popularity of this topic. For example, there are sizable reviews in anthropology (Schwartzmann, 1978), biology (e.g., Fagen, 1981), education (e.g., Christie and Johnsen, 1983), history (Sutton-Smith, 1981), and psychology (Rubin et al., 1983). The intent of the present review was to stimulate serious thinking and research on the role of recess in schools. Given the importance of the topic there is a relative paucity of empirical research on children's recess. This lack of descriptive and predictive work is indeed surprising in light of the popularity of recess in school curricula (Blatchford, 1998; Pellegrini, 1995b). The research that does exist, however, tells a rather consistent story. Timing and duration of recess relates to playground activity, and possibly to subsequent classroom behaviour, in ways which interact with age, gender and temperament. Recess behaviour is also a generally positive predictor of children's, and especially boys', social cognitive development. Thus, it seems to have educational value and certainly has considerable educational relevance. There are clear lines of future research that could be both theoretically interesting and practically important.

There are difficult issues concerning the management of breaktime in schools. A main problem, we would argue, arises out of a tendency toward growing restrictions on pupils' unsupervised activities within school, on the one hand, and the likely benefits of these activities for their social, physical and even cognitive development, on the other hand. There is a tension, in other words, between a greater control of pupil behaviour and the likely value of pupil independence. This is connected to views concerning the role of adults with regard to breaktime. There appear to be two main views: first, an 'interventionist' view, involving more deliberate management of pupils' behaviour at breaktime and playground environment changes, and, second, a 'non-interventionist' view which sees little need to do more than check the physical safety of children on playgrounds. Blatchford (1998) has argued that it is important to seek to reconcile the value to pupils of breaktime with the understandable wish of schools to ensure control over behaviour and learning. Unfortunately teachers in schools seem to see the value of breaktime in fairly low level terms (Blatchford and Sumpner, 1998), rather than in the more fundamental social and cognitive terms reviewed in this chapter. There are, then, few signs of an appreciation in schools of the value of breaktime and yet, as we have seen, in some schools breaktime is being reduced.

Lastly, the situation with regard to breaktime in schools needs to be seen alongside changes to the opportunities for peer interaction *outside* school.

There are signs in a number of countries (e.g., England and Australia) that children of primary school age have fewer opportunities out of school for interacting freely with peers. Children are far more likely to be driven to school, rather than walk. This emphasizes the likely importance of interaction at breaktime in schools, which for a growing number of pupils may be the main opportunity for them to meet relatively freed from adults.

6 Aggression in school: the specific case of bullies and victims

Violence is a major problem in elementary and secondary schools around the world. Problems range in severity from acts of physical aggression, such as shoot-outs in school yards, to acts of verbal aggression, such as teasing and shunning. While aggression has an unfortunately long history in urban schools (e.g., The 'Blackboard Jungles' of 1950s American schools), the problem has crept into the seemingly such 'peaceful' settings as rural Scotland and rural Arkansas, as well as schools in Norway and Sweden. Indeed, the prevalence and intensity of the problem of school aggression in countries such as Norway and Britain has lead to national campaigns to remediate the problem.

School aggression is first identified in elementary schools and becomes particularly acute, in terms of frequency and severity, in middle or junior high schools (National Center for Educational Statistics, 1995). Both perpetrators and targets of various forms of aggression are at risk, respectively, for incarceration and depression/suicide (Olweus, 1993b). Cases of teenage suicide in Norway, apparently precipitated by being victimized spurred campaigns to stem the tide against school violence. More recently, in America a 15-year-old boy with a long history of being victimized has been accused of killing his mother and three peers. Clearly there is a real problem. Unfortunately, the same scenario continues to re-play in America's schools. In order to begin to remediate these problems, it is especially important to identify them at the most stressful periods in youngsters' lives, such as making the transition to adolescence and to a new school.

In this chapter we discuss one important dimension of the problem of school violence: bullies and victims. Bullying is defined, following Olweus (1993b), as instances of negative actions being directed at a specific youngster or group of youngsters repeatedly and over time. Negative actions are broadly defined in terms of physical aggression, for example, hitting, verbal aggression, such as name calling or social exclusion, and indirect/relational aggression (Crick, 1996; Crick and Grotpeter, 1995; Lagerspetz et al., 1988). Bullies are the perpetrators of these actions and victims are the targets.

Because of our limited empirical knowledge of this problem in schools, much of this chapter is couched in tentative language. Additionally, we make suggestions for ways in which this problem can be more thoroughly studied. This empirical base, we feel, is necessary to guide school policy.

Much of what we know about bully and victim relations in childhood and early adolescence is based on self-report methodology. For example, the work of Olweus (1993b) has children answering a series of questions which results in their being classified as a bully or a victim. Perry and colleagues (Perry *et al.*, 1990) asked children to nominate peers whom they thought met victimization criteria. Crick and Gropeter (1995), too, use peer nomination methods to identify perpetrators of relational aggression or aggression used to manipulate social relationships (e.g., shunning). This methodology has provided valuable descriptive information on the rates of bullying and victimization. The motivation for using self-report questionnaires is certainly clear enough: aggression is a rare event and one that typically occurs in the absence of adult observers.

Another group of researchers, associated with Kenneth Dodge's laboratory (e.g., Schwartz *et al.*, 1993; Schwartz *et al.*, 1997), have begun to study the behavioural processes associated with bully and victim status using the contrived playgroup paradigm. In this procedure, previously unacquainted youngsters (typically boys) are observed interacting in small playgroups. Simultaneously, they are asked to nominate playmates they like and dislike, as well as those who are aggressive and targets of aggression. This research has provided useful information on the ontogeny of bullying and victimization status. For example, non-assertive and submissive behaviour are precursors to victimization (Schwartz *et al.*, 1993).

In this chapter we will review the literature on bully–victim relationships, describing bullies, victims, and aggressive victims. This latter group of youngsters is both aggressive with and victimized by their peers. This comorbid behavioural constellation puts these youngsters at great risk for internalizing (e.g., depression and suicide) and externalizing (e.g., aggression) disorders. Because of these risks and the limited observational work with this group, we outline a process by which the problem can be studied. We also consider some associated ethical issues.

Bully and victim status and differential use of aggression

A substantial portion of school violence involves bullies systematically targeting a group of victims (Perry *et al.*, 1990). That is, much school violence is perpetrated by a specific group of youngsters: bullies. The target of much of this aggression is also limited to a specific group: victims. The research of Olweus (1978, 1993b), with Scandinavian youngsters, Perry (e.g.,

Boldizar *et al.*, 1989; Perry *et al.*, 1990), with middle class American young-sters, and Smith (Smith and Sharpe, 1994) with a diverse group of English children, have provided much information on bullies and their motives for targeting specific children. We consider possible antecedents and conse-quences (in terms of cost and benefits) of behaviours which lead to bully-ing and victimization. This process is an important first step in addressing the problem.

Bullies

Bullies are youngsters who systematically and repeatedly target another group of youngsters towards whom they are either directly and physically aggressive (e.g., hitting), or indirectly and relationally so (e.g., shunning). Bullies are typically bigger and stronger than their targets (Olweus, 1993b). Boys, more than girls, have been identified as bullies (Olweus, 1993b), especially those using physical aggression. They are also non-compliant and aggressive in other aspects of their life (Olweus, 1993b). Bullies represent about 7–15 per cent of the sampled school-age population (Olweus, 1993b; Schwartz *et al.*, 1997; Smith and Sharpe, 1994).

More recently, researchers have identified another form of aggression, which seems to be a particularly female form of aggression. Relational (Crick, 1996; Crick and Grotpeter, 1995) or indirect (Lagerspetz *et al.*, 1988) aggression involves the negative uses of peer relations, such as shun-ning or maligning a peer. While this line of research has not typically been framed in bully–victim terms, it should, when it occurs persistently, be con-sidered a form of bullying.

Socialization research suggests that the families of bullies are conflictual and often their parents use aggression and other power-assertive techniques to manage behaviour (Loeber and Dishion, 1984; Schwartz, 1993). Fol-lowing exposure to adults using such power-assertive strategies and expo-sure to violence in the media, these youngsters have learned that aggression can be used instrumentally, in the service of obtaining desired goals (Ban-dura, 1973; Dodge, 1991; Schwartz *et al.*, 1997), as a way in which to secure reinforcement and get things done. For example, bullying may boast social status within a group of aggressive youngsters. Unfortunately, we have only limited observational data to substantiate these claims. For example, pre-school children's bullying behaviours are often reinforced by victims' responses of pain and submission (Patterson *et al.*, 1967).

Older youngsters (i.e., during early adolescence) may use physically assertive behaviours as a way in which to publicly display dominance over weaker peers or rivals (Pellegrini and Smith, 1998). Observations of boys in early adolescence on the school playground provide further support for this claim. Boys ascending in the dominance hierarchy (that is, boys mov-ing up in status from less to more 'tough' or 'hard') initiate physically vigorous interaction with peers of both higher and lower dominance status in an effort to gain status. On the other hand, boys declining in dominance status (that is, boys moving down in status) limit physically vigorous initiations to lower status peers (Pellegrini, 1995a). Further, in the initial stages of group formation these physically vigorous encounters result in aggression at statistically reliable rates (Pellegrini, 1995b). By that we mean aggressive boys often turn seemingly playful, but rough, interaction into aggression. Targets of this rough interaction are rated by their teachers as victims (passive and aggressive victim status was not differentiated in this work).

The aggressive behaviour of bullies often results in general unpopularity, or rejection, with peers; that is, they tend to be more frequently disliked than liked by peers in their classrooms (Dodge, 1991; Olweus, 1993a). However, among other aggressive youngsters, bullies tend to be popular (Cairns et al., 1988; Pellegrini et al., 1999). Their facility in using certain forms of aggression may relate positively to their peer status within such deviant groups. This represents a commonsensical picture of a 'gang' leader: tough and a leader of his peers.

In short, bullies are aggressive youngsters who use aggression in a systematic and calculating way against a group of weaker peers. As we will discuss, this target group is unpopular with their peers and consequently the costs associated with this type of aggression (e.g., disapproval by one's peers) are limited.

Victims

Unlike bullies, victims are a much more heterogeneous group, being composed of passive victims, representing about 10 per cent of the sampled population of school-age youngsters (Olweus, 1993b; Pellegrini et al., 1999; Schwartz et al., 1993; 1997) and aggressive victims, representing 2–10 per cent of the population (Olweus, 1993b; Schwartz et al., 1997). Passive victims tend to be physically slight or frail, and in middle school they tend to be average or poor students and not popular with peers (Olweus, 1993b). Behaviourally, these youngsters are not assertive; for example, in relation to non-victims, they initiate social conversation and persuasives at lower rates (Schwartz et al., 1993). In response to peers' initiatives and persuasives they are more submissive than are comparisons (Schwartz et al., 1993). In the absence of bullies they blend into classrooms like other youngsters and they are not victimized as adults after they leave school (Olweus, 1991).

Aggressive victims too, are systematically bullied by their peers, yet they display a hostile style of social interaction (Perry et al., 1990). Additionally, these youngsters are 'hot tempered': they use aggression reactively, not instrumentally, in response to provocation or after losing control (Schwartz et al., 1997). Descriptively, these youngsters are nominated by their peers as those who both 'start fights', 'say mean things', 'get mad easily' and 'get picked on, teased and hit or pushed' (Schwartz et al., 1997).

Aggressive victims are both similar to and different from both passive victims and bullies. Like bullies they are aggressive but their aggression is reactive, not instrumental; passive victims are not aggressive. While bullies are described by peers as starting fights and victims are described as getting picked on and teased, aggressive victims are described as both starting fights and being picked on. Unlike bullies, however, aggressive victims are not popular with any particular clique of children. Indeed, aggressive victims are the most rejected members of their peer group. Extreme rejection, in turn, puts this group at extreme risk of negative developmental outcomes, such as dropping out of school, behaviour problems (Parker and Asher, 1987) and, in extreme cases, homicide, as may be the case with the American 15-year-old described at the beginning of this chapter.

The socialization histories of aggressive victims, like those of bullies, are also typified by adversative and power-assertive interactions. However, aggressive victims describe their parents as inconsistent and are sometimes abused (Bowers *et al.*, 1994). Further, aggressive victims perceive their families as low in warmth and parental management skills. In short, they view the world as a hostile and untrustworthy place (Bowers *et al.*, 1994) and, based on these hostile attributions, these children often react aggressively to others' provocative social behaviour. For example, an aggressive victim would typically attribute hostile and aggressive intent to a peer accidentally bumping into him.

Aggressive victims, unlike bullies, use aggression 'reactively' (Dodge, 1991; Schwartz *et al.*, 1997), not instrumentally. As illustrated above, they often use aggression in retaliatory circumstances, in response to what they perceive as threat. It may be an emotional response, not a calculated initiative. Unlike bullies, these children may not systematically choose weaker children as targets of their aggression. These youngsters may use aggression as a result of losing self-control.

Additionally, aggressive victims may associate with bullies because they are reinforced by the bullies for doing so. That bullies exhibit pro-social behaviour at rates similar to their non-aggressive peers (Pepler *et al.*, 1993) suggests that they may be reinforcing victims during interaction. Relatedly, victims often imitate bullies (Dodge and Coie, 1989). It may be that bullies and aggressive victims choose to interact in similar activities, like rough games, and bullies occasionally dispense pro-social behaviour to victims as reinforcers; only occasionally are they aggressively victimized by bullies. Aggressive victims may also imitate bullies' tactics and later use them with less dominant peers. Thus, bully–aggressive victim interaction may be mutually reinforcing.

How do bullies and victims establish and maintain their relationships?

Social exchange theory predicts that bullies seek out targets for whom the negative consequences (or costs) of aggression are minimal in relation to the benefits. The victimization process may begin at transitional points between schools, when children are establishing relationships with a new peer group; for example, when a child enters a school or a classroom in the middle of the school year. Bullies may initially 'sample' a wide variety of peers for potential victimization; targets become less varied as victims are identified (Perry *et al.*, 1990). Bullies may interact with a variety of children during recess. As part of this process they identify those children whom they know they can and cannot intimidate. Those children who can be intimidated become 'their' victims.

This 'sampling hypothesis' clearly needs further empirical testing. Not only do these results need replication with bullies but we should also determine the extent to which aggressive victims are the targets of these behaviours. To date we only know that aggressive victims are aggressive; we do not know the identity of the targets of their aggression.

It may be that bullies and aggressive victims are attracted to the same peer group because their behaviours are mutually reinforcing. It may be that each group accrues some benefits from interacting with each other. Determination of potential costs and benefits associated with the bully and aggressive victim roles is consistent with theories (e.g., Bandura, 1989; Dunbar, 1988) which state that aggression is likely to occur when rewards are probable (e.g., when others value, or do not discourage, aggressive acts) and costs (e.g., school sanctions and retaliation) are minimal.

Benefits and costs of aggression to bullies

It has been demonstrated that some bullies are reinforced for being aggressive towards some, but not all, children. Specifically, pre-school bullies are reinforced when their victims visibly express pain and submission (Patterson *et al.*, 1967). Further, primary school children attend to public bully–victim displays (Schwartz, 1993). It may be the case that such public displays of dominance by bullies raise their status with some of their peers.

Dominance status in the peer group is especially important for boys, especially when they are making the transition to a new classroom or a new school (Pellegrini, 1995a). By dominance status we mean, by virtue of an individual's leadership and 'toughness', 'hardness' or fighting ability, he is ordered hierarchically in a peer group and that order determines access to resources valued by the group (Pellegrini and Smith, 1998). Based on dominance status, individuals gain access to resources, such as notoriety among peers, monetary rewards (in cases of extortion), and access to favours (such as not having to wait in a queue). Both passive and aggressive victims may be targets of these dominance displays.

Victimized youngsters (passive and aggressive victims have not been differentiated in this research) and bullies often seek out each other for rough play even though the victims are hurt by the bullies in this context (Pellegrini, 1995a). Interestingly, aggressive victims and bullies do not dislike each other more than children having a less destructive relationship (Dodge and Coie, 1989). More troubling is the fact that the observed aggression against victims is not de-valued by most children; classmates witnessing these episodes *do not* think badly of the bullies for hurting this particular group of children (Perry *et al.*, 1990); similar aggressive acts against non-victimized children, on the other hand, are viewed negatively by most children. Thus, bullies seem to use aggression instrumentally against a specific target group (victims), to gain in dominance status (considered 'benefits'), with few associated costs.

What are the costs and benefits of aggressive victim status?

We noted that bully–victim relationships function as a way in which bullies acquire resources, or benefits. Benefits must be balanced with costs if the relationship is to continue. Though it may seem counter-intuitive to think that victims accrue any benefit from such a relationship, there are hints in the literature to suggest that aggressive victims may do so.

It may be that victims are aggressive with their weaker peers in order to acquire resources, such as social status (Dunbar, 1988). If aggressive victims *initiate* aggression against less tough peers, rather than against someone 'tougher' (i.e., of higher dominance ranking), it suggests that the victims may be using aggression instrumentally, to dominate less tough peers.

This display of dominance may provide the aggressive victim with social status, particularly if the target of the aggression shows signs of submission. Consequently, behavioural responses to aggressive acts provide an insight into the motives for the aggressive acts. Exhibition of pain, cries, or submission to aggression all reinforce aggression and can be viewed by perpetrators as benefits associated with aggressive acts against specific targets. Specifically, when a young child inflicts pain on a peer and that pain is visible to the perpetrator and his peers, that act of aggression is reinforced. Signs of submission, such as crying, are public displays that the perpetrator is dominant in relation to the target. For some youngsters, such exhibitions are important for peer group membership. As noted above, membership in some peer groups, like gangs, is limited to highly aggressive youngsters (Cairns *et al.*, 1988).

If, on the other hand, aggressive victims *respond* aggressively to others' aggression, aggression may be 'reactive', possibly a result of their losing self-control. This scenario may occur in the context of aggressive victims responding aggressively to bullies' aggression. The research of Schwartz and colleagues (1993, 1997) suggests that this may be the case for aggressive victims. In this case, their use of aggression may be less calculating and benefits, too, may be less apparent.

In summary, we suggest that bullies and victims have relationships with associated costs and benefits. The benefits for bullies are high and the costs are low. For aggressive victims, the costs of their relationships with bullies are high and the benefits low.

Contextual variation in bullying and victimization

The occurrence of bullying and aggression in schools is a result of both personal and contextual variables. As noted above, there are certain individual differences associated with bullying and aggression. For example, youngsters with social information processing deficits are likely candidates for aggressive victimization. Both aggressive victims and bullies have temperaments which predispose them to aggression, being highly active and emotional.

These individual differences are exacerbated in specific circumstances. For example, aggression is likely to occur as children make the transition to a new school, such as moving from primary to secondary school. Children often use bullying tactics to establish their status in a new peer group (Pellegrini *et al.*, 1999). Further, within certain peer cliques, aggression is differentially rewarded as it is related to peer status. Specifically, in peer groups comprised of aggressive youngsters, aggression is positively related to popularity and friendships, whereas in groups of non-aggressive youngsters, aggression is negatively related to popularity and friendships (Pellegrini *et al.*, 1999).

Another transition which is related to aggression is the transition from childhood to adolescence. Adolescence has been described as 'brutal' (Cairns *et al.*, 1988) because of the frequency and intensity of observed aggression. This period witnesses rapid changes in body size, social roles (from sexually immature to sexually mature) and institutional placements (moving from primary to secondary schools). These individual changes correspond to changes in peer groups. Typically children move into a larger, more diverse and less familiar peer group. These factors necessitate re-negotiation of status in these new peer groups. Adolescents, especially boys, often use aggression to attain peer status (Pellegrini *et al.*, 1999).

There are also some global school level factors that merit discussion.

Generally, aggression occurs in those places in the school with little adult supervision – toilets and unsupervised play yards are prime venues. When supervision is instituted, bullying declines (Olweus, 1993b). Olweus' (1993b) extensive survey work in Scandinavia is also informative for pointing out some school levels which do not support bullying. For example, he has found that there are no differences between large and small schools or between urban and rural schools in predicting bullying and victimization. What does support it is lack of supervision and a climate which tolerates aggression (e.g., teachers being abusive to children, not punishing aggressive children, ignoring children's and parents' concerns with children being victimized). It might be tempting to feel that simply cutting out those contexts within which bullying is most likely to take place – for example, breaktime – would effectively reduce the amount of bullying. However, as argued in the last chapter, it is important to weigh this against the benefits of breaktime. It is not just the contexts *per se* that are crucial, but also the lead given by staff and the way behaviours such as bullying are dealt with (Blatchford, 1998).

Methodological issues

As noted above, the vast majority of research in this area has been conducted with questionnaire methodology. Questionnaires are useful for studying aggression, and other infrequently occurring behaviours, with a large number of subjects. Questionnaires limit our understanding of events, however, to what respondents choose to tell us. This limitation may be particularly problematic in this area where respondents (that is, both children and school authorities) may be less than forthcoming with the facts.

For this reason we suggest that bullying and victimization should be studied using direct observation methods. Inferences about possible costs and benefits of behaviours can be made by observing the peer groups in which aggression occurs. This perspective on inferring the meaning of behaviour leads us to directly observe youngsters in situations where they are minimally supervised and are free to interact with peers on their own terms. Interesting venues to observe include the lunchroom, recess, hallways, cafeteria, on the school bus and in the playground. The commonality among all these venues is that children are minimally supervised by adults. When there is neither adult supervision of peer interaction nor sanctions against bullying, aggression is likely to occur because there are low costs and high benefits associated with committing these deeds.

Correspondingly, observers should remain as unobtrusive as possible. In some cases, observers have remained out of sight of children by using various 'remote recording' techniques, such as videotaping children in the playground from a window overlooking the ground and taking notes on or video recording children's playground behaviour from a car parked adjacent to a school playground. The obvious limitations to this sort of procedure is that children's language cannot be recorded. This limitation should be overcome in that language, in the form of threats, ridicule, and teasing is often used in bullying bouts. Indeed, without close proximity it is often difficult to differentiate rough play, from real aggression. Further, bouts of relational aggression would be difficult to record.

To remediate this problem, Pepler and Craig (1995) suggest using remote video cameras in conjunction with radio microphones. To minimize reactivity Pepler and Craig also use 'dummy' microphones on children not being observed. These small and rather inexpensive microphones (around $100) can be worn on children's shirts or jackets. Pre-school children usually habituate to wearing these devices after two or three observation sessions and play as if they were not wearing them (Pellegrini, 1996). Older children, however, seem to be more self-conscious. Pepler and Craig (1995) note that by 11 to 12 years of age, youngsters seem reticent when wearing microphones. It is important for future research to document if children of this age do habituate to this apparatus and, if they do, the duration.

Videotaping bullies and victims interacting with each, as well as other children, and then having them and their peers view the videotapes is an interesting way of determining the value to the participants of these interactions. With this procedure, children are asked to describe the events and discuss possible benefits and motivations for participation.

This strategy has been used successfully with children to identify the benefits of rough-and-tumble play and aggression (Smith et al., 1993). Youngsters provide insight into the meaning of various sorts of behaviours by classifying the bouts as aggressive or non-aggressive, describing the behaviours as they occur indicating if they enjoyed that sort of interaction and why they 'played' with those specific youngsters.

Interestingly, this research suggests that showing children bouts in which they participated provided different information from that given by children who did not participate in viewed bouts. Participants in these bouts, compared to non-participating classmates and teachers, provide consistent (i.e., reliable over a two week period) information on the meaning of the bouts. That is, when participants in bouts were interviewed separately they agreed with each other on the meaning and value of the behavioural bouts. These classifications differed significantly from those generated by non-participating peers and teachers.

This is an important methodological lesson for a number of reasons. First, showing children films in which they did not participate and asking them to interpret them will provide limited information. Second, the idea that children perceive some events differently from teachers was not supported here. The argument of a 'peer v. teacher' culture seems to miss the mark. Peers interact differently with each other depending on the nature of their relationship. Relationships between participants, such as friendships, are crucial to understanding the meaning of events, especially those which may be ambiguous and provocative (e.g., exploitative v. non-exploitative). Youngsters who interact with each other in certain ways, such as bully–victim patterns and rough-and-tumble play, probably also have a specific sort of relationship, maybe even a close relationship.

Close relationships are defined as reciprocal and dyadic (Hinde, 1976). Bullies and victims exhibit some of the properties of close relationships: they choose to engage in certain forms of reciprocal play together and they do not dislike each other. This relationship with each other may be responsible for their unique insights into the nature of their interaction with each other. Only aggressive victims and the children with whom they interact, for example, may know why they interact with bullies in aggressive or rough play bouts. These reasons are not apparent to others not having a close relationship, or previous history of interactions, with those specific partners.

Lastly, it is important to determine the extent to which aggressive victims attribute aggressive intent to social interaction. As noted above, some aggressive children (aggressive victims) view their worlds as hostile, threatening places. When presented with an ambiguous social provocation situation, such as a rough-and-tumble play initiation, they assume the act is aggressive and respond accordingly (Pellegrini, 1988).

In cases where direct observation is difficult (e.g., on the school bus) or impossible (e.g., in toilets and gym locker rooms) student diaries are useful (Pellegrini, 1996). With diaries, considered an indirect form of observation, students keep a daily record of their interactions (with particular attention paid to aggressive acts), participants in the interactions, and locations. A glossary of words to be used in the recording helps to standardize the language.

Conclusion

We have outlined some important questions that might help alleviate the problem of school violence by reducing bully–victim aggression. We know a great deal about bullies and victims from studies conducted in Europe and North America with youngsters from middle and lower socioeconomic groups. We know substantially less about the specific behaviours and peer group dynamics of these children. Thus we call for more research to help guide policy. Theory and emerging research should be a joint venture between behavioural and social scientists and professionals working in the field. In this way theory, data, and programmes can help shape effective policy.

To this end we suggest two possible 'models' which might explain bully–victim relations and should guide this research. In one case, bullies may be using aggression instrumentally against weaker peers. Part of this research endeavour is to discover possible benefits to the bullies for this sort of behaviour. We suggested dominance theory might be a useful construct in guiding this research.

A second 'model', for aggressive victims, suggest that they use aggression reactively, not proactively. It may be the case that these children view their worlds as hostile places and 'lash out' aggressively when they lose control. So rather than using aggression in a calculating way to secure resources, these youngsters use it by default.

7 Classroom environments

The school and the classroom are particular contexts with particular features which will have an impact on and meaning for pupils and teachers. Minuchin and Shapiro (1983), in a pioneering paper, show how the school context is likely to change with the stage of education. They distinguish three broad stages which are organized differently and in which different aspects of social behaviour are expressed. They argue that the youngest children (in pre-schools) will have little concept of the school as an organized society, and interactions are predominantly with one or two female teachers and small groups of peers. Pre-school children behave in ways still very close to the family context and there will be an emphasis on establishing viable social behaviours (though elsewhere in this book we will see that even young children have a surprising degree of social competence with peers and knowledge of social status and friendship relations). At primary or elementary school, the classroom is still the main context and is now experienced as a social unit, with social expression and learning more complex. By the middle years of childhood, children are likely to have their feet equally in two worlds – teachers still give leadership and authority, but the peer group now functions as a social group independent of adults. As Minuchin and Shapiro say: 'The peer group is the social frontier in the classroom.' By high school or secondary school the social field becomes the school as a whole rather than a particular classoom, and the adolescent student comes into contact with a variety of teachers (male and female) and peers.

In this book we are mostly concerned with the younger children in school, that is, children of primary age and are mostly concerned therefore with the classroom context. This does not mean that school level environments and policies are not important. It is clear from research on school effectiveness that there can be important differences between schools – including primary schools – in their effects on pupils' educational progress, and some of the constituent factors in successful schools are well understood (Mortimore *et al.*, 1988; Stoll and Mortimore, 1995). In this sense, Minuchin and Shapiro's stages are probably too severe. However, as Doyle (1986) has argued, there are boundaries separating the classroom from the school. This is partly because the two environments have been studied separately. School effectiveness researchers do not always study classrooms closely, and classroom research has not often studied school level effects. But beyond this, classroom contacts between pupils and teachers are qualitatively different to those in other school contexts. 'Classroom contacts between teachers and students differ on such dimensions as duration, familiarity, substance, and purpose from those that occur in other school contexts.' (Doyle, 1986, p. 393). In particular, the classroom is still the main academic and social context in primary school pupils' lives, and in this chapter we look at several main features of this environment.

One orientating point, basic to social psychology, is that behaviour is affected by both individual personality and situation. This idea goes back to Lewin in the 1930s, and the idea that the environment and its interaction with personal characteristics of individuals were important determinants of actual behaviour. This was expressed in the basic formula $B=f(P,E)$, that is, behaviour is a function of both person and environment. Ross and Nesbett (1991) show how easy it is to underestimate the effect of the situation on behaviour – this is the 'basic attribution error'. When applied to classrooms, the basic idea is that different classroom activities and structures have forces, different to other contexts, which pull events and participants along with them.

An early, influential conception of the immediate environment as a factor in everyday behaviour was the ecological psychology of Barker and Wright and their colleagues (Barker, 1968). They showed ways in which different contexts – classroom, home, street, as well as smaller, within-school class contexts such as different activities, could be seen as niches or settings with predictable and systematic consequences in terms of teachers' and pupils' behaviour. As we shall see below, it was Paul Gump (1967) who did most to show how the stream of behaviours that make up a day in the classroom can be segmented into behavioural settings.

Another early and influential conception of the ecological context of behaviour is that of Bronfenbrenner (1979). He is often credited with assisting the recognition that psychology needs to concern itself with naturally occurring behaviour and the effects of contexts within which behaviour takes place. He was one of the first to offer a nested or multilevel hierarchical model that is now commonplace in more recent statistical modelling of influences on behaviour, for example, as seen in school effectiveness research (Goldstein, 1995). He identified an immediate context (microsystem), for example, the family or the school; a mesosystem, which involved links between microsystems, for example, those between home and school; an exosystem, which would include parents' conditions of employment; and a macrosystem, which could include government policy on employment and working conditions. Like many seminal ideas, the basic structure of Bronfenbrenner's model has been influential, even if the vocabulary has changed. For example, a recent thorough review of factors influencing school progress made a distinction between 'distal' and 'proximal' variables (which in Bronfenbrenner's terms roughly translates as macro- and micro-systems) arguing that the former, for example centralized curriculum reforms, were much less important than the latter, such as teaching and learning processes in classrooms (Wang *et al.*, 1993).

Even this system needs to be adapted. The school can be seen as one type of microsystem, but within this level there will be units, such as the classroom and the playground, which are parallel to each other and which, as we see throughout this book, are very different contexts with qualitatively different sets of relationships, rules and dynamics. In addition, some contexts are nested within these sub microsystems; for example, within a class of children there are often separate groups of children within which children work. As we shall see, these groups can differ in terms of the types of relationship, tasks and adult role.

There has been a tendency in educational psychology and educational research to consider the effects of teaching and teacher–pupil interactions independently of the environment in which these interactions occur. As we shall see in the next chapter, research on teaching has tended to view classroom processes in terms of teachers' actions toward pupils and pupils' learning or attainments, rather than in terms of wider, contextual dimensions affecting pupils and teachers together. Teachers do not meet pupils individually out of context – rather, it is the group nature of classroom life that shapes the nature of the tasks and the interactions between teachers and pupils, and defines the kinds of interactive skills or competencies that pupils and teachers need. In terms of research design, this turns on its head the usual way of conceiving classroom effects; that is, in terms of teaching (the independent variable) affecting pupil learning or attainment (the dependent or outcome variable). In this chapter we consider interactions and behaviour as dependent variables, with the context or environment of the focus of attention as the independent variable. Another way to view this is to say that the teacher is not viewed just in terms of attempts to teach or socialize children, but as someone who necessarily adapts to the demands of the classroom environment (Weinstein, 1991). Simultaneously, this reversal of 'independent' and 'dependent' variables makes an important point: people and contexts affect each other in a variety of ways. It is not simply a matter of X affecting Y.

In this chapter we will review some of the ways in which classroom contexts have been conceived and researched. The literature overall is vast and we can only provide a selective review. We will do this in two main sections. First we look at class level contexts, such as the physical layout of classrooms, the number of pupils in a class, the interactive and social characteristics of classrooms, and the classroom psychological environment. We then look at units within the class, such as segments, activities and tasks, and within-class groupings. We will highlight current research, taking place at the Institute of Education, on class size differences and within-class grouping practices.

Class level

Physical environment of the classroom

Perhaps the most obvious way of looking at the effects of the classroom environment is in terms of its physical nature (see reviews by Arends, 1994 and Doyle, 1986). One possibility is that the layout of the classroom, for example, in terms of circles, U shape or in traditional rows, can affect behaviour within it. It is also possible that the organization of the classroom environment in terms of, for example, divisions created with bookcases to produce separate areas, could affect things like the density of students and interaction patterns. Ecological psychologists used the term 'synomorphy' to refer to the compatability between the design of a setting and the activities and actions in that setting.

Classroom physical arrangements do not appear to affect student achievement (Arends, 1994), but there is some evidence of a connection with student behaviour and attitudes. Here is a quote from Waller in 1932 (in Weinstein, 1987):

> In the front row is a plentiful sprinkling of overdependent types, mixed perhaps with a number of extraordinarily zealous students. In the back row are persons in rebellion. . . .. Quantitive investigation of these phenomena would be long and difficult, but not impossible.

Early observation research by Adams and Biddle (1970) was one of the first to make use of videotapes for research purposes and showed that such work was indeed possible. They found that when arranged in traditional rows there was an 'action zone' comprising pupils in the front and centre of the classroom. Other research has found that pupils in this 'social-consultative' zone had a more permissive and interactive style of contact with the teacher, whilst those in the 'public zone' (middle and back of the room) had more lecturing from, and one-way communication with, the teacher. It would be instructive to compare in a systematic way these location–interaction effects in more contemporary classroom layouts, to see what effect recent policy and curriculum reforms have had.

There also seems to be a connection between student choice of seat and feelings about school, but there are difficulties in explaining the connection between the two. It is not clear to what extent the association between seating position and attitudes and behaviour is because particular students select their position in class or to what extent their position in class affects their attitudes and behaviour (Weinstein, 1987, p. 547). Walberg (in Weinstein, 1987) found that students who preferred to sit at the front generally expressed positive views, whilst those sitting at the back expressed negative views, about school, studying and their capacity for success. It also seems that some pupils actively seek out locations in the classroom which enable them to participate more. Weinstein (1987) has concluded that characteristics of seating and the individual pupil both contribute to student participation, but that pupil attitudes are predicted by seating (being nearer the teacher enhances affective outcomes).

Another body of evidence has experimentally manipulated physical arrangements. Several studies have compared pupils' work and behaviour in traditional rows as opposed to other configurations. Axelrod et al. (1979) found more disruptive and less on-task behaviour in groups. Wheldall et al. (1981) in Britain observed two year 6 classes for two weeks each in groups, then rows and then groups again. The results showed an increase in on-task behaviour when children were in rows. Bennett and Blundell (1983) found a marked improvement in the quantity of work when seated in rows. The quality of work was the same when in rows as opposed to groups, and there was a less marked decline in quantity when reseated in groups. Teachers in this study thought classroom behaviour improved in rows, followed by an increase in talking when reseated in groups. Pupils' reactions were more mixed in that some liked the quieter atmosphere in rows, but others did not like restrictions on space available. However, other studies report opposing results with more off-task and less on-task behaviour in rows as well as more student withdrawal (Rosenfield et al., 1985; and Weinstein, 1987).

Another body of research, concerning the physical dimensions of schools, has examined differences between traditional classrooms with open plan designed schools (see reviews in Bennett, 1987; Doyle, 1986; and Weinstein, 1979). Gump (1974) researched primary (first and second) and intermediate (fifth and sixth) grades in two open plan and two traditional school buildings. This research tradition clearly conceptualizes the environment as having a 'main effect' on behaviour. In Barker's terms, environments are 'coercive'. Differences were clearer at the primary stage, though the small sample makes such findings tenuous. At primary level, students in open plan settings occupied a greater variety of sites than students in traditional classrooms, and also more time in settings in which they worked together. More time in open settings was spent in transitions, waiting and organizing.

Bennett (1987) reviewed research in this area in the UK and also reports more time wasting in open plan settings. Overall, he concludes that physical differences in teaching areas do not differentiate teaching practices. There is much agreement that no architectural solution can work without considering what use teachers make of it. There is not a simple relationship between design and teaching. Teachers have been found to adapt open spaces to form discrete areas and reclaim their own space, and one reason for this might be that work loads and preparation appear to increase in open plan settings. Bennett also reports that studies suggest that conventional school designs result in pupils with higher achievements. There seems to be an interaction between physical design and social class of pupils, with pupils with low ability or low socioeconomic status doing worse in more open settings, and better in more structured settings.

Number of children in the class

Another strand of research at the classroom level has been on the effect of the number of pupils in a class. There has been for many years a vigorous debate about the educational effects of class size differences. It is probably true to say that the overwhelming professional judgement is that, other things being equal, smaller classes will enable teachers to provide a better quality of educational experience for pupils, and hence better educational attainments. However, such research that has been done in the UK has suggested little connection between size of class and children's performance, or even more puzzlingly, that children in large classes do better.

The likely importance of class size differences in the everyday experience of teachers and pupils, and the vast resource and policy implications involved, mean that the lack of systematic research is worrying. Educational research can never be the only, or even the main, basis of policy, but it is rare to find such an important aspect of education so uninformed by any research evidence. Given the enormous resourcing implications connected to reductions in size of class it is no surprise that until recently politicians seized on inconclusive findings from much research. There is now, though, a Labour Government in the UK and a Democrat as President of the US who both seem persuaded that smaller classes are preferable on educational grounds. In the UK, the Government are committed to reducing all classes at Key Stage 1 (5 to 7 years), or at least setting a maximum of 30 in a class. However commendable this policy may be, there is still little direct research evidence on the effects of class size differences.

There are three key areas: first, how large are classes, second, what are the effects of class size and adult–child ratios on educational progress, and, third, what classroom processes mediate any effects found.

How large are classes in schools?

A main conclusion from an examination of official statistics on class sizes and pupil teacher ratios (ptrs), is that at primary level in the UK they are large, and have been growing over the past decade or more. Class sizes differ between primary and secondary sectors. In 1996, for example, the average class size in England at primary was 27.5 and at secondary level 21.9. There are more than four times as many large classes in primary schools (see Blatchford *et al.*, 1998, for a more detailed analysis of the official figures). International comparisons appear to be only available in terms of ptrs. At primary level the UK comes out badly. In 1994 it had one of the worst ptrs – 21.7:1 compared to the OECD average of 17.5:1. There is a need to obtain measures that more validly describe size of class as experienced by teachers and pupils rather than on the register (see Blatchford *et al.*, 1998). We also need to be clearer about different adult to child ratios. There is a need to differentiate between teachers, different forms of adult help, and parents (see below). These limitations in published class sizes and adult–child ratios are not trivial; measures must be closely tied to a child's experience if they are to be precise enough to be examined in relation to educational progress.

Does the number of pupils in a class affect pupils' educational attainment and progress?

This is perhaps the most commonly asked question about class size in schools. It is a deceptively simple question, and it is frustrating to many people that the clear answer likely to be given by teachers and others is not matched by research findings. There are several reasons why research findings are unclear. With regard to the UK, a main problem is that we have simply not carried out research which is able to answer the question. Such research as has been done has not employed designs and measures precise and strong enough (see Goldstein and Blatchford, 1998). Earlier British research, which looked at naturally occurring associations between size of class or ptrs and pupils' performance, tended to find little or no relationship between class size and outcomes in terms of attainment or found that pupils in larger classes did somewhat better than pupils in smaller classes (see review in Blatchford and Mortimore, 1994). But the now well understood problem with this kind of research is that we often do not know whether the results can be explained by another factor, for example, that poor attainers tend to be allocated to smaller classes, or more experienced teachers are given larger classes. In other words there may be reasons which could explain the results other than the unlikely conclusion that large classes are better for pupils.

A review of research on class size and its effects on educational achievements by Slavin (1990a) identified eight studies of value, all of them from North America. Generally, they show a moderate effect on pupil attainment (0.2 standard deviations on average) in favour of classes of less than 20. The recent STAR research in Tennessee, in the US, has done much to renew interest in research evidence on class size effects. This is a large scale experimental study that has provided evidence that small classes do have benefits for young children in schools (Word *et al.*, 1990), and this has influenced policy in the USA and other countries, including the UK and The Netherlands (Bosker *et al.*, 1999). Though there are important questions about the validity and generalizability of results from the STAR project (Goldstein and Blatchford, 1998; Mitchell *et al.*, 1991; Prais, 1996), it suggests, along with reviews of the literature (e.g., Blatchford and Mortimore, 1994; Glass *et al.*, 1982; Robinson and Wittebols, 1986; Slavin, 1989), the most solid conclusion that can be drawn: the largest effects have been found with children soon after, or at the point of entry into, the school system. There is also evidence that class size has most effect in the case of disadvantaged children (see Blatchford and Mortimore, 1994; Goldstein and Blatchford, 1998).

There appears to be an important connection between the age of child and class size reductions. The STAR results show that class size reductions have an effect if experienced from school entry. Discussion about the benefits or not of class size reductions cannot be divorced from the age of pupils concerned. There is no evidence we know that class size reductions on their own are effective as an initiative with older children who have been in school for some years. This is one reason why class size changes are more relevant to primary, and particularly the infant school years – Key Stage 1 – than secondary schools. As the STAR team have said, class size reductions are effective as a policy of prevention, not remediation (Blatchford and Mortimore, 1994).

Are processes within classrooms affected by class size differences?

If it can be shown that class size differences have an impact on pupils' academic progress, this still leaves unanswered questions about what mediates the effect. In other words, the association between class size and outcomes in terms of pupils' attainments *has* to be explicable in terms of some other changes within classrooms. Unfortunately, we have little systematic information on what processes might be affected. Although the STAR project found differences in the attainments of children in small and regular classes, the researchers were not asked by the state of Tennessee to enquire about processes underlying the effect, and so we do not know *why* small classes were effective.

It is also helpful to understand more about the classroom processes in cases where size of class does not seem to be related to outcomes, for example, in terms of pupil attainment. It may be, as Shapson *et al.* (1980) suggest, that teachers do not alter their style of teaching when faced with a smaller class, so missing opportunities it provides. Another possibility is that larger classes do not have an adverse effect because teachers alter their style of teaching, for instance, in large classes teachers may feel they have to teach more formally to the whole class, and perhaps restrict the curriculum covered to the 'basics' of reading and maths. This may boost scores in these areas but may adversely affect other aspects of pupils' development, which may not be measured in the research. Another possibility, as we shall see below, is that teachers compensate for the potentially adverse effects on children, though this may have costs in terms of their own well being.

To help explore some ways that classroom processes might be associated with size of class, we examine three main areas, suggested by reviews of the research in this area (see Blatchford and Martin, 1998).

The nature and quality of teaching

When asked to comment on ways in which size of class affects classroom life, teachers often cite the nature of classroom interaction and teaching. However, it needs to be said that research has provided only limited support for the commonly held view that the amount and quality of classroom interactions differ in small and large classes. There are difficulties in interpreting many previous studies of classroom interaction, for example, because of their anecdotal nature, small numbers of classes, and the nature of research designs (see Blatchford and Mortimore, 1994). Finn and Voelkl (1992) conclude that the classroom processes that distinguish small from large classes are far from clear.

A controversial report from OFSTED (1995) used Inspectors' gradings of the quality of teaching and learning seen in lessons. At Key Stage 1 both the quality of learning and the quality of teaching were rated as better in smaller classes, and lessons rated as 'less than sound' in terms of teaching and learning were seen less often in small classes. There were no clear differences in favour of small classes at Key Stage 2.

A main difficulty is that, although many would claim to recognize good and poor teaching, it has proved difficult to find a way of reliably recording and measuring quality of teaching. For this reason it is worth starting with more easily measured aspects of classroom behaviour and interaction. If there is one aspect which, on commonsense grounds, one would expect to be affected by size of class it would be the amount of individual attention a child receives from teachers. This, indeed, seems a logical consequence of reducing the number of pupils to teachers.

Research documenting teachers' comments also points to the increased opportunities for more individual attention and more individualized teaching that result from smaller classes (Blatchford and Martin, 1998). Pate-Bain et al. (1992) report, on the basis of teacher interviews conducted at the end of each school year for STAR research, that teachers felt they were better able to give individualized instruction, and interact more frequently with each child (1992, p. 254). Bennett (1996) reports that teachers and headteachers thought the main adverse effect of large classes was the decreased amount of individual attention.

Teachers' reports are supported by the meta-analysis by Glass and Smith who found that smaller classes resulted in greater teacher knowledge of pupils, frequency of one to one contacts between teachers and pupils, variety of adaptation of teaching to individual pupils, and talk to parents (see Cooper, 1989). Shapson et al. (1980) found that one of the few observation measures on which there were differences was the proportion of pupils addressed by teachers as individuals. This increased in a linear way as class sizes decreased. Finn (1996) concludes from his review that interactions between teachers and individual pupils are more frequent and longer in smaller classes. In a large scale observational study in Britain, pupils in smaller classes were found to experience more teacher attention than pupils in larger classes (Galton *et al.*, 1980).

In a recent small scale study commissioned by the National Union of Teachers, Galton *et al.* (1996) examined how competent teachers behaved when faced with a large class and then a small one. It was concluded that teachers with small classes are more likely to engage in behaviours that typify effective teaching, that is, more challenging questions, more feedback on work, and more sustained interaction. Although suggestive, there are limitations to this study – only a small number of teachers were observed, for a short time, when in an unusual situation, and the authors admit that none of the results reached statistical significance.

Shapson *et al.* (1980) have been influential in indicating that although teachers may feel small classes have beneficial effects on their teaching, this is not necessarily borne out by direct observations of their classrooms. This suggests again the complex way in which the classroom environment and teaching behaviour are related. The 'effect' of class size reduction may well be potential, rather than actual; it may also vary according to the nature and attitude of the teacher. It also suggests that class size reductions are unlikely to be marked unless teachers alter their style of teaching to exploit the opportunities of smaller classes and groups.

Pupil attention in class

Regardless of any connection with class size, there is a good deal of evidence that pupil attentiveness in class is a major variable having positive effects on pupils' achievement (Rowe, 1995). It seems likely that pupils' will learn to the extent that they are attentive to the topics being discussed, or to the work presented to them. In studies of classroom processes related to pupil achievement, dating back to the 1970s, it was found that pupil attentiveness, reflected, for example, in the notion of 'time on task' (see Shulman, 1986), was a mediator of academic success at school. Time on task often has a key role in models set up to explain factors influencing pupils' educational progress (e.g., Creemers, 1994; Dunkin and Biddle, 1974).

It seems likely that, other things being equal, in a smaller class children will be able to concentrate more. This could be for a number of reasons, including the likelihood of less disruption and distraction, and the likelihood that teachers will be able to uphold continuity of involvement. There is some research evidence to support these claims. Finn (1996) has argued that pupil engagement in class mediates the effect of smaller classes on achievement. Several studies indicate that pupils in smaller classes attend and participate more and spend more time on task (Cahen, in Cooper, 1989; Carter, 1984 in Cooper, 1989; Klein, 1985). In explaining why small classes might be linked to attentiveness, Cahen *et al.* (1983 in Cooper, 1989) argue that pupil attention is greater because pupils are not lost in the crowd and have more opportunities for participating. Once again, though, the evidence is not always clear; Shapson *et al.* (1980), in a systematic observation study, did not find that pupils in smaller classes participated more in assigned tasks.

Pupil adjustment to school

Adjustment to school can be seen to have two main components. First, and most obviously, adjustment can be seen in terms of academic progress, for example in terms of progress in literacy and in numeracy. This is the kind of adjustment that has most commonly been examined in relation to class size. Other aspects of academic adjustment have been less often studied, no doubt because they are more difficult to measure. For example, it might be expected that in larger classes it is more difficult to help children become independent in the classroom and resourceful, though this would be difficult to test.

Second, adjustment to school can be seen in terms of social and behaviourial adjustment. A child who does not adjust well to the classroom routine and other children in school is unlikely to do well academically. It seems plausible that, other things being equal, with fewer children in the class teachers will be able to settle them more easily, reassure and draw out quieter children, nurture immature children toward participation in class and deal more effectively with the demands of more troubled children who might otherwise affect the progress of others. Bennett (1996) reports that teachers believe larger classes adversely affect behaviour in class.

The importance of a child's early adjustment to school has been recognized in Britain for some time. Research was conducted at the end of the 1970s on factors influencing successful transition into infant and first school (e.g., Cleave *et al.*, 1982) and nursery school (Blatchford *et al.*, 1982). But a number of factors in recent years have led to a renewed interest in more precisely describing children's adjustment to school. These include recent initiatives regarding school entry assessments, concerns with behaviour and indiscipline in school, and moves toward greater integration of children with special needs into mainstream schools. Moreover, recent research in US developmental psychology has helped provide a conceptual and empirical basis for understanding children's transition into school settings and the important influence of peer relations and friendships (Ladd *et al.*, 1996).

As we have said above, the age of the child is crucial when considering class size reductions. The STAR project indicates that smaller classes are likely to be effective only if experienced by children from the point of school entry. Mosteller (1995), in a sympathetic review of the STAR project, offers an explanation for why class size seems important in children's initial adjustment to school.

When children first come to school, they are confronted with many changes and much confusion. They come into this new setting from a variety of homes and circumstances. Many need training in paying attention, carrying out tasks, and interacting with others in a working situation. In other words, when children start school, they learn to cooperate with others, to learn to learn, and generally get orientated to being students.

So here the explanation of the class size effect cannot be separated from the age of the children; small classes work in the case of young children because the children are new to school, and because small classes offer the children opportunities to learn how to learn – to learn how to be students. This view is plausible but it has not been properly tested. If true it may be particularly relevant in the case of England and Wales where children enter school earlier than most other countries. In some schools children are entering school in September or in January in the year in which they are 5, and may therefore be just 4 years of age on entry. Such children can therefore face the double difficulty of adjusting to a more formal reception curriculum (when a few years ago they would have been in nursery or playgroup), and a large class. To use Mosteller's term, this will make the 'start up' even more difficult for the child.

Though far from clear, some research supports the connection between class size and social aspects of adjustment and behaviour in class. A main theme of several studies is that in smaller classes classroom management is easier, and children's behaviour better (Cahen *et al.* in Cooper, 1989; Carter in Cooper, 1989; Filby in Klein, 1985). Glass *et al.* (1982) found in their meta-analysis that there were fewer misbehaviours in smaller classes. Finn (1996) concludes that in smaller classes less time is spent in classroom management. Finn and Voelkl (1992), in a follow up study of the STAR cohort when in the 4th grade, found that pupils who had been in smaller classes displayed more effort to learn, and less non-participatory or disruptive behaviour. However, in the STAR research itself, smaller classes did not seem to affect levels of classroom discipline (Nye *et al.*, 1992).

Perhaps the strongest evidence connecting larger class sizes and social adjustment to school concerns the quality of relationships between children in the class. Research on children at nursery level indicates that less favourable staff–pupil ratios can lead to more negative relations between children, including more aggression, annoying and teasing (Russell, 1985; Smith *et al.*, 1989). Other research with older pupils has found that in smaller classes they are more appreciative of each other and show an increased desire to assist one another. However, Shapson *et al.* (1980) found no difference in conflicts between pupils.

Teachers in a large scale longitudinal study of class size differences at Key Stage 1 reported that their ability to socialize or 'nurture' children into school life was easier in smaller classes because there were fewer children to get to know, and children were able to get the teacher's attention more regularly (Blatchford and Martin, 1998). Existing research and theory, as well as teachers' experiences, therefore suggests the importance of social aspects of adjustment to school, and the possible links with size of class. However, this link has not been explored directly in the UK, and in the current Institute of Education research, just cited, this is being studied. The conceptualization of adjustment to school in the study takes account of research on children's social and behavioural difficulties and research on social relationships, referred to above.

Social and psychological dimensions of classrooms

The two areas looked at so far – the physical nature of the classroom and the number of pupils – represent only part of the way that classrooms may have effects. There are a number of other ways that classrooms may be looked at. Unfortunately, a bewildering set of concepts and vocabulary has evolved, stemming from quite diverse disciplines – not just educational and social psychology (including ecological psychology) but microethnography and sociolinguistics – making summary very difficult.

Perhaps because we have all spent many years in classrooms, it is very easy to take characteristics of classroom environments for granted and not look objectively at their distinctive nature. Weinstein (1991) describes classrooms as 'crowded, competitive, coercive'. Doyle (e.g., 1986) has been very influential in showing how there are important elements in place over and above the characteristics of particular teachers and pupils. He identifies six elements as follows:

Multidimensionality

The classroom is often a crowded place, and there a large quantity of events and tasks in the classroom. Events have to be planned to meet individual requirements and changing demands. There are many management functions, records to be kept, resources to be ordered and planned for.

Simultaneity

Many things happen at once in classrooms, perhaps especially in primary schools with the tradition of helping individuals and groups working at different paces and tasks. But even in a whole class setting an eye has to be kept on whether students are following, whilst watching for misbehaviour, whilst answering pupil questions, whilst trying to keep the logic of the presentation going, and so on.

Immediacy

There is a rapid pace in classroom events. Gump and Jackson have separately estimated that a primary school teacher has 500 exchanges with individual students each day. There is little time to reflect on practice!

Unpredictability

Classroom events often take unexpected turns. Interruptions are frequent, and it is not easy to anticipate how an activity will go on a particular day with a particular group of students.

Publicness

Classrooms are public places, and events are often witnessed by most of the pupils. If a teacher fails to notice a pupil's behaviour this is likely to be noticed and acted on by other pupils.

History

Classes accumulate a common set of experiences and norms which provide the foundation for future actions. Classes are affected by new arrivals and the departure of students.

Doyle feels that these six dimensions create pressures that shape the task of teaching. Their effect varies no doubt but the pressures operate in all classrooms regardless of how teachers organize activities.

Classroom psychological environment

Another way of conceiving of effects at the classroom level, which has received a good deal of attention going back many decades, is the 'classroom psychological environment'. The theoretical roots of the concept comes from Kurt Lewin. The concept is rather abstract but refers to the climate or atmosphere of the class as a social group, which can influence what students learn. Paradoxically, given its abstract nature, it is usually measured in very concrete, psychometric terms by asking students to rate psychological characteristics of their class on questionnaire items. Dimensions include cohesiveness, satisfaction, goal direction, difficulty, competitiveness and friction. There are overlaps with the term 'classroom climate', though this tends to be drawn from observational measures and is more linked to process product research (see Chapter 8 of this book). From the late 1960s on, researchers have sought to link classroom environment to learning outcomes. Key research programmes have been conducted by Marjoribanks, Walberg, Moos and Frazer. Reviews by MacAulay (1990) and others conclude that many studies have shown that classroom environments have important influences on student achievements and self concept. There is also agreement that it is important to consider the person-environment 'fit', that is, students achieve better when there is a higher similarity between the actual class environment and that preferred by students. This also suggests that different types of pupils, for example, in terms of temperament, will perform in different ways, and react differently, in different classes.

Classroom task and reward structures

Another direction of research on classrooms has conceived of the class in terms of task or goal structures. One version of this can be found in the work of the Johnsons (Johnson and Johnson, 1987) who were interested in the way students related to each other in terms of the degree of interdependence they sought while working toward instructional goals. Goal structures could be cooperative, competitive, or individualistic (see review in Arends, 1994). A connected notion concerns the extent to which reward structures are cooperative, competitive or individualistic (Slavin, 1983, in Arends, 1994). The way teachers organize goal and reward structures determines which types of goals are accomplished.

An allied area of research, but stemming more from theory and research in the area of motivation, has made much progress in linking classrooms to the kinds of goals students pursue. Again this is a huge area of research and its coverage and theoretical underpinnings can only be hinted at here. One central theme has been the extent to which classrooms encourage 'mastery' or 'performance' orientation. The basic notion is that classroom environments should encourage students to be independent and in control of their learning. In a statement of immense relevance to current trends in education in England and Wales, Eccles and her colleagues have concluded: 'In general, environmental settings which emphasize evaluation, social comparison, and competition appear to increase self-focus or an ego-involved orientation' (Eccles *et al.*, 1984, p. 307). Eccles and others argue that schools typically are not well matched to student's needs as learners. Eccles' work is grounded in Atkinson's expectancy value model (see Pintrich and Schunk, 1996). Other research stems from a goal theory approach to motivation. Again the distinction between task mastery/ intrinsic interest v. ability/self focus is key. Ames (1992) has shown that if there is a stress on ability relative to others' grades and performance, then students will adopt ability focused goals, while emphasis on mastery, effort and improvement are likely to lead to task focused goals. There is an overlap here with Doyle's (1979, in Arends, 1994) view that the primary feature of classroom life are rules concerning how students 'exchange (their) performance for grades' (in Arends, 1994, p. 108).

Participation structures

Other ways of viewing classroom environments have come from microethnographic and sociolinguistic analyses of classroom interactions, for example, concerning rules governing speaking, listening and turn taking. Sinclair and Coulthard (1975), Mehan (1979) and many others have shown the ubiquitous place in classrooms of the three-part move of teacher initiation–student reply–teacher evaluation or follow up. McHoul (in Doyle, 1986) has described the difference between teacher–pupil verbal interactions and conversation in other contexts. The former is highly ritualized and, despite its taken-for-granted nature, rather odd when looked at analytically and in relation to other kinds of dialogue; for example, because the teacher is in control, turn taking is limited, students do not usually select another pupil to speak, and the student normally has to wait for the teacher to select. Because of its constraints, the three-part move probably helps continuity in classroom discourse and avoids overlap and confusion (see Doyle, 1986, for coverage of other analyses of rules of class-room interactions).

A central theme in this area is a view of the classroom as a communica-tive setting and of the social or 'communicative competence' that is required there. It has also been called the 'hidden curriculum', that is, through implicit rules of authority and classroom order pupils are social-ized into the rules and power structures in the wider adult society. Know-ledge about rules in classroom discourse has helped understanding of the difficulties that some children have if they are used to different systems of rules. Pupils are quick to learn what seems appropriate in different settings within school, but some, because of their home and community experi-ences, find this easier. Low ability, working-class, and ethnic minority stu-dents seem to be most likely to have problems in comprehending the largely middle-class rules that operate in classrooms. If pupils' home and pre-school experiences are not congruent with the rules operating in school classrooms then it will be difficult for them to follow lessons and proce-dures and gain access to instruction. Because these pupils may show diffi-culties in class, teachers may come to expect these pupils to fail academically. Often cited studies are Phillips (1972) who studied difficul-ties of native Americans in school, Heath (1982) who studied why poor black children were failing and not participating in school, and Willes (1983) who explored difficulties one might expect children starting school to have in understanding interactional demands of the classroom.

One strategy has been to compare natural language use in out-of-school contexts with that used or needed in school contexts. This helps get a hold on what is distinctive about the social and interactive nature of the class-room. Interestingly, when one considers that many initiatives in early and pre-school education have been based on the view that home environments can be culturally or linguistically deficient, and that school environments can offer a necessary educational corrective (in the US, compensatory pro-grammes such as Head Start were based on this assumption), this research has tended to put interaction patterns at school in a poor light in compar-ison to those at home. A good example of such research is Tizard and Hughes (1984) study of English working-class and middle-class 4-year-old girls at home and at school. They found children who could appear lin-guistically incompetent and monosyllabic at school and did not impress teachers could, when in the familiar home context, engage as a matter of course in conceptually rich and complex exchanges with their mothers.

Examples in the study include discussions at home about a sloping roof, shopping and the window cleaner, and these are analysed to show they involve more child input, are more geared to child concerns and involve discussion about knowledge (rather than play in the hope of conceptual development that was prevalent in the nursery environment).

We have in the first part of this chapter examined a wealth of research on the classroom context. We have covered the physical layout of classrooms, the number of pupils, the psychological environment, classroom task and reward structures, and participation structures. It is now time to focus down more closely on contexts within classrooms.

Contexts within classrooms

Some of the most interesting research on classrooms has been an attempt to locate and study meaningful units below or rather within the level of the class. The importance of this is that different contexts within classrooms may place different interactional demands on participants, and the educational effects may need to be examined in terms of these units or contexts. Classrooms are composed of numerous sub-settings that vary in rules that are appropriate and in the behaviour they elicit from teachers and pupils. Hargreaves *et al.* (1975) showed that classroom rules had to be understood as operating within contexts, or phases of lessons. Five phases were identified: entry, settling down or preparation, the lesson itself, clearing up and exit. Students were typically allowed to speak quietly amongst themselves during entry and preparation, but after the signal that the lesson proper had begun they were expected to attend to the teacher and not talk to each other. There may also be phases within lessons, for example, recommendations for the literacy hour to be divided into discrete phases – whole class teaching, ability groups, etc..

A review of research relevant to this section is again made difficult by the variety of different approaches, often from quite different academic disciplines and literatures. One approach again has its roots in the ecological psychology of Barker and Wright. Segments of classroom life are identified on the basis of painstakingly collected narrative records of the classroom 'behavioural stream'. In analysis, the continuous temporal record is divided into segments that are natural units of action, and these segments are identified on the basis of, for example, changes in participants (small group to whole class), resources used in the lesson, roles of participants (e.g., verbal answering to writing) and rules governing behaviours (talking allowed v. silence during individual work). A change in one of these can mean a change in the nature of the segment (see Doyle, 1986; and Gump, 1967). Once the segments have been identified the kinds of behaviours, particants, etc. that occur within them can be examined.

The basic unit of classroom organization is often seen to be the activity

(Doyle, 1986), that is, short blocks of classroom time during which students are arranged in a particular way. Researchers have calculated the number of activities typical during the school day to be more than 30 in an average elementary school class (Ross, 1984 in Doyle, 1986). Activities can also overlap with each other. Doyle, following Gump (1967), states that this is rarely more than two at one time but in some primary school classes in the UK there can be four or five activities running parallel to each other at one time.

Segments, as used in ecological psychology, are units resulting from the cutting up of the temporal stream of behaviour, but other analyses of settings within classrooms refer to settings that operate at particular moments in time. Doyle (1986) and Weinstein (1991) have summarized research on different activity types. Berliner's (1983 in Doyle, 1986) list is typical of US research: reading circle, seatwork, one way presentation, mediated presentation (for example, involving tapes), silent reading, construction, games, play, transitions and housekeeping. Weinstein (1991) organizes her review around the following activities: recitation, teacher directed small groups, seatwork, student directed small groups. In US research a few activity types seem to dominate, with 'seatwork' taking up the bulk of time, followed by whole class presentation and then transitions and other housekeeping events (Gump, 1967). Similar results come from observational studies in English junior and infant schools (Blatchford *et al.*, 1987; Galton *et al.*, 1980). It would be interesting to see to what extent recent curriculum reforms in the UK and the emphasis on whole class teaching and the introduction of literacy and numeracy hours have affected the types and durations of different activities.

The point of relevance to this chapter is that different activities or segments can demand different kinds of behaviours from both teacher and pupils. Mehan (1979) showed how competent participation in classrooms requires an understanding of what context one is in and when contexts change, as well as what behaviour is appropriate in different classroom contexts. Gump (1967) (in Doyle, 1986) found that teachers engaged in more acts in whole class than reading groups, and dealing with difficulties in pupils' behaviour may be more common in some segments than others. Bossert (1979 in Doyle, 1986) found that teachers were more inclined to seek control in larger groups and so were more concerned with controlling misbehaviour. Understandably, teachers provide more individual help during seatwork, though Galton *et al.* (1980) showed that the cognitive level of language use can be higher in whole class settings. Research on the nature of teacher language in classes with overlapping activities (Bossert, 1979) indicates that the frequency of reprimands is less in multitask classrooms than whole class settings, though this may just mean there are less interactions overall. Blumenfeld *et al.* (1983 in Doyle, 1986) found teacher talk in 'open activity structures' (that is, where students work on different

activities at the same time) was less negative, more about academic performance, and was less about procedure, than teacher talk in single task classrooms. The extent of multiple tasks is likely to vary between countries.
There has been a tradition in some English primary schools of parallel and
different activities in small groups. This may mean that recent reforms have
made multitask classrooms less common.

Student behaviour can also vary by activity type. Gump (1967) found
that pupil involvement was highest in teacher-led small groups, then whole
class recitations and teacher presentations, and was lowest for individual
study and pupil presentations. Also, behaviours seen as problematic can be
affected by activity type. Silverstein (1979 in Doyle, 1986) in a study of
fourth grade classes found such behaviours (from daydreaming to disruption) more common during seatwork and less common in small group and
whole class settings. Gump (1967) examined behaviour during the opening
part of segments – the first four minutes – and found involvement significantly lower than during the remainder of the segment. So here there is
variation by phase of segment. Students did most of their work near the end
of a segment, if a product or end product was required.

Blatchford *et al.* (1982), on the basis of an observational study of two
nursery classes attached to London primary schools, examined behaviour
of newcomers in two main types of activity: free play and so called
'directed' sessions. Interest was in how such young children, new to school
settings, would behave in the more formal, directed settings. Five such sessions were examined: register, milk, story, rhymes and music. For the most
part children behaved 'appropriately' in all five sessions, though there was
rather less attention in register, probably because their attention wandered
after their name had been called. In one class this session was much more
concerned with individuals rather than the whole group and this would
explain the increase in 'move away' and 'lost' behaviour in this session.
More inappropriate and disruptive behaviour occurred in rhymes and
singing sessions, most probably because children had difficulties with the
words and actions, and in one of the nursery classes this appeared to go on
too long. Some directed sessions were therefore less prone than others to
hold children's attention. These kinds of results are useful if it is agreed that
newcomers to school will become more easily assimilated if there is a continuity and focus to events.

There may also be systematic associations between sequencing of activities and pupil involvement. Gump (1967) found that involvement in the
beginning phase of seatwork was especially low after recess/breaktime (see
also Chapter 5). Krantz and Risley (1977 in Doyle, 1986) found off-task
behaviour was high when story time occurred after recess – which may be
one reason why staff can find afternoon play disruptive and why it is being
eliminated in some English schools (Blatchford and Sumpner, 1998). One
of us was very struck by the evaluations of a recent course he ran for

teachers and educational psychologists. It was clear the sequencing of events affected the participants' attention: the session straight after a full lunch was much less successful than the rest of day. Being psychologists and teachers, there were also plenty of suggestions in the evaluation forms about how the 'graveyard slot' could be better organized to avoid loss of attention!

Tasks

We shall see in the next chapter that there has been increasing interest in teachers' subject matter knowledge. There has also been interest in ways in which subject matter content is enacted in classrooms. One approach to this has been to see the classroom 'task' as the unit of analysis. Doyle (Doyle, 1986; Doyle and Carter, 1984; see also Bennett *et al.*, 1984 in the UK) have used the notion of the 'academic task' to account for how the curriculum becomes a programme of action in classrooms. So subject matter appears, or is manifested, in classrooms as work. Key dimensions in this model include 'accountability' (e.g., evaluated strictly by the teacher) which will affect the seriousness with which such tasks are taken by pupils. Another dimension is ambiguity and risk, so that higher cognitive tasks requiring understanding, reasoning, and problem formulation are high in ambiguity and risk for students because the correct answers cannot be so obviously predicted and so failure is a possibility. This will affect pupils' attitudes to work, so that pupils may be more positive toward tasks which are low on challenge but low on risk. Doyle and Carter (1984) in a study of three junior high English classes, found tasks involving descriptive or expository writing were difficult for the teacher to manage. They could extend over several days, involved frequent student questions, and clarification and assistance, while, in contrast, more predictable and less ambiguous tasks involving recall or predictable algorithms, e.g., as found in vocabulary or grammar assigments, proceeded smoothly and efficiently. This situation will presumably be affected by the way ambiguity is dealt with by teachers, and also by individual differences between pupils. There are surely tasks that may be challenging but also carry more reward. As Doyle says, safe can be boring.

Within-class groupings

All pupils in classes are grouped in some form or another, and different groups may affect their learning. The benefits or disadvantages of grouping practices have aroused a good deal of comment and research. While a balanced view has been expressed: HMI (OFSTED, 1995) recommended that 'teachers employ different teaching methodologies to achieve different objectives' (p. 6), and that teachers 'deploy an intelligent balance of grouping strategies' (p. 6) rather than following doctrinaire methods for the handling of classroom groups, it is also true that 'progressive' primary education practices, including groupwork, have been criticized as being ineffective (Alexander et al., 1992; OFSTED, 1995), and it has been recommended that teachers adopt 'whole class' teaching methods, albeit tempered with a recognition that pupils need to be interactive rather than passive.

Some research on groupings at primary level reveals a negative picture, as seen, for example, in studies that have shown that the quality of talk and work in groups can be relatively low level (Bennett et al., 1984, Galton; 1990), and that pupils may not always be confident about what is required of them (Galton, 1990). Research (Dreeben, 1984; Galton, 1990) has shown that pupil groupings are often chosen to meet the needs of classroom organization and physical structure rather than to promote children's learning. Being seated around tables does not mean that pupils will or can work as a small group. Galton and Williamson (1992) showed that teachers do not always coordinate learning task and type of groupings. Bennett et al. (1984) found an individual approach to cognitive enhancement often hindered effective development of learning from taking place amongst pupils.

Grouping of pupils is connected in a more positive way to current theories of learning and development, for example, the benefits of peer interactive groupings (Doise and Mugny, 1984; Howe et al., 1992; Rogoff, 1990; Vygotsky, 1978). Experimental research on cooperative group work also paints a more positive picture (Slavin, 1990b; Johnson and Johnson, 1987). Studies generally show that cooperative groups have positive effects on student achievement, race relations and concern for others. Although widely cited, such studies are difficult to interpret in the sense that they may not reflect the everyday conditions in classrooms, and can demand a good deal of preparation for teachers. Doyle (1986) argues that there is little information on problems classroom teachers have in managing cooperative team learning.

If teachers are to be effective in their classrooms and 'deploy an intelligent balance of grouping strategies' (OFSTED, 1998, p. 6), they must be aware of the potential for learning and have the ability to bring these 'pedagogic groupings' into practice in their own classrooms. However, to date, research, while useful in pointing out the inadequacies of particular groups or the relationship of tasks assigned to groups, has been less successful in showing which of these groupings have been most effectively tied to specific types of classroom learning tasks and with what frequency (and purpose) teachers use the range of small groups available to them. Surprisingly little is known about about the nature of groupings used in an everyday way in classrooms (Blatchford et al., 1999b).

Perhaps most attention has been paid to the composition of groups. Teachers necessarily have to make decisions concerning who should be in groups, taking into consideration various factors including ability, sex distribution and friendships between pupils. One major problem for any teacher is how to distribute the range of pupil ability amongst groups; whether to use same or mixed ability groups for particular curriculum tasks. Research has concentrated almost exclusively on ability mix (Webb *et al.*, 1997). Ability based groups are currently recommended by school inspectors (OFSTED, 1998), though there is little research on the effectiveness of this form of grouping in primary schools. Other features of group composition may also be important, including sex mix (Bennett and Dunne, 1992; Howe, 1997) and friendship (see Chapter 3).

But there are a number of other features of groupings within classrooms that require more attention. In a recent study at the Institute of Education, the multidimensional nature of group characteristics has been systematically described using a novel form of teacher completed maps of classroom groupings at particular points in time (Blatchford *et al.*, 1999b). For each group in the map, group composition in terms of ability, sex and friendship mix was documented, but this was accompanied by information on the size and number of groups in class, the curriculum, task and activity type, the role of adults and support of groups. One focus was on the interconnections between these different features of groups. Another key interest was developments with age over the primary phase (grouping practices were studied in a large-scale survey of reception (4/5 years), Year 2 (6/7 years) and Year 5 (9/10 years) classes). Over the whole stage, small groups of 4–6 pupils dominated, but with age there was an increased usage of smaller groupings, a reduced availability of adult support, and a greater emphasis on the extension and generalizing of skills. These changes in grouping practices reflected the increasing autonomy of pupils with age (see Blatchford *et al.*, 1999b).

Contrary to the common view that mixed ability teaching dominates in early primary education, the majority of groupings were composed on the basis of similar ability. Indeed, there was more of a balance of mixed and similar ability groupings with the older children, in Year 5. There was a larger proportion of boys than girls working individually, and this may reflect issues of behaviour and attention control, and special needs considerations. This possibility is further indicated by the high level of adult presence with these groupings. The predominance of triadic groupings, where boys were in the majority, could be cause for concern (Tann, 1981). Typically, pupils worked alone but on the same task as others in their group. There was very little interactive (cooperative) group work.

Grouping practices within classes and class size

The class and the group can be thought of as two types of environmental contexts within a classroom, with the group level usually nested within the level of the whole class (except when the children are all working together – with whole class interactive teaching there is only one group!). It is likely that the two levels are connected. It might be expected, for example, that in a large class the teacher would be forced to organize the children into more and/or larger groups. One aspect that may be important, therefore, is the connection between the size of class and grouping practices within the class. We end this chapter by examining recent research which has been attempting to show the nature of the links between the two levels and the educational implications for teachers and pupils.

Some teachers in the Institute of Education study seemed clear about the connection (see Blatchford and Martin, 1998). In response to a question asking them to explain how they felt the quality of teaching and learning in their class this year had been affected by the size of class, they wrote:

> I try to keep working groups to around eight maximum – but ideally I would like only six in a group. I like to value every child's contribution to group work and smaller groups make this possible.

> Quality of teaching/learning has been much more effective as group sizes have been much smaller.

> Some of my groups have 10 children – and I often have them working around a large table. It's much harder to control this size group which must affect learning.

However, as far as we know, this possibility has not been looked at systematically before. It has been possible to study this in a systematic way in the Institute of Education class size study, and the parallel project on grouping practices, described above. Connections between class size and grouping practices in terms of number and size of groups, group composition, presence of adults, and the nature of the curriculum, task and activity type were explored at reception, Year 2 and Year 5 age levels. As might be expected, results showed that class size increased with age of child; the youngest children in school (in reception classes) were in smaller classes. Class size was found to constrain within-class groupings in several fundamental ways. Surprisingly, given the expectation that in larger classes teachers would be forced to use more whole class teaching, it was found that there was a greater use of whole class interactive teaching in *small* classes. Contrary to expectation, the number of very large groups, including whole class teaching, *decreased* with size of class. What increased with size of class was the increased use of large groups of 7–10 pupils (Blatchford *et al.*, 1999b). Teachers therefore appear to prefer to organize learning in terms of groups, but because of the number of children, they are forced to teach to larger groups than they would like (Blatchford *et al.*, 1999a).

Conclusions

The review in this chapter has necessarily had to cover a wealth of research, often from very different conceptual and empirical research traditions. Enough, though, has been covered to illustrate the importance of considering the classroom context. The chapter was structured in two parts: first, in terms of ways of conceiving contexts at the class level, in terms of the physical layout of classrooms, the number of pupils, the psychological environment, classroom task and reward structures, participation structures, and, second, in terms of within-class contexts such as behavioural segments, tasks, activities and within-class groupings. Finally, we looked at just one way that the different contexts can be linked through the connections between class size and the size and number of within-class groupings.

Several conclusions might be drawn from the research reviewed here. One is the main point that classroom contexts can be influential in affecting teachers and pupils and educational interactions between them. The research on class size and within-class grouping just cited, for example, is suggestive of ways in which teachers and pupils will necessarily adapt to class level and within-class levels, suggests ways in which the two levels will interconnect, sometimes in surprising ways, and also shows ways that these connections will vary according to the age of the child.

One avenue for future research is on identification of other links between class level and within-class level contexts. Staying with class size, this could include links between class size and the nature and effectiveness of learning tasks in different groups. It may be that given a class of a given size (a large class of 32, say) then certain consequences may then follow in terms of the size and number of groups, and these in turn may affect the educational experiences of pupils in those groups.

This examination of the effects of classroom contexts, and connections between levels, could well be extended to forge links with research on effectiveness in schools. We have shown throughout this chapter that there are differences particular to the classroom level, and research could be insightful when considering ways in which schools are more or less effective. As we said at the beginning of this chapter, researchers interested in school effectiveness have tended not to conceive of the classroom context in the same way as we have in this chapter. But school and teacher effects will necessarily be mediated through activities within classrooms.

Attention to classroom contexts at both the class and within-class levels is important theoretically but future research could seek to be clearer about implications for practice. One challenge is to seek a fuller conceptualization of ways that experiences in classroom contexts connect with academic development. We have looked at this in a limited way, for example, in terms of groupings in class and class size effects, but more could be done in terms of conceptualizations involving other within-class settings.

There are also methodological issues related to identification of class-room contexts. Interestingly, Dunkin and Biddles' early (1974) review still seems relevant, indicating that there are still important issues to resolve, for example, ways of recording the sequencing of segments, and teacher and pupil behaviours. Again, links with effectiveness research are important. This kind of research, with close and systematic attention to segments and activities, is difficult and time consuming to collect but could be helpful for teachers. One possible line of enquiry would be differences in sequencing between effective and ineffective, or experienced and beginning, teachers.

This chapter has focused on academic aspects of classrooms, but it is important to recognize that

the classroom is not simply a social context in which students learn academic lessons. It is a social context in which students also learn social lessons – lessons about appropriate behaviour in various con-texts, about one's self as a learner and one's position in the status hier-archy, about relationships with students from other ethnic and racial groups, about the relative value of competition and cooperation, and about friendship. Experiences in activity segments influence the con-tent of these lessons.

(Weinstein, 1991, p. 520)

The classroom context is therefore of importance for academic and social development, and in various ways throughout this book we have sought to review current knowledge on both. It should be clear, though, that there is still much work to be done.

8 Interactions in the classroom: teacher–pupil interactions

The actual problem to be solved is not what to teach, but how to teach.

Charles William Eliot, 1869 Inaugural Address Harvard College
(in Gage, 1985)

Arends (1994), in an essential book on teaching, has argued that teachers, regardless of the age of their pupils, their subject areas, or the types of schools in which they teach, are asked to perform three important functions: first, executive (providing leadership to students); second, interactive (face to face instructions with students); and third, organizational (working with colleagues, parents and others). In this chapter, and in line with the focus of this book, we are concerned with the second of these, that is, with the interactive function of teaching. Approaching this from a somewhat different direction, if one considers the nature of classroom life – all the myriad events and interactions that take place – one main feature is the interactions that take place between teachers and pupils. Though there are a range of new developments in education, for example, those involving computing and distance learning, face to face interactions are still a main feature of most classrooms and still lie at the heart of the learning process, and this is likely to be true across all types of schools, subject areas and age of child. Gage's conclusion in the mid-1980s still stands: 'Teaching is the central process of education' (Gage, 1985).

There has been an enormous amount of research on face to face interactions between teachers and pupils. This research has had a variety of purposes and stemmed from a range of different theoretical and conceptual frameworks. It is not intended (or possible) to review all of this work in one chapter. The aim is to concentrate on work which has had an interest in the effects, and more specifically, the effectiveness of teaching interactions. Though not an exact match, this concern has tended to be informed by a psychological orientation. This work is of importance in its own right but is also interesting because of the way it highlights debates about the merits of different paradigms of research on classroom interactions, that has applications beyond the school setting. There are, for example, informative but relatively unexplored parallels between research on teacher–pupil relations and parent–child relations. It is probably true to say that developmental psychologists are not as familiar as they might be with research on classroom interactions, but in turn educational psychologists tend not to be familiar with developmental research on parent–child interactions and peer interactions. This is unfortunate because there are many conceptual and methodological overlaps between the two kinds of research, and much that each can learn from the other. In this chapter we will seek to bring out some general conceptual and methodological issues.

In research on teaching there has been recognition of difficulties with the notion of a 'science of teaching', not the least because it begs questions about the nature of 'science' with regard to teaching, and suggests, at least to some, a now outmoded positivist approach. Some time ago it was recognized that there was a gap between research on teaching and research on learning (e.g., Bennett *et al.*, 1984). Recently there has been renewed interest in 'pedagogy' and an attempt to show the necessary links between teaching and learning. Biggs and Moore (1993), for example, have identified ways in which conceptualizations of learning and conceptualizations of teaching are linked. Watkins and Mortimore (1999) however, have shown the problematic nature of 'pedagogy' and the links between teaching and learning.

While recognizing that there are important connections between teaching and learning and also the value of an appreciation of pedagogy, this chapter will focus more narrowly on *interactions* between teachers and pupils rather than with psychological and learning processes in the child. In this sense the chapter is more limited than a full coverage of pedagogy as described by Watkins and Mortimore (1999). The chapter will also be selective in its approach to interactions, drawing more on observational research and from psychology, than, for example, sociology and other disciplines. In line with Gage's delineation in his 1985 monograph, in this chapter we consider classroom teaching in terms of such things as: 'lecturing and tutoring but all other types of interactions such as teacher–pupil questioning, pupil responding and initiations, as well as pupil work at tables and desks, and the managerial activities that maintain the whole process.'

We will be concerned with attempts to describe the nature of interactions, to look at developments with age and by school sector, and also the effects of these interactions, both short term and long term, on pupils' school attainments. Specifically, the chapter has two main sections: first, descriptive research on the nature of interactions in classrooms and, second, the effects of these interactions on educational outcomes. The chapter ends by looking more generally at issues involved in research on teaching and discusses competing ways in which teaching has been researched.

Descriptive research on teaching

One of the main directions of research on teaching has been the search for valid and insightful descriptions of the nature of teacher–pupil interactions. Some of the seminal studies in the literature have provided new ways of looking at teaching and classroom interactions. To select but a few works, books by Adams and Biddle (1970), Dunkin and Biddle (1974), Flanders (1970), Jackson (1968), Kounin (1970) and Sinclair and Coulthard (1975) have all contributed in very different ways. These studies had very different conceptual and disciplinary roots, including sociology, sociolinguistics and ethnography, as well as psychology. As we shall see below, there are fundamentally different approaches to knowledge and research, and currently an acrimonious debate, between competing 'paradigms' of classroom research. This is one reason why knowledge in this area of educational research has not built up through a collective dialogue and accumulation of findings. This is not helped by some contemporary views, which disparage the whole notion of educational research developing and building knowledge and theory (Costas, 1998).

As an example of one research approach to the description of teaching, we look at perhaps the largest and most ambitious study conducted in Britain. This is the so-called ORACLE study, based at Leicester University, from which have come a number of books and papers (e.g., Galton *et al.*, 1980, and Galton and Simon, 1980). The aim of the study was to describe teacher and pupil classroom interactions and activities in a sample of junior school classrooms and then relate these to pupils' progress in school. The study involved the use of two carefully designed schedules – a teacher record and a pupil record. The teacher record comprised 27 mutually exclusive categories of teacher behaviour: statements, questions, silent interactions etc., as well as categories denoting whether interactions were in a class, group or individual setting. The pupil record was based on earlier US observation systems, and involved a number of sub-sets of categories within which there was a further choice of categories. The research used a form of time-sampling involving a series of snap shots every 25 seconds ('instantaneous time sampling') at which points teacher and pupil behaviour was coded.

There were many such observations – 18 lessons throughout the school year. Pupil observations were conducted with a sub-sample of children – four boys and four girls in each class. The first book (Galton *et al.*, 1980) gave basic descriptive information. It confirmed that the basic interactive processes of classroom life are not always apparent to informal acquaintance and would certainly not be apparent if one only attended to political rhetoric of the time. The study was done in the context of a backlash against the Plowden Report in the late 1960s and the supposed dominance of child-centred progressive education in schools. A couple of schools had collapsed in a clamour of right-wing recriminations about the state of public education. This movement led to Prime Minister James Callaghan's Ruskin Lecture, the so-called 'Black Papers', and to the widely held view that progressive ideas had led to chaos in schools, out-of-control children and ineffectual teaching, with little work on the 3 Rs. Such views are still heard today.

We feel that observational research of classroom interactions, like that in the ORACLE study, can make a modest, perhaps, but none the less important contribution. For instance, the ORACLE study showed that the premises of the view just outlined were almost entirely wrong. It showed the value of collecting in a careful way information on classroom interactions and behaviour. In contrast to the view just expressed, the researchers found that around three quarters of classroom time was spent on curriculum related activities, lessons were dominated by basic skills of number and language, and there were very low levels of disruption. In one of the interesting findings, the 'asymmetry' of teacher–pupil contact was highlighted. That is, from the teacher's point of view she interacts with children a lot, and often with individuals, but from an individual pupil's point of view, s/he often works alone, interacting with the teacher in only one sixth of lesson time, and even then most often as but one pupil in the whole class. In general, there was a good deal of individual work, but little individual attention or instruction, and little cooperative group work. Critics such as Barrow (1984) sought to undermine the results by claiming they are obvious or logically necessary, or missed important features of teaching, such as creativity, or important background pupil characteristics, such as home support, but research has to be selective and results can often be seen as obvious in retrospect. One value of the ORACLE study is that its limitations are obvious because of the overt nature and description of its methods.

Although the common right wing criticism expressed in the 1970s was shown to be unfounded, a similar view is still heard today. Those with a political axe to grind will always be selective in their examples and evidence; but it is unfortunate that the kind of evidence which would give the lie to extreme views is still so limited. Interestingly, if anything, the ORACLE project showed a restricted, rather dull coverage of the curriculum, an over-reliance on unstimulating worksheets and, more impressionistically, an absence of flair in classroom interactions.

A later study, this time involving younger, infant school-aged children (5 to 7 years), also involved a substantial direct observational component, and although there were differences in terms of location and social background of schools, it provides the basis for a general account of changes from the infant stage (Key Stage 1: 5 to 7 years), and the junior stage (Key Stage 2: 7 to 11 years), that is, over the whole primary stage. This was a longitudinal study of children's progress in London schools from school entry (Blatchford et al., 1987; Tizard et al., 1988). Children were followed through to the end of secondary school (at 16 years), but observations were only conducted during the first (reception) year and then in Year 1 and Year 2. Observations were conducted during classroom learning time (excluding, for example, times out of the classroom in assembly, swimming, music and movement, and register and break). An observation system was devised which covered individual children's behaviour in five main areas: settings (individual work, group work, play etc.); school subjects (maths, language etc.); interactions with their teacher; interactions with other children; and behaviour when not interacting. Within each of these last three 'social modes', there were categories denoting whether work or play was on task, procedural (e.g., sharpening pencils), social (e.g., discussing TV programmes) or 'task avoidance' (e.g., disruptive, disengaged or aggressive). Each child was observed for six 5-minute periods each day, divided into consecutive 10-second time intervals. Within sets of behaviours, choices for each time interval were made on the basis of which categories occurred for the longest length of time (sometimes called 'predominant activity sampling'). This kind of observation work is extremely time consuming to conduct and process. Some measure of this comes from the total number of observation (and therefore data) points – 93 990 10–second intervals in the first year, 55 680 in the second and 46 740 in the third year of school. Full details of the schedule and more details on the research can be found in Blatchford *et al.* (1987).

General results showed that children were for the most part found in individual work, and that group work occurred rarely. These findings are similar to those in the ORACLE study. The proportion of times children were in a setting with the teacher was around a quarter of all observations. Again like the ORACLE study, while it was found that individual work was common, individual *teaching* was not. In most contacts with teachers they were one of a class; in only 1 in 5 contacts, whether in a class, group or individual setting, were they the main focus of a teacher's attention. One to one contacts between teacher and child only occurred in 17 per cent of contacts between them. The most common type of behaviour was what was called 'task teach' – communicating facts, ideas or concepts by explaining, demonstrating, questioning or suggesting. If we include times when the teacher organized and prepared children for work this figure rose to 80 per cent – indicating again the business-like and work-orientated nature of classrooms. It is worth remembering that this study involved the youngest children in schools. The child's active contribution to teacher–pupil interaction – that is, the total number of child responses or initiations to the teacher – actually decreased over the first three years (9 per cent, 7 per cent and 6 per cent of all observations for the three years) – indicating a progressively passive role for pupils in relations with their teachers. Interestingly, we found that more emotionally charged behaviours, like praise and disapproval/criticism, were very rare, as were disruptive comments to the teacher. It was found that the total of all on-task behaviours (across the three social modes) was 61 per cent, total procedural behaviours 13 per cent, total social behaviours 5 per cent, and all task avoidance/off-task behaviours 9 per cent. Results on sex and ethnic differences can be found in Chapter 12.

In summary, this exhaustive observation study showed that for the bulk of their time children, even at this tender age, are busy and involved mostly in individual work in the basics of language and mathematics. Interactions with their teachers are predominantly business-like and concerned with the basic areas of reading, writing and maths.

Both studies are rather dated now. They are described here because they illustrate the role of basic descriptive observational research on interactions in classrooms, and also because, as mentioned above, there have not been more recent studies that update the picture. Interestingly, Galton (1998, in TES 3 July) has provided a brief description of main results from a follow-up study, carried out in 1996–7, involving 38 primary schools, most of which figured in the original study. This showed that work with groups and whole class teaching had nearly doubled (7.5 per cent in 1980 report to 14.6 per cent in 1996 for group work, and 15.1 per cent to 31.3 per cent for class teaching). The reason for this difference is not clear but is likely to be in response to changes in educational and curriculum policy; it may, of course, owe something to the original report and the interpretations for practice, for example the value of interactive whole class teaching. However, children still spent most time working on their own, and most contacts with their teachers are as a member of the class. It was also found that the ratio of teacher statements to questions had not changed; thus the increase in class teaching had increased the amount of talking *at* pupils.

It may well be that main aspects of classroom interaction change little over time, and this is because they are connected to some main features of classroom environments (see Chapter 7) and these remain fairly constant over time. These would include a certain number of children, in a room of a similar size, with a trained adult with broadly constant educational aims. As Watkins and Mortimore (1999) have remarked, in a mass education system, with its roots in Victorian times (and earlier), the one to many, teacher controlled, school subject-dominated nature of classrooms imposes a similarity in pedagogy across the age phases. They question whether this is appropriate in today's schools, though in some respects there is a trend at present in England and Wales toward an even more traditional emphasis.

Research on the effects of teaching

So far we have concentrated on the nature of interactions between teachers and pupils. However, much research has sought to go beyond this in order to examine the *effects* of such interactions on pupils' educational progress or achievement. This is an important developmental topic, and well as one of the most obvious and basic questions asked in educational research: that is, to what extent are differences between teachers, in their interactions with their pupils, related to differences in their pupils' educational progress. Teaching is here considered as an independent variable, with pupil educational attainment or progress the outcome or dependent variable.

Early research on teaching

To understand developments in research on teaching one has to be aware of what were seen as weaknesses in earlier research. Around the beginning of the 1970s there was a general recognition that research needed to shift from teachers' personal traits, and effectiveness in terms of global ratings, to teachers' actual behaviour in classrooms (e.g., Brophy, 1986). The earlier concerns were teacher's personality, attitudes, values, interests, needs, etc. By the time of the third edition of *The Handbook of Research on Teaching* (Wittrock, 1986), review chapters were immersed in observational studies of teaching (e.g., Brophy and Good, 1986a).

The well-rehearsed problem with the earlier approach is that there does not appear to be a clear connection between the personality, experience, ability and emotional and social characteristics of teachers on the one hand, and effectiveness in teaching on the other. The approach to effectiveness is indirect. To take an obvious example, teachers' attitudes may not be a good guide to what they actually do in the classroom and the nature of their interactions with their pupils.

Process-product research on teaching

It was the response to limitations in early research that led to advances in understanding effects of teaching, but also led to, and served to highlight, important differences in approaches to research on teaching. In line with the seminal paper by Shulman (1986), these different approaches can be considered in terms of different 'paradigms' of research. Reviewers have not used the same terms for these different approaches, but there is general agreement that quantitative, behavioural approaches can be distinguished from qualitative, more interpretative approaches. It is process product research (a main form of quantitative research) that has been most directly concerned with the effects of teaching and, specifically, teacher–pupil interactions. As we have seen, the limitations in early research led to a realization that one needs to look at what teachers actually *do* in order to understand effects on children's attainments in school. In the language of this approach, one needs to examine the interactive 'process' in relation to the pupil outcomes or 'product'. The obvious methodology for studying and measuring interactive processes was seen to be naturalistic direct observation. There were parallels at the same time (1970s) in developmental psychological research on mother–child interaction (see e.g., Clarke-Stewart, 1973; Blurton Jones, 1972a).

An influential review (Dunkin and Biddle, 1974) brought together early research and organized it in terms of a much-quoted model of influences. There were four groups of variables – first, 'presage' variables (e.g., teacher formative experiences, training and properties such as skills, intelligence, motivation); second, 'context' variables (e.g., social class, attitudes and abilities of pupils, and school and classroom contexts such as class size); third, 'process' variables (such as teacher and pupil behaviour); and fourth, 'product' variables (e.g., attainment in school subjects). This model provided a vocabulary that has been widely used in subsequent research in this tradition. According to Shulman (1986), the characteristics of process product research has been: a concern with teaching effectiveness; teaching measured on the basis of observation of behaviour in naturalistic classroom settings; the use of 'low inference' categories of behaviour (as opposed to 'high inference', more subjective categories like warmth); the use of relatively large samples over periods of time; and numerical analysis of data in terms of correlations between measures of the frequency of teaching behaviours like question types, lecturing, praise and measures of outcomes in terms of pupil achievement test scores. So effectiveness in teaching is assessed in terms of correlations with indicators of achievement, relatively independent of particular classrooms and contexts such as particular school subjects. The implicit aim was the search for laws to describe generalizable relationships between teaching and pupil outcomes. In this sense it was a positivist agenda.

Given the later criticisms of this approach it is worth pointing out why it was an advance. The advances have been summarized by Shulman (1986).

1. It rebutted the depressing implications of the Coleman Report that teachers made little difference and provided the impetus to look more closely at teacher effects. It showed that teachers *did* make a difference, that is, variations between teachers in their classroom behaviour were related to variations between students in their attainments.
2. The metaphor of teaching as a bundle of skills, that could be broken down into observable sub-skills, was compelling. This kind of applied behavioural analysis seemed to be successful in work in other areas, e.g., for second language learners, radar technicians, mechanics, so why not teaching?
3. It moved research on teaching into real classrooms, with teachers and pupils behaving as they would normally, rather than in artificially created situations.
4. The implications for practice seemed relatively straightforward, in the

sense that correlations between teacher behaviours and attainment could be easily translated into action. Although researchers like Brophy (1986) warned against simplistic prescriptions, research findings were translated into 'teacher should' statements (Shulman, 1986). Shulman concludes that the approach worked. Teachers who behaved in ways identified by the research seemed to have students who did better. It was also credible with teachers and, in the wider context of the US during the 1970s, it was consistent with a return to basic education and concern with achievement in basic skills.

A main feature of this approach is therefore the use of direct systematic observation, and this led the development of sophisticated observation systems and a concern with methods (Croll, 1986; Galton, 1987; Medley and Mitzel, 1963; Simon and Boyer, 1970). In this regard there are similarities again with research in developmental psychology (e.g., Bakeman and Gottman, 1986; Blurton Jones, 1972a; Hutt and Hutt, 1970; Pellegrini, 1995b), which has been similarly concerned with observation methods. In both, there has been much concern with reliability of observation systems. Early on, it was realized that high inference categories, such as enthusiasm, warmth and clarity of presentation are problematic, as they are difficult to code reliably and require interpretation on the part of observers. Low inference categories are often favoured because they require less interpretation and are therefore more reliable. Though this is often examined in terms of observer agreement (which is limited as an approach to reliability – see Blatchford *et al.*, 1987), there were more sophisticated treatments of the topic as far back as Medley and Mitzel (1963). Some critics argue that reliability is often achieved at the expense of validity, that is, high reliability may mean that observers agree on how to code a set of categories, but these categories may be relatively superficial and miss important aspects of teaching.

Findings

As said above, it is not intended or possible to review findings from this research. There are particular difficulties in any case, because of a tendency for results to be in terms of a list of correlations between behaviour categories and measures of attainment, and for these not to be guided by a theoretical or conceptual framework. In this section we seek to provide an overview of main findings.

Rosenshine and Stevens (1986 in Wittrock) offer a straightforward summary of research in this tradition. On the basis of their review they identify the following 'fundamental instructional "functions" '

1. review, check previous day's work (and reteach if necessary)
2. present new content/skills

3. guide student practice (and check for understanding)
4. offer feedback and correctives (and reteach if necessary)
5. encourage independent student practice
6. conduct weekly and monthly reviews

The single most comprehensive overview of research in this tradition is probably provided by Brophy and Good (1986a). A shorter paper covering the same material is by Brophy (1986). In a later paper, Brophy (1989a) concluded that process-outcome (as he calls it) research firmly established three general conclusions about teacher effects on students:

1. Teachers make a difference; that is, some teachers bring about greater gains in student achievement than others and these differences in student achievement gains are related to differences in the teacher's behaviour in class.
2. Achievement gains are related to classroom differences in exposure to academic content and opportunity to learn, e.g., teachers who produce most gains place more emphasis on developing student mastery, maximize classroom time for activities designed to foster such mastery, and organize and manage effective learning environments.
3. As well as maximizing 'time on task', successful teachers spend much time actively instructing their students, so there are more interactive lessons, featuring teacher–student interaction and less time on independent 'seatwork'.

Brophy (1986) reminds us that the teacher will always have an important role, over and above specific curriculum initiatives. So-called 'teacher proof' curricula, that depend on curriculum approaches or computer programs to carry the content to children, are insufficient. Education needs to work *through* teachers, not around them.

In general, US reviews (e.g., Brophy, 1986) support the notion of 'active teaching', that is, whatever the grouping arrangements – group or whole class – there should be a good deal of teacher talk, which is academic rather than managerial or procedural, and which involves much asking of questions and giving of feedback rather than extended lecturing (Brophy, 1986). A similar notion is what Rosenshine (1987 – in Creemers, 1994) called 'direct instruction'. Creemers considers this a form of explicit stepwise instruction, emphasizing student learning and cognitive achievement. It is summed up succinctly by Rosenshine: 'If you want students to learn something, teach it to them directly' (Rosenshine, 1987, p. 258 in Creemers, 1994).

On the basis of his review, Creemers (1994) summarizes effective teaching in basic skills in these terms:

1. structure learning experiences
2. proceed in small steps but at a brisk pace

3. give detailed and redundant instructions, explanations and examples
4. ask a number of questions and provide overt student practice
5. provide feedback and corrections, especially in the initial stages of learning new material
6. have a student success rate of 80 per cent or higher, especially in initial learning
7. divide assignments into smaller assignments, and find ways to control frequently
8. provide for continued student practice

Creemers reminds us that direct instruction is probably best equipped for well-structured school subjects like maths, which can be divided more obviously into small, discrete units. Stemming as it does from the behaviourist roots of the process product research tradition, it is most applicable to basic skills and cognitive knowledge. These are obviously very important, especially in the early years of school, but teaching also needs to be directed at promoting higher cognitive processes such as learning strategies, problem-solving and meta cognitive strategies, which will require more strategic teaching methods. Creemers feels that direct instruction which was used only to achieve specific objectives is now best seen in the context of, and used to serve, more complex and overarching teaching strategies which are concerned with basic skills but also provide scaffolds (such as how to proceed, modelling, thinking aloud and social support from peers) to support meta cognitive knowledge and skills.

A feature of Creemers (1994) review is that it emphasizes European research. He points out that in Europe there is a more obvious pedagogical background to educational research and there has been more attempt to combine research on teaching with pedagogy of education. Being more recent, his review also includes research from other, more cognitively orientated, and meta cognitive models, as well as meta analyses of research. Results, though, according to Creemers, are consistent with earlier process product research. On the basis of his review, he formulates a basic model of educational effectiveness, one component of which concerns teacher behaviour. Aspects in this component include: management/orderly and quiet atmosphere; provision of homework; high teacher expectations and belief of their ability to affect students; clear goal setting (restricted set of goals, emphasis on basic skills, emphasis on cognitive learning and transfer); structuring the content (hierarchically ordering goals and content, use of advance organizers, use of student prior knowledge); clarity of presentation; more questioning (both high and low order questions); immediate exercises after presentation, checking for understanding; and evaluation of whether goals are achieved and corrective instruction if not (Creemers, 1994, p. 89).

As for UK research, the one most seminal study is again the ORACLE study. On the basis of the observation schedules described above, teaching behaviours were grouped into teaching styles. As we have seen, a problem with much process product research is the tendency toward analysis of associations between many separate teaching behaviours and pupil outcomes. This becomes rather unwieldy and tends to cut up teaching into tiny parts, when there may be interconnections between them. In an attempt to overcome this problem, a statistical technique called cluster analysis was used to group teachers after data collection on the basis of their similarity across a number of teaching behaviours. This resulted in six teaching styles: individual monitors, class enquirers, group instructors, infrequent changers, rotating changers and habitual changers, and associations were then examined with progress in mathematics, language and study skills. The authors claim that results do not show any one style is better than others, though they do find that 'class enquirers', who carried out above average amounts of whole class teaching, were most likely to use challenging questions and reduce intermittent working in pupils, and had pupils who made more progress. 'Individual monitors' who engaged in most conversations with pupils had pupils who did better in reading tests. The least successful style was that of 'rotating changers'.

In recent years quantitative research involving classrooms has shifted much more toward studies of school effectiveness (see Stoll and Mortimore, 1995). Creemers (1994) has said that although the focus of attention in school effectiveness studies is the school, many findings seem actually located at the classroom level. Ironically, given the use of multilevel statistical techniques and the expressed need to be clear about different levels of analysis (child, class, school etc.), effects at the class level, including classroom interactions and face to face teaching, are not always easy to identify. One pioneering study in this tradition examined progress in a sample of London junior schools (Mortimore *et al.*, 1988). It made use of the same observation instruments as used in the ORACLE study, and although individual correlations between observation categories and progress are not presented in full, results in general supported the findings with regard to the importance of whole class teaching and maximizing the quantity of teacher talk to pupils, and higher order communications in particular.

Most research on teaching has been correlational in the sense of looking at associations between naturally occurring behaviours in classrooms and outcomes. In some studies (reviewed in Brophy, 1986; Gage, 1985), experimental designs were employed to test these associations more precisely. Usually these involved the training of teachers in instructional practices, known to correlate with achievement, followed by an evaluation of their success in terms of changes in student achievement and teaching behaviours (see Gage, 1985).

It was soon realized that the basic process product paradigm, with its focus on teaching behaviours, needed to be supplemented. As Shulman

(1986) has shown, these developments had much to do with advances in other areas, e.g., cognitive and information processing theories. There is space here to mention just a few developments. One main extension was a concern with student mediating factors, particularly, student 'academic learning time' ('ALT' – Fisher *et al.*, 1980 in Brophy, 1986). The now familiar notion was the importance of maximizing student time engaged in work, and organizing the classroom efficiently so that activities run smoothly, transitions are brief, and little time is spent getting organized and dealing with misconduct. As originally conceived there was an additional notion of high success rates. A consistent finding is the connection between high student task engagement and student achievement though this still leaves a number of questions about the causal connections involved. There are also still problems in dealing with issues of instructional quality. As Gage (in Shulman, 1986) has said: 'time is an empty vessel'.

There has been attention to other mediating factors which extend the basic model of teaching effects. These have included pupil cognitive processes and teacher decision-making (see Shulman, 1986). Other mediating factors, such as within-class curriculum coverage, have also been found to be important (Tizard *et al.*, 1988). Alternative approaches with their roots in sociology, anthropology and linguistics (which Shulman, 1986, collects together under the label 'classroom ecology') have served to extend the vocabulary of concepts and terms in the study of teaching. Work on classroom environments, including that of Doyle (1986 – see Chapter 7 of this book), and the Dunkin and Biddle model described above, have been influential in extending conceptualizations of classrooms beyond the strictly interactive nature of teaching. As we shall see below, conceptualizations of classrooms, with roots more in anthropology and linguistics, introduced a concern with individuals in context and the meanings they shared and made (see Erikson, 1986; Shulman, 1986).

Putting together the US and European research, perhaps the one main conclusion to be drawn concerning the effects of face to face interactions on pupils' educational progress is support for interactive teaching – what might be seen as modified traditional class teaching, with a stress on whole class teaching, higher order questions and statements and sustained interactions. When the focus is on individuals, time is wasted and lost, and interactions can – surprisingly, given the greater attention that might be expected – be more concerned with routine matters and more low level. There is consensus that it is a mistake, especially with young students, to allow them to work for too long on their own. In this respect there is a good deal of agreement, from an array of different starting points, that earlier child centred notions of discovery based learning, where teachers were conceived as facilitators who only indirectly conveyed information, were misguided. Even bright students will develop erroneous ideas if left on their own too long. Brophy (1989b) makes the point that in practice individualized instruction shifts too much of the burden for planning and managing learning to the pupils themselves, and requires a combination of sustained motivation and independent learning skills unlikely in young children. It also tends to shift too much of the burden for successful instruction to the materials and curriculum content. This is likely to be successful only if the teacher has considerable time to supervise and offer immediate feedback – unlikely with class sizes of 30 or more.

It needs to be said that these results tell only part of the story. They only relate to the interactive nature of teaching, and are particularly relevant, as we have seen, to basic skills as an outcome. Although, as we said at the beginning of the chapter, we are mainly concerned with the interactive nature of teaching, there is clearly more to teaching and learning than this. We just mention here one important aspect. A good deal of research and theory shows the importance of developing within children resources and motivational processes that equip them to be independent learners. One commonly used distinction is between 'mastery' and 'performance' orientations, that is, between the confidence to seek mastery and understanding of a task, as opposed to simply striving for good grades. There is much consensus that in the long run performance orientation is dysfunctional, and that teaching should aim to encourage a 'mastery' orientation (see Pintrich and Schunk, 1996 for a review). Such an aim is different to the aims of teaching considered in this chapter, but should not be seen as contradictory. There is space here to do no more than assert that encouraging child responsibility for learning is as important as the 'how' of teaching. Teaching interactions must not be at the expense of directed and independent learning; rather, there is a need for balance between teaching and pupil motivational considerations.

It is difficult to be precise about the current state of research on teaching. This is because influences from different approaches have merged and separate threads, such as process product research, are more difficult to identify. Concerns have also become more localized, e.g., by curriculum area. There has been more attention to context and 'more fine-grained' approaches. The previous tendency to average across teaching situations, over months or weeks, and then relate measures to achievement test scores has been questioned, and there is more recognition of the need to study more subtle and qualitative aspects of teaching. There is more recognition of the value of subject-specific research, for example, mathematics and writing (see Brophy, 1989b), more concern with goals of instruction, and concern with teachers' subject matter knowledge (Arends, 1994), teachers' professional 'craft' knowledge (e.g., Cooper and McIntyre, 1996) and teachers' planning and management of learning tasks and activities. Research on more generic aspects of teaching has combined with the literature on curriculum areas and instruction in particular subject areas. Following Shulman's (1986) conclusions, there has been attention to the nature of teachers' cognitive understanding of specific subject matter content. There is also more understanding of the contextual and 'situated' nature of learning (e.g., Brown, 1989), and more attention to the views of practitioners' about learning (e.g., Weinstein, 1998), and more concern with pupils' views (e.g., Blatchford, 1996; Ruddock *et al.*, 1996).

Important as these various developments have been, it is difficult not to feel that one consequence has been a loss of direction for research on teaching. The present, more fragmented, state of research has moved attention away from the 'big picture'. In particular the localized focus in terms of school subject area has many strengths, and historically was necessary, but one danger is the loss of attention to teaching issues that might cross school subject areas, and the view that expertise in school subjects is the main aspect of teaching – to the exclusion of other interactive aspects of teaching, and an understanding of learning (see Watkins and Mortimore (1999) on Chris Woodhead Chief HMI – who has said that an understanding of learning is not necessary for teachers). This trend toward greater fragmentation may in some cases be deliberate, but much has occurred incidentally. Whatever the reason, the effect has been a neglect of more generic, cross-subject area issues concerning teaching and classroom interactions.

Issues in research on the interactive nature of teaching

There are some important issues of research design and analysis, arising out of research on teaching. The review by Dunkin and Biddle (1974), as well as the paper by Medley and Mitzel (1963), still repay careful reading concerning issues related to observation methods. In this section we select three general issues for discussion.

How to assess the 'effects' and 'effectiveness' of teaching?

On what basis should effectiveness in teaching be judged? This is a large and difficult question that can only be touched on here. One debate has concerned the general way in which the study of teaching should be conceived, and this has much to do with the underlying conception of teaching. One distinction is between whether teaching is best seen as a set of skills or has more in common with artistry. We return to this distinction below. Biggs and Moore (1993) identify at least three conceptions of teaching: transmission of knowledge, efficient orchestration of teaching skills, and facilitation of learning (connected to quantitative, institutional and qualitative conceptions of learning respectively).

It has been much easier to conceive of research on teaching and implications for practice on the basis of a quantitative conception of teaching because there is a more obvious expression of what is learnt and the criteria by which it could be assessed. Despite Gage's (1978) brave attempt to seek a reconciliation between these two views (the title of his book reveals the intention – *The Scientific Basis of the Art of Teaching*) the tension between competing models of teaching still underlies much debate about research on teaching.

There is much agreement that an exclusive concern with academic outcomes, usually maths and language, and in terms of test results, is too narrow. There are other aims and subject areas in education, and these need to be considered. There are other areas, e.g., citizenship and moral development, and other attributes, including problem-solving, independence, study habits and quality in social relations. However, although there has been, and is currently probably too much, preoccupation with basic skills in maths and language, this does not now mean that these things are not important.

There has been, as we have seen, a general weakening of the assumption that the interactive nature of teaching is important. Along with a recognition that children spent most time engaged in individual work (see above), attention shifted to the tasks pupils were engaged in rather than the relatively rare interactions that took place. Again this is understandable, but does not mean that these interactions are not important.

What is the appropriate level of analysis in assessing differences between teachers?

When seeking to describe teaching, how useful and reliable are dichotomies such as formal v. informal? Bennett *et al.* (1976), before the ORACLE researchers, sought to overcome the limitations of simple dichotomies by using cluster analysis to group teachers. However, the statistical technique was questioned and subsequent reanalysis, using a more sophisticated technique, did not replicate the original results. Also, although the cluster analysis produced 12 styles, it was decided to use only three of these in the analysis comparing groups, making it difficult to know how representative the comparisons were.

An underlying issue relates to the tension in research on teaching between measurement in terms of smaller more 'atomic' units, as in much process product research, and more general 'molecular' categories, such as 'formal' v. 'informal'. Given the difficulties with both types of measurement, it is understandable that the ORACLE study sought a compromise by constructing more molecular constructs (i.e., styles) out of atomic units of behaviour. However, there are costs, in that it can, as in the ORACLE study, become difficult to know which of a cluster of behaviours contributed to any associations found and which, if any, behaviours interact with each other. The psychological reality or validity of the clusters is also unclear. There are again parallels to observational research in developmental psychology, e.g., research on mother–child interaction (Bakeman and Gottman, 1986).

One problem, when seeking to move beyond smaller individual features toward more general and larger units, concerns whether it is valid or meaningful to consider teaching in terms of 'styles', that is, in terms of stable and reliable differences between teachers. As Watkins and Mortimore (1999) argue, simple polarizations such as quantitative v. qualitative, teacher centred v. pupil centred are inadequate, though they do unfortunately tend to match everyday conceptions of learning and teaching. In 1986, a House of Commons Select Committee wrote: 'we hope the simple argument between styles, whether formal or informal, individual or class teaching, child-centred or subject-centred, can be left behind: none is sufficient by itself' (p. 115 – in Watkins and Mortimore, 1999). This is probably correct, but is more a judgement of a committee than a conclusion grounded in evidence. Although Mortimore *et al.* (1988) used the ORACLE observation schedules, in contrast to the ORACLE researchers, they rejected the aim of identifying teaching 'styles':

> in fact, we found no evidence of readily identifiable teaching styles at all. We feel that teaching is far too complex an activity for it to be categorised in this way. On the contrary, our results indicate the value of a flexible approach, that can blend individual, class and group interaction as appropriate.
>
> (p. 254)

Once again, though, it is not clear whether this opinion is based on the failure through statistical analysis of their data to identify styles, or is a more impressionistic or professional judgement.

Identification of styles can carry with it a notion of teaching as somehow involving fixed behaviours and also stable differences between teachers, though much depends on the way in which, and the level at which, teaching is defined. For example, teaching could be defined not so much in terms of particular behaviours (as ORACLE) as in terms of broader dimensions like flexibility, that is, units that are more dynamic (though also inevitably more 'high inference'). For some, the conception of teaching in terms of a 'repertoire' is more attractive and, as Arends (1994) has argued, is more conducive to the idea that teaching behaviours should be used strategically for particular contexts and purposes, and curricular areas. However, again, it is not clear to what extent this view, that is, the advantages of a repertoire notion of teaching, can be supported empirically.

How best to research effective teaching?

A main difference in research on teaching is between quantitative approaches and more qualitative approaches, and we return to this difference below. Research designs have also differed between those that sample teachers in a more or less random way, in order to capture differences as they occur naturally or selecting teachers in order to study aspects more precisely, e.g., studies of expert v. novice teachers.

Another kind of choice concerns the nature of data. In this chapter we have concentrated on data drawn from observations of interactions in classrooms, but alternatives are possible, for example those that make use of pupil views on good and bad teaching. In Bennett *et al.* early study of teaching styles (1976) questionnaires were used.

One of the characteristics of quantitative approaches to teaching, and one of their limitations, according to Shulman (1986), has been their 'unabashedly empirical and non-theoretical' nature (Shulman, 1986, p. 13) – an emphasis on what worked rather than why it worked. Quantitative research on teaching has also typically measured teaching in terms of frequencies of occurrence. Findings therefore say more about the amount of teaching behaviours than the quality of instruction, for example, what form it takes and how well it is implemented (Brophy, 1989a). One consideration, to which all can no doubt testify, is that even infrequent teaching behaviours may be influential. It is possible, for example, that just one praise or comment, concerning a child's work, can have a lasting impression on that child.

Problems can arise when teaching is conceptualized or at least measured in terms of a continuous variable; for example, it may not be easy to get at differences between teachers who are outstanding and those who are merely adequate. In other words, there are problems, in searching for linear associations between frequencies of occurrence and other variables like outcomes. Other ways of treating distributions may need to be considered. Also, prescriptions should remain within a certain range (though this may be difficult to establish); because a particular behaviour is related to achievement does not mean a huge increase in it will produce similar gains – indeed it is easy to think of examples that may be counter-productive (e.g., too much homework, too much praise or criticism). It is worth reminding ourselves (as Brophy, 1986) that findings from research are only strictly generalizable to other similar classes and may not therefore generalize to other different classrooms, e.g., from mainstream to special education.

Effective teaching may be revealed in more complex ways than frequencies of behaviours. As Dunkin and Biddle (1974) realized early on, it is important to examine sequences of behaviours as well as individual occurrences, but this is difficult to do in terms of observation techniques and statistical analysis of data once collected, and has proved to be problematic in research on teaching and other social relations, e.g., mother–child interaction. Even sequences of behaviours may miss the strategic nature of teaching, for example, in terms of the enactment of lesson plans or instructional intentions.

'Paradigm wars' in research on teaching

In this chapter we have touched on differences in views about the best way to research teaching and in this final section we look more deliberately at this issue. In seeking to understand research on teaching, it is vital to be aware of the arguments between alternative approaches to research on teaching, or, to use Gage's term, 'paradigm wars'.

If, as Shulman concluded in 1986, the process product paradigm was 'losing intellectual vigour within the research community', by the end of the 1990s, judging by contributions to the AERA journal *Educational Researcher* it and allied quantitative approaches seem to have lost much credibility in US educational research. Interestingly, and over and above any judgement about its correctness, this extreme rejection of quantitative approaches seems exclusive to educational research. It perhaps reflects the peculiarities of education and educational research, for example, in terms of the extent to which it can be considered a distinct discipline or is dependent on other disciplines such as sociology and psychology. The argument does seem to be, at least in part, between disciplines, particularly between sociology and psychology. Perhaps it reflects, therefore, the lessening influence of psychology in educational research. Gage (1985) also makes the point that the 'war' has been at heart a battle between disciplines, with psychology informing process product research, anthropology spawning the interpretative-qualitative approach, and sociology, economics and political theory underlying what he calls 'critical' theory.

It is interesting to read Nate Gage – perhaps the foremost commentator on research on teaching over the past four decades – as his views have altered in tone over the same period of time. In the earliest commentaries there is the excitement of realizing a new programme of research with much potential to improve teaching and achieve conceptual advances. This was followed by scholarly reviews of the growing literature and a wideranging discourse on the art and science of teaching (Gage, 1978). But then the tone changed. There was first a robust defence of process product research, with an attempt to show the complementarity between quantitative and qualitative approaches (Gage, 1985), but this was followed by an apocalyptic vision of what would happen if the qualitative and critical approaches were allowed to dominate (Gage, 1989). Since then the debate between paradigms has rather left positivist/quantitative research behind – as we see below.

But first we look at the case against quantitative research because we feel some of this criticism is unnecessary and unhelpful, and because we feel that the issues raised have a general application to research on interactions in schools.

The 'ethnographic' critique

A main plank in the problems faced by quantitative research and a main contribution to the paradigm wars has been the 'ethnographic critique'. There is no one definitive expression of this view and it comes in many guises and from many starting points and authors. In the UK, one of the most influential expressions of this view was the paper by Delamont and Hamilton, first published in 1972, but then revised in 1986. This was an attack on systematic observation methods in particular, but, as we have seen, this is the main research technique employed in process product research and to a large extent synonymous with it. They acknowledge that there have been some changes since the appearance of their paper in 1972 and that there are differences between observation work in UK and US research, but they still feel much of their original critique stands. To summarize their criticisms, they take issue with the use in structured observation of prespecified categories used in statistical analysis, the ignoring of context, a concern only with overt behaviour and a neglect of intentions, in terms of small and arbitrarily defined bits of behaviour, rather than global concepts, which therefore provide only a partial description.

Barrow's (1984) critique of systematic observation is also a critique of quantitative research more generally, and the ORACLE research in particular. Some of Barrow's criticisms are on closer inspection trivial. One example is the problem raised by Barrow concerning teachers both praising work and offering ideas and the difficulties he feels this then raises if the categories are mutually exclusive and only one category is therefore coded. In fact, this problem would appear to be easily overcome by the use of subsets of mutually exclusive categories which would enable different aspects of the same behaviour to be coded. There is not space here to deal fully with Barrow's paper – see Croll (1986).

In a carefully argued paper, McIntyre and MacLeod (1986) respond directly to Hamilton and Delamont's critique. While recognizing the limitations of systematic observation, they argue that the use of predetermined categories is defendable and show this need not impede theoretical development; selective observation is inevitable and necessary; access to mental states and shared meanings is difficult for *any* approach; many studies have carefully defined units of behaviour (i.e., not arbitrary); and, damningly, qualitative/ethnographic research in fact often uses quantitative, although implicit and untested, statements as findings.

In addition, identification of pre-existent (v. emergent) categories, and statistical analyses, as distinctions between quantitative and qualitative research represent poor criteria. To take the case of ethology: Ethologists studying children, (for example, Smith and Connolly (1980) and Pellegrini (1995b)), typically share a Darwinian theoretical bias and are interested in studying children in their natural habitats as these are the circumstances under which adaptation took place. Further, they also induce categories of behaviours in those contexts. Does the fact that they use factor analyses to define their categories separate them from ethnographers who also use numbers? Is Heath's (1983) *Ways with Words*, not a qualitative study or ethnography because summary statistics are used? In short, such distinctions are not good ones, and while they do much to fracture and divide scholars, they do little to advance our understanding of children in schools.

But perhaps the most coherent and even-handed account of the differences between quantitative and qualitative approaches is by Gage (1985). He characterizes what he calls the ethnographic-sociolinguistic paradigm as seeing teaching as an instance of symbolic interaction, that is, the process by which people (teachers and pupils) develop meaning in terms of situations (mainly classrooms) and their own actions. The concern of research in this tradition is with meanings participants have about their situations. Such research, in contrast with process product research, seeks 'thick' and critical descriptions, on the basis of qualitative and interpretative methods. Research in this tradition has dealt with a variety of aspects of classroom discourse, participation structures and so on (see reviews by Cazden, 1986; Erickson, 1986). Ethnographic-sociolinguistic research is 'ideographic' in seeking (at least in terms of Bolster's formulation) to understand particular cases.

In seeking to identify the scientific basis for what he quite readily sees as the 'art' of teaching, Gage employs the distinction between 'ideographic' knowledge, which, as we have just seen, applies to the understanding of a particular event or individual, and 'nomothetic' knowledge, which is general across individuals and is identified with the scientific method, usually producing knowledge about relationships between variables. Gage is fully aware that in the case of research on teaching we are often applying nomothetic knowledge to the ideographic, that is, to a particular situation or teacher; indeed, Gage argues this is just what engineers, physicians and other scientists do all the time – they just differ in the amount of nomothetic knowledge available to them. All of us, including teachers, must compensate for the inadequacies in our nomothetic knowledge, which in the case of knowledge on teaching is relatively large, by the use of artistry and craftsmanship. The distinction (nomothetic/ideographic) is useful in helping to place usually opposing perspectives (quantitative/positivist v. qualitative/ideograph) into one framework, and emphasizes their complimentarity.

Conclusions

Gage calls for more integration of process product/quantitative and ethnographic research approaches. This conciliatory tone seems, in the light of subsequent events, rather to imply wishful thinking. But it seems to us that this kind of rapprochement is vital if research on teaching is to recapture its sense of direction. We should, though, heed Shulman's warning (1986): while it is tempting to say that if separate paradigms of research are separately insufficient we should seek a more eclectic strategy, Shulman cautions against what he calls a 'goulash' approach, that is, one in which different types of research are thrown together with little thought for their different assumptions and purposes.

The trouble is that educational research is in danger of losing out in two areas: first, the belief that research of any sort is useful, and that there are questions and issues that can be addressed empirically, and second, some educational research is losing contact and credibility with policy makers and teachers. It seems to us that energies spent in battles between paradigms could be redirected at research on teaching. This is important not just because it would help researchers but also because it is necessary to counter the kind of general uninformed comments on pedagogy that are now current. It is unfortunate that a lot of educational discussion and initiative is built on informal notions of effective teaching and pedagogy and is quite separate from research on teaching going back, as we have seen, four decades. It is important that efforts are made to show that there *is* a body of debate and knowledge that relates to real issues in classrooms and, though there is of course disagreement, there is much that research can contribute to teachers and policy makers.

Currently in the UK there is renewed questioning of the value of educational research. This is largely about whether research on teaching is useful and necessary. Chris Woodhead, who at the time of writing is still the Chief HMI, has argued that education and educational research cannot be considered a distinct discipline, has not produced works and research of any use to teachers and its claims on school effectiveness, for example, do not 'stand serious scrutiny'; indeed it 'seeks to render the straightforward complex: to mystify the business of education and the job of a teacher'. Woodhead feels that educational research is saying no more than the obvious: 'I am simply not convinced that research of this kind generates additional insights that justify the considerable sums of taxpayers' money spent on them' (Chris Woodhead, *Guardian*, 15 December 1998, p. 17 – at time of *Guardian*/Institute of Education Debate).

Given what has been said above about the present state of research on teaching, it is tempting to say that educational researchers have only got themselves to blame for this situation. But perhaps the best response to Woodhead is again the reasoned and even-handed approach of Nate Gage, who in 1985 sought to counter similar views on the value and obviousness of findings from educational research. Gage made the point that findings may appear obvious but this does not seem to have led to them being put into practice. All correlations between practice and outcomes necessarily provide evidence that, however obvious findings about effective teaching might be, teachers still *vary* in their teaching practices. After the fact, findings from educational research can seem obvious, but some teachers do these things less often than do teachers who have been introduced to previous research and theory.

It is important to seek to show those who criticize research on teaching (like Chris Woodhead) that, although there are examples of mediocre and downright bad research, there do exist useful and insightful studies, and also useful commentaries (such as Gage, Creemers) which draw out messages and implications from this research. There must be a deliberate effort to counter the view that teaching is purely a practical activity, that subject matter knowledge is sufficient, and which cannot be informed by evidence and research on teaching. There is a need to show the value of evidence-based comment, the fallacy of the view that all research on teaching is flawed, and the strength of the view that research needs to be considered alongside professional experience.

9 Literacy learning in the social-developmental context of school

In this chapter, we will limit our discussion to the initial stage of becoming literate – what has been labelled as 'emergent literacy'. This entails the ways in which aspects of children's oral language relate to initial phases of reading and writing. A basic premise of this chapter is that becoming literate in the schools of most industrial societies involves learning a variety of language we have called 'literate' or 'school' language which in many ways resembles an 'elaborated code', as described by Bernstein (1971). Learning the school language register, however, seems to be an important precursor to becoming literate in schools simply because of the similarities in the design features between home and school language. Neither is intrinsically more abstract or logical than the other. We argue that literate language is a very early form of school-based literacy, given their shared design features: it is the form that literacy takes before formal reading instruction.

Discussion of the ways in which literate language relates to school-based literacy may be particularly important to the ways in which literacy is taught in most North American and European countries. Discrete dimensions of language, such as sounds and letter names, are extracted from language and put up for examination by children and teachers. In the same way, literate language takes aspects of language, such as making meaning clear, and puts them up for examination, as evidenced by the central role of the use of 'meta' language in literate language. The importance of this sort of talk for early literacy has been repeatedly demonstrated by the fact that it relates to knowledge of literacy conventions (such as letter names, sounds and phonemic awareness), which, in turn, relates to more traditional measures of reading and writing (Pellegrini *et al.*, 1995c; Pellegrini *et al.*, 1998).

This orientation also has a developmental dimension. As noted in Chapter 1, a developmental orientation involves a search for patterns and changes across the life span. It is a search for continuity and discontinuity within individuals across childhood, as well as continuity and discontinuity across different situations. To this end we will present a conceptual model of children's literacy learning from the pre-school through the early primary grades, both at home and school. An important initial consideration is the way in which 'literacy' is defined. As we noted above, a developmental orientation suggests that literacy may be defined differently for individuals at different ages and in different contexts.

Our developmental orientation also includes consideration of the social ecological niche of literacy learning. Briefly, we consider the transactional relation between children and their environments, both in and out of school. We stress the ways in which social interaction between children and adults and children and peers structure children's social behaviour and language. Continuity or discontinuity between home and school interaction patterns should predict, at least to some extent, school success or failure respectively.

A developmental orientation

It is important to stress our developmental orientation because it has implications for the ways in which we define, measure and eventually teach literacy in schools. Probably the most basic principle guiding our developmental orientation is that children are qualitatively, not quantitatively, different from adolescents and adults. Such a notion is made clear in most stage theories of development that specify defining characteristics of children at different 'stages'. Applied directly to literacy, quantitative differences in children's and adults' literacy status would be gauged in terms of degree. For example, children's literacy might be defined in terms of recognizing letters and a limited number of words. Adults, on the other hand, are able to read more words. In short, quantitative differences as applied to literacy would have children possessing fewer skills than adults. Pedagogical implications of this theory would have the adult model of literacy being broken down into its component parts. Children are then taught the individual components, from simple to more complex. Literacy is achieved when the individual parts sum to the adult model.

Qualitative differences between children's and adults' literacy assumes that child and adult literacy are different constructs, altogether; they involve different skills. Children's skills are useful for their solutions to problems presented within childhood, as well as being useful for developing adult forms of literacy. Teaching children in this mode entails having them use literacy to solve their local problems, such as scribbling an imaginary grocery list or retelling a story. In short, qualitative differences are more basic. We will argue that literacy for young children (infant school children) is defined in terms of a variety, or register, of oral language.

It becomes a developmental task to chart the ways in which these seemingly different constructs that change across time, at the same time have a thread of continuity. In the specific case of literacy development we suggest that there is a continuity in the design features of children's oral language, especially the sorts of language used when children are being read to and when they are engaged in social pretend play, with similar features in school-based literacy.

We note, however, that similarity between sets of design features does not guarantee that they are functionally related. The antecedent may lead to a consequence that does not resemble it. Similarly, consequences could have origins in antecedents with which they do not share design features. In the next section we discuss different definitions of literacy and their (often implied rather than explicitly stated) theory of learning or development.

Individuals' contributions

Another basic tenet of a developmental orientation, as outlined in the chapter on development, is that despite regularities in development as indicated in stage-like progression, individual differences exist; individuals and their environments influence each other in a dialectical fashion.

Not all children proceed through the developmental process in the same way or at the same rate. By extension, not all children become literate in the same way. The systems theory notion of equifinality posits that there is more than one route to competence. Equifinality reminds us again that the relations between antecedents and consequences are very complex.

Our conceptualization of development also recognizes the unique contributions that individuals make to the developmental process. Individual differences, often expressed in terms of children's temperament, mediate the transaction between children and their social and physical environments. We must take account of individuals' contributions if we consider development something other than a uni-directional, cultural reproduction process. Cultural reproduction models of development are uni-directional to the extent that the values and practices of society are directed at and internalized by children with little consideration for the ways in which individuals (independent of society) affect their environments.

Temperament is an excellent construct to gauge individuals' contributions to the developmental process in that it has a biological expression, appears very early in life and is stable across the life span. Children with a certain temperament, for example sociable, extroverted children, may seek out a number of different social partners with whom to interact. These children might come to learn literate language by interacting with a variety of others and taking on a wide range of roles. By interacting with others from a variety of backgrounds children learn to explicate the meaning of their messages so that they can be understood even by those with whom they do not share a common background.

Children who are less sociable, and introverted, may interact with fewer social actors than their more social counterparts. The social relationships may be characterized as intensive or 'close relationships', such as friendships. Children may learn literate language in this sort of relationship through the conceptual conflicts and resolutions of conflicts that typify close relationships (Hartup, 1996). That is, friends, compared to acquaintances, are more likely to disagree with each other. These disagreements, because they are important to the participants, are closely monitored, remembered, and usually resolved in the interest of maintaining the relationship. By monitoring conceptual conflict and working toward resolution children become aware of their friends' feelings and needs. They, in turn, monitor their own behaviour so as to accommodate to those needs. This sort of perspective taking is an important psychological precursor to effective communication, both oral and written (Jones and Pellegrini, 1996; Pellegrini et al., 1984) and subsequent literacy (Pellegrini et al., 1997, 1998). That is, the perspective taking associated with conceptual conflict relates to children's ability to reflect upon language and its use. This 'meta' perspective on language is realized in children's talk about talk, which, in turn, predicts school-based literacy (Pellegrini et al., 1997, 1998).

Of course individual differences are mediated by larger societal factors. It may be the case, for example, and following Bernstein (1971), that in some groups, children are discouraged from taking a variety of roles. Instead, they might be 'restricted' to a limited number of roles. As we will discuss below, 'positional' socialization orientations limit children's role experiences: children are restricted to certain roles, due to their being a 'child' or a 'girl'.

Transaction between individuals and the environment

The final aspect of development that we will discuss is the dialectical relation between individuals and their environments. Socialization theories of development posits a uni-directional force from society to the children. Instead, we consider development a dialectical, or transactional, process. Children influence their environments and their environments influence them. Some of the best examples of this transactional relation come from the child language literature (Ninio and Bruner, 1978; Pellegrini et al., 1985; Pellegrini et al., 1995b) and the mother–child interaction literature (Snow, 1972). In cases where mothers read and talk to their children they gauge the sophistication of their interaction strategies and talk to children's levels of sophistication.

When we consider the twin notions of child effects on the environments, in conjunction with individual differences, a clearer picture of the transactional nature of development emerges. Individual children self-select themselves into environments which are supportive of their temperament, for example, by choosing a certain peer group. In this way they affect their environment. The environment, which might be composed of certain children, in turn affects the child by providing models for social behaviour.

To conclude this section, development involves children changing across time. The nature of the change, we think, is qualitative in the sense that children at different periods of life see the world as different places. Individual development is embedded in an ecological matrix where children and their social and physical environments affect each other. We consider in detail the ways in which literacy develops and the ways in which individual children learn literacy at home and at school.

What is literacy?

Literacy, as Wolf (Wolf *et al.*, 1988) and colleagues at Harvard Project Zero note, can be defined very broadly, in terms creating and interpreting various symbol systems, such as maps, music scores, graphs, as well as traditional alphabetic scripts. In this chapter we are only concerned with literacy in alphabetic scripts, and in particular, we are concerned with the specific form of alphabetic script used in schools. At the simplest level, literacy in this context means being able to read and write school-based texts. Part of this process invariably involves children being able to use the sorts of oral language that characterizes literacy instruction. Moving beyond this simple (and probably too simple) level, we must ask ourselves what exactly do we mean by reading and writing. We suggest that the nature of literacy varies in functional terms, as well as according to the developmental status of the learner.

By 'functional' we mean that literacy has many different uses and, consequently, is defined differently in different communities. So reading (in the form of singing) from a hymnal is one form of literacy that differs from reading required on a standardized test or in a children's book at school. Similarly, for writing, the variety of writing required to convey a telephone message to a friend is very different from that required in a school essay. Scribner and Cole's (1978) categorization scheme for literacy among the Vai captures this functional variety quite nicely. One level of literacy is not learned in school and is used for personal needs. Examples of this include writing to complete an application, to make a grocery list, or used as a mnemonic aid. Another form of literacy is that which is used in religious ceremonies, such as Koranic literacy or Scripture reading. This sort of literacy is learned across a long period of time in formal settings but is different from school literacy or the type of literacy taught in Western schools.

School-based literacy is also taught across a long period of time but it entails reading and writing about specified topics.

School literacy is taught, not acquired

Being literate in one area often does not preclude similar levels of facility in another area. Applying these findings to children in Western schools, there are instances where children and mothers are literate in one area (reading toy adverts in a newspaper) but they are not very facile with school-based texts (Pellegrini *et al.*, 1990). The rules for interacting with the print and the participants, that is, the design features, in these two literate events are dissimilar.

School-based literacy is something that must be taught either implicitly or explicitly. It is not 'acquired' in the same sense that oral language is acquired. Virtually all individuals (under conditions ranging from highly supportive to highly restrictive) acquire aspects of oral language (specifically syntax) that render them functional. Biological theories explain the incredible ease with which syntax is learned through an innate Language Acquisition Device (Chomsky, 1965) or a Darwinian mechanism by which language is used in order to keep track of our social partners so as not to be exploited (Dunbar, 1993). The process of acquiring syntax is largely complete by the time children are only just beginning to read.

With reading, on the other hand, many individuals do not become literate. Further, no scholars, to our knowledge, have suggested a biological programme for literacy as they have for oral language development. Where literacy seems to be learned 'naturally', as in cases of precocious readers described by Durkin (1966) and Clark (1976), the home environments in which literacy is learned is very close to the environment of school. For example, these children are read to frequently by parents, the books that are read are similar to those used in school literacy events and the sort of talk that surrounds home literacy events is similar to the talk of school literacy events (Bernstein, 1960, 1972; Cook-Gumperz, 1977; Heath, 1983). In this case, the design features of school and home literacy are isomorphic. The same types of books are read at home as at school and parents talk to children in ways similar to teachers; for example, they ask them identification and recall questions about the text.

Thus, school-based literacy is only one very specific variety of literacy, much like an oral language register. It is no better or worse than other types of literacy; it just happens to be used by a certain social group. Access to this register is necessary for success in school and probably in society at large.

The specific case of school-based literacy

When we speak of literacy we typically mean school-based literacy. Even when 'functional' definitions of literacy are proffered, such as UNESCO's (Harman, 1970), school grade level criteria are stipulated: 'A person is literate who can, with understanding, read and write a short, simple statement on his everyday life' (Harman, 1970, p. 226). This functional definition is often coupled to a grade completion criterion of fourth or fifth grade.

An all too simple definition of literacy in school often involves defining it in terms of some performance outcome on a measure, such as a norm-referenced 'grade equivalent score' or a criterion-reference list of skills. While some tests can and indeed do measure early school-based literacy we suggest that defining literacy in terms of these scores on these measures is limited. It is limited, we think, because it confuses the directionality in defining a psychological construct, such as literacy, with the instrument used to measure it. Psychological constructs should be defined theoretically before they are defined, and measured, psychometrically. Psychometric definitions, such as NRT or CRT scores used to define literacy, reverse this logic: it takes test scores or other discrete skills that are indicative of literacy and uses them to define the construct, literacy. Thus literacy becomes defined as the ability to recognize letters and produce their corresponding sounds.

While phoneme-graphic recognition is an important component in learning to read and write, it is only one small correlated dimension of the larger social cognitive process of learning literacy. This larger process is what needs defining before we can develop measures to assess it.

The type of literacy taught in schools has often been described as 'decontextualized' in the sense that meaning is conveyed primarily through linguistic means, with minimal reliance on contextual cues and shared assumptions. If a speaker, for example, wanted to identify a car in the car park, literate language would encode critical information about the car (make, year, colour) as well as the location (lot A, aisle 5, in the middle). More contextualized language might rely on shared knowledge (e.g., it's in the place we parked yesterday) or context (e.g., pointing to the location).

Literacy also entails the decontextualization of the 'self'. This involves treating one's self, as well as others, as generalized others, with whom one shares little knowledge. The communicative implication of this stance is that meaning must be 'lexicalized', or explicitly encoded in language. The ability to distance from and reflect upon one's audience is crucial to literacy (Applebee, 1978). The literate communicator conveys meaning so that this generalized other can comprehend the message. Because of the generalized and distant nature of one's audience, communicative strategies which rely on shared knowledge assumptions and gestures do not effectively communicate meaning.

Literate events in school or those events where individuals interact around print are typically characterized by 'literate language'. The language of the books that children read and the language that children produce both in writing and while talking with teachers and peers during literacy events is also 'literate'.

Take the example of children's reading books. In texts for young children, pictures are the supportive context which help children decode meaning expressed in the lexicon. As children progress through school, this supportive context is minimized, as meaning must be inferred from the text primarily. Similarly, when talking to the teacher about a story with which both teacher and child are familiar, the child should assume the teacher is naive, and explicitly encode meaning.

These two aspects of the social context of school literacy (decontexualized and assuming a fictionalized self) have an affect on the structure of language that occurs there. At the word level, fictionalized others are encoded in third person pronouns and individual words which reflect a common theme, for example, lexical cohesion (Halliday and Hasan, 1976). At sentence level, syntactic structure (subject/predicate) reflects the information structure of the message: background or given information is encoded in the syntactic subject, and new information is encoded in the predicate. At the text level, meaning in one sentence is tied to other sentences, for example, 'The *car* is black. *It* is in row A'.

As children learn to use language for different purposes and in different situations, they reflect upon the language system *per se*. In order to produce and comprehend the sorts of language that minimally rely on context and maximally rely on linguistic features, children must choose from a variety of linguistic options to realize their meaningful intentions. Thus, decontextualization and fictionalized self-features of literate language should have the correlated benefit of stimulating children's metalinguistic awareness, or awareness of the rules and options governing language and its use in a social context. Children's awareness of language and literacy can be inferred from their use of terms about language, for example, *talk, say* and *listen*, and literacy events, for example, *book, pencil* and *read* (Pellegrini *et al.*, 1995c). As noted above, this sort of talk is indicative of metalinguistic awareness, a powerful predictor of later reading proficiency (Adams, 1990).

There is another design feature which is particularly important in primary school children's literacy events and that is the rhetorical genre of the typical literacy event: narrative. Children in the early years of school are exposed frequently to texts written in the narrative, or story, mode. Stories, like literate language, have fictionalized characters, are written using richly descriptive language, and are temporally and causally motivated. In short, the stories that children read and write should be cohesive and have noun phrases elaborated with adjectives, and use various types of conjunctions to conjoin phrases (Pellegrini *et al.*, 1984).

Table 9.1 Design features of school-based literacy

Design features	Linguistic realization
Decontextualization	New/old syntax Cohesion Adjectives
Fictionalized self	Third person pronouns Cohesion
Metalanguage	Language about language and literacy
Narrative structure	Varied use of conjunctions Adjectives

The design features of school-based literacy and the ways in which they are realized linguistically are displayed in Table 9.1.

Variety of social roles and the use of literate language

Our social ecological orientation guides us to examine the locations in which and processes by which children learn to use literate language. This involves a search of home and community speech events that share design features with literate language. Social scientists, most notably Basil Bernstein (1960, 1972) and his students (e.g., Cook-Gumperz, 1977) and anthropologists, such as Gumperz (1986), Heath (1983) and Schieffelin and Cochran-Smith (1982) have examined the socialization of what we have called literate language. There is striking similarity across these discussions of language, school and literacy to the extent that they all define school-based literacy as a linguistic register indigenous to main-stream culture.

These scholars argue that literate language and school-based literacy are extensions of the ways in which children are socialized to interact with each other and adults and the ways in which they convey meaning. The rules of these 'speech events' (Hymes, 1967) are learned by children so that they know how to act and speak in specified situations. Thus, competence in lan-guage use is not determined in terms of some abstract and implicit knowl-edge of syntactic rules, but instead in terms of role appropriate, communicative competence (Bernstein, 1972; Hymes, 1967). Commu-nicative competence involves knowledge of the socially accepted options for social behaviour and language in a variety of situations. These situations, or speech events, are rule governed in terms of social and linguistic norms. Similarity in design features exists between speech events, generally, and literacy events specifically, in most middle-class homes and schools. Similarity exists between home and school for the social roles that children take and the forms of language that children use.

One of the most thorough, and perhaps one of the most controversial explanations for the socialization of literate language comes from Basil Bernstein (1960, 1971, 1972). He suggests that conveyance of meaning is determined by one's role assignment and flexibility in the socialization context. He specifies four socialization contexts: the regulative context (where the child is made aware of the moral order and rules), the instructional context (where children learn skills and about objects and people), the imaginative context (where the child is encouraged to experiment and re-create the world in his/her own terms), and the inter-personal context (where the child becomes aware of his/her own and others' affective states). Children in different groups are socialized to take different roles in these contexts.

These different socialization practices have direct implications for children's language use. Take the regulative context. If children are treated according to a 'positional' orientation, their language and social experiences are limited to culturally determined roles; for example, children must always obey parents, without question. Parents set out guidelines without providing rationales or expecting feedback from children. The implication of this orientation is that children do not have to explicate meaning verbally in order to be understood: meaning can be conveyed by virtue of one's assigned social role. Such limited role experiences (they are only recipients of orders) and the language they use in these situations may evidence a paucity of appeals based on reasoning and causal conjunctions (e.g., Do this *because* it's your turn). These sorts of socialization contexts are typified by strictly defined power relationships. Parents, by definition, give orders and children, correspondingly, comply without question; this is exemplary of Bernstein's notion of strong classification (Bernstein, 1972).

By contrast, a person-centred orientation involves looser power relationships. Roles are more likely to be based on reasoning, not assigned position. Consequently, in a regulative context children must define their social role by appropriate social and linguistic behaviour; they cannot merely step into a positionally defined role. Part of the process of defining role, according to Bernstein (1972), entails making role relationships opaque. Children in these circumstances reflect upon their roles and those of the interlocutors and follow role appropriate social and linguistic rules. In short, the person-centred orientation socializes children to a 'fictionalized self' orientation, to explicate meaning verbally and to reflect upon the rules of different speech events.

When children from positional and person-oriented traditions go to school they often encounter an institution that does not encourage (or indeed tolerate) deviations from accepted social behaviours and registers; this is Bernstein's (1972) notion of a strong frame. Thus, children who have learned the language of school are speaking the socially accepted register of school; other language varieties are not tolerated. The implications for school success then becomes painfully clear and predictable.

That these socially accepted registers can be learned in school is a powerful dimension of Bernstein's theory. Unlike more fatalistic theories which put forth a variant of the 'critical period hypothesis' (i.e., if you haven't been socialized to learn school language by the time you enter school, it is nearly impossible to learn it), by weakening the frame and classification systems in schools and by experiencing other socialization contexts (e.g., churches, youth groups) children can learn the register of school as well.

Earlier we noted that Bernstein's theory was controversial. Much of the controversy related to discussions of class differences and socialization contexts. Bernstein's theory stimulated a massive amount of research in the UK (e.g., Tizard and Hughes, 1984; Wells, 1986) and in the US (Hess and Shipman, 1965) and in many cases the hypothesized class differences (in the UK) and the hypothesized class and race differences in the US were not supported. A more basic dimension of the theory has been supported, however. That dimension relates to the way in which children's socialization contexts affect social behaviour, language and school success. Research in this area, does support Bernstein's basic notion of role assignment and flexibility.

Drawing from the literature on family interaction, a consistent picture emerges. Children reared in homes characterized as authoritative (Baumrind, 1989) are more socially competent (this includes school-based achievement) than children in other socialization arrangements. Authoritative parenting practices are generally defined as responsive to children's needs, yet demanding. Steinberg and colleagues (Steinberg et al., 1992) have further illustrated that autonomy granting and democratic orientations within an authoritative style are particularly important in predicting school success. Examples of democratic and autonomy-granting orientations include parent–child joint decision-making. This orientation is strikingly similar to Bernstein's person-oriented socialization style. Also like Bernstein, Steinberg and colleagues suggest that children can learn these orientations at home or in their peer groups; thus they are not 'trapped' by their home context.

Close relationships and literate language

In the preceding section, we suggested that the flexibility and variety of roles which children took facilitated children's learning literate language. The nature of specific relationships between individuals, too, influences the sorts of language as well as other behaviours that children generate. Relationships, following Hinde (1976), are interactions between individuals across time. Thus, Jack and Sam have a history of interactions and special relationships; they are friends. Jack's interactions with Sam will differ from his interactions with Joe, who is an acquaintance, not a friend. Knowing about relationships helps us understand and predict the nature of individuals' interactions in different social arrangements. Close relationships, such as friendships, sibling relationships and attachment relationships are characterized by an emotional component that distinguishes them from other social arrangements.

Close relationships of the sort noted above are typified by an emotional component indicative of trust and investment. When friends or a securely attached child and his/her mother interact together, they trust each other and they enjoy each other's company. This emotional component may be particularly important for children learning literate language to the extent that these relations afford opportunities to disagree and resolve disagreement and then reflect upon social interactive processes and corresponding language forms (Pellegrini *et al.*, 1997). As noted above, the ability to reflect upon language and social processes is an important component in literacy development. Specifically, friends, compared to non-friends, tend to disagree and then compromise frequently (Hartup, 1992). Further, children in close relationships tend to monitor and remember the details of their interactions (Dunn, 1988; Dunn and Slomkowski, 1992). Evidence of children's monitoring of the social interactive processes includes children's talk about 'internal states', such as emotions and language. Talk about emotional states also tends to 'cool' the high emotionality surrounding disagreement between friends and enables them to reflect upon the interaction process. It is this disagreement/resolution, monitoring, cooling and reflection process that leads directly to friends' use of literate language (Pellegrini *et al.*, 1997; 1998). Friendships in school are discussed in greater detail in Chapter 3.

While we have argued that close peer relationships and their corresponding forms of reciprocal interaction foster 'meta' processes, it is also the case that close adult–child relationships, and their complementary interaction styles, also afford children with opportunities to reflect upon the social interactive process. We know from the attachment literature (Bus and van IJzendoorn, 1988) for example, that interactions between securely attached children and their mothers are coordinated and mothers' adjust their styles so as to maximize children's participation in the interaction process. This process of children 'appropriating' task responsibility is an important precursor of metacognitive processing in Vygotskian theory (Wertsch, 1979). For example, when mothers talk with children in story book reading contexts they often ask children to plan (What comes first?) and to evaluate information (e.g., Did he really say that do you think?). Mothers also model cognitive and linguistic terms which children then use later (Pellegrini *et al.*, 1995b). In short, children learn to 'go meta' on the literacy events through interactions in close relationships. In close peer relationships, conflicts and resolutions seem to facilitate reflection. In close adult–child relationships, mothers' ability to engage children in literacy events may effect reflective processes.

Conclusion

In this chapter we have discussed school-based literacy from a social developmental perspective. We defined school-based literacy in terms of facility with language characterized by 'meta' talk, fictionalized self, verbally explicated meaning, often embedded in narratives. We posit that children's socialization histories, both in the home and with their peer group, have important implications for the social role and rules they learn. These socialization experiences in turn affect children's learning of literate language. Following Bernstein's theory, we would expect children socialized to take on different roles and interact with a variety of people to develop literate language as a consequence of these varied social experiences. It may also be the case that the quality of the social relationships are important, rather than just diverse experiences. In close peer and adult relations children learn to monitor the interactive process such that they treat the rules of literacy as opaque and consequently are capable of 'going meta' on these rules. This 'meta' ability is crucial in school-based literacy learning.

10 School-based mathematics

A basic orientation of this book is that children are developmental beings and as such they are different from adults. Second, our notion of development is that it is a transactive process between organism and environment, with each affecting and responding to each other. As such, this notion of development presumes varied developmental trajectories depending on a number of characteristics with the children and with his/her environment.

Just as we specified this process for literacy learning, we will do so for school-based mathematics learning. There is, however, a crucial difference between our understanding of children's development of literacy and mathematics. Simply, we know much more about the former than the latter. Indeed, we know very little about the social contexts and processes, outside of school, which develop into school-based mathematics. Because of this dearth of information, we will present a general model for understanding children in a developmental niche (Pellegrini and Stanic, 1993; Super and Harkness, 1986). We will then use this model to make specific inferences about their learning of mathematics both in and out of school.

Because contrasting cases help us understand the developmental process more clearly we will examine social economic status (SES) differences in children's developing mathematical competence. SES is important because children's competence in school subjects generally and school mathematical competence specifically varies as a function of SES, where lower socioeconomic status (LSES) children systematically do worse than their middle socioeconomic status (MSES) counterparts (Carpenter *et al.*, 1987; Reyes and Stanic, 1988; Saxe *et al.*, 1987; Yando *et al.*, 1979). In American schools this disturbing trend is detected in the pre-school years, in informal mathematics tasks (e.g., Saxe *et al.*, 1987) and continues through the elementary grades and beyond.

The lack of perceived adaptive value of school mathematics has been proffered as a reason for such widespread variation within American society (Lave, 1988; Ogbu, 1988). That is, where children do not see the value of a subject, they will not be motivated to learn it. Where the value of certain types of mathematics is clear, children do become competent, as in the case of Saxe's (1991) Brazilian candy sellers. The nature of school and standardized mathematics tasks and the ways in which mathematics is taught seem to be of little use and value to many segments of American society.

Indeed, SES differences are minimized on school-like tasks when familiar elicitation strategies are used (e.g., Ginsburg and Russell, 1981; Pellegrini *et al.*, 1990). We will argue that SES differences in school mathematics are due, in part, to different contextual features between everyday and school mathematical events.

It seems to us, as it does to others (e.g., Saxe, 1991), that an important step in the effort to improve children's school-based mathematics is to locate children's levels of mathematical competence in their everyday lives before they encounter formal schooling. Such descriptions of the utility of mathematics in various out-of-school, work place settings could also be useful in redesigning school curricula (Heath, 1989; Shapin, 1992). This is not to say that transfer of competence from home to school, from school to home or from school to work place is a matter of simply identifying similar routines in both settings. While general similarities may exist between home and school mathematical events, such as an adult encouraging a child to count, closer examination of the social roles, motivations and expectations in each setting reveal clear differences which may be responsible for home–school differences (Snow, 1992; Walkerdine, 1988). Children's counting, for example, may be encouraged by mothers as part of a practice routine whereas teachers may encourage counting routines as part of an evaluation, or testing, situation (Walkerdine, 1988).

Such differences are partially responsible for the lack of concordance between everyday competence and school competence (Lave, 1988; Snow, 1992). As Lave (1988) has shown, adults use very different methods to solve mathematical tasks in supermarket than they use to solve school mathematics problems; it is as if they are solving different problems. Thus, it is not surprising that they could solve supermarket problems virtually perfectly, yet this competence was minimally related to measures of school mathematics competence. Thus, individuals can be competent in mathematics out of school, but not competent on seemingly similar aspects of school mathematics. It may be, as Snow has suggested, that transfer lies in the ability to see 'affordances', i.e., recognize and use similar person/environment features, between everyday and school tasks. Different levels of mathematical competence at school and in everyday settings seems, in turn, related to SES. For example, there is a relation between pre-school children's SES and performance on standardized achievement and aptitude tasks (e.g., Elardo *et al.*, 1975) and, specifically, on standardized mathematics tasks (Saxe *et al.*, 1987).

As noted above, when mathematics tasks are made more familiar to LSES children, SES differences are minimized (Ginsburg and Russell, 1981). This suggests a concordance between MSES or mainstream culture and the culture of school mathematical competence, given the ways school mathematics are typically measured. In this chapter, we draw on prior research to support the thesis that children from culturally different families possess everyday mathematical competence (e.g., Carraher *et al.*, 1985; Lave, 1988; Saxe, 1991) before they enter school (e.g., Ginsburg and Russell, 1981; Walkerdine, 1988) which is relevant to their everyday lives. Yet as culturally different children, that is, primarily LSES children, progress through school, they lose ground in relation to their MSES counterparts (Carpenter *et al.*, 1987; Yando *et al.*, 1979). For this reason, it seems particularly important to attend to the transition from pre-school to school. We will argue, following others before us (Cole and Bruner, 1971: Laboratory of Comparative Human Cognition, 1983), that the increasing differences in school mathematics performance are probably due to the contextual differences between mathematics in school and everyday mathematics.

Descriptions of children in various settings in school and out of school, it should follow, are necessary to understand children's mathematical competence. We, like many others (e.g., Saxe, 1991; Snow, 1992), suggest that children's mathematical competence varies according to the social and physical arrangements of their environments. Specifically, where children have varied experiences which overlap with school-like mathematics experiences, they are more likely to be successful in school than those with less varied experiences. Explication of similarity between these diverse contexts is necessary for the transfer of competence from everyday to school mathematics. Also like Snow (1992), we suggest that mathematical competence at home and school involves the ability to find and match the physical and social resources in the different contexts.

In this chapter we will put forth a model by which such competence can be located. The difference between our approach and those taken by others is that we explicate the ways in which children's mathematical competence develops by their interacting with and re-formulating specific aspects of their environments. The specific interactive elements of the environment to be discussed are based on Super and Harkness's (1986) developmental niche model and include the physical setting, the child-care customs, and the psychological beliefs of child-care takers.

Ginsburg and Russell (1981), Saxe (1991), and Saxe *et al.* (1987) have conducted important, initial research on the issue of differential mathematics competence of young children in different segments of American and Brazilian society. Additionally, Ginsburg and Russell (1981) showed minimal SES differences in many areas of pre-school children's mathematical competence, while Saxe *et al.* (1987) showed minimal mother–child interaction differences between MSES and LSES whites from intact families. More specifically, Saxe *et al.* showed that mothers' specification of goal structure level for counting and numerical reproduction activities varied as a function of children's ability. Relatedly, children adjusted their levels of interaction to mothers' instructions. Thus, both MSES and LSES mothers exhibit child-sensitive teaching strategies. These studies corroborate the point that pre-school-age children from both MSES and LSES backgrounds possess mathematical competence. Indeed, Saxe's (1991) work with Brazilian candy sellers is similar to what we propose here to the extent that he identified the social and physical dimensions of children's environments that were important in their establishing mathematical goals. These dimensions varied as a function of children's everyday experiences, for example, whether they were candy sellers or not.

Mathematical competence during the pre-school period

Researchers have defined mathematical competence of pre-school children in terms of counting, generally, and the following specific components: protoquantitative schema (e.g., making quantity judgements such as 'lots'); counting skills, including the production and comprehension of counting words; cardinality (e.g., labelling a set after counting); ability to perceive more and less; and adding and subtracting (Gelman and Gallistel, 1978; Ginsburg and Russell, 1981; Resnick, 1989; Saxe *et al.*, 1987). The constitutive elements of mathematical competence that we will examine do not reflect all areas of mathematics, yet they are commonly applied to the development of an important aspect of young children's mathematical competence: counting ability (Sternberg and Powell, 1983). Because the development of young children's counting ability is the central thrust of early school mathematics we will focus on the five components listed above. Further, aspects of spatial perception, a somewhat neglected aspect of school mathematics, may represent a separate 'intelligence' from the more logico-mathematical intelligence (Gardner, 1985).

The development of these components of mathematical competence is such that, with age, pre-school children's facility with each component increases (Saxe *et al.*, 1987), though the age effects are mediated by cultural variables, such as social class and family constellation variables (Ginsburg and Russell, 1981; Saxe *et al.*, 1987). Specifically, Ginsburg and Russell reported SES differences on cardinality and perception of more/less while Saxe *et al.* also reported SES differences on cardinality. It has been suggested by some scholars (e.g., Saxe, 1991; Saxe *et al.*, 1987; Walkerdine, 1988) that these levels of competence are, in turn, a result of children's experiences in specific social contexts or the physical arrangements of specific environments.

In this chapter we will outline a heuristic by which to study the social *and* physical contexts in which children's mathematical competence develops. Expanding on Saxe's (1991) notion of 'goal structure' analyses, we apply Super and Harkness's (1986) developmental model for locating children's mathematical competence in their everyday context. This examination involves descriptions not only of the social and physical dimensions of the different environments but also of the differing social roles and expectations or beliefs which determine the ways in which children construct mathematical concepts. Thus, what Super and Harkness (1986) call the *developmental niche*, as it is conceptualized here, describes the interactive aspects of physical and social dimensions of the environment. Environment, as we define it, is not 'coercive' (Barker, 1968); individuals contribute to the definition of environment. Indeed, individuals create their own niches, they do not only move from one to another.

The developmental niche (Super and Harkness, 1986) is more akin to Saxe's (1991) three component approach for the study of cognition and culture to the extent that we are concerned with identifying the social and physical aspects of the environment that children use to develop mathematical competence (Saxe's component 1) and the ways in which these components relate to school mathematics (Saxe's component 3). Thus, these models attempt to explain cultural differences in the ways in which mathematical competence develops. For example, and as Saxe (1991) found, different groups may use different signs to represent numerical values. In such cases it would be extremely difficult to assess and compare groups on common criteria for mathematical competence. While recognizing that cognitive 'universals' may exist (e.g., Klein and Starkley, 1988), a role of the developmental niche, then, is to explicate where similarities and differences exist.

Our approach extends the work in the field in that the five components of mathematics listed above typically have been assessed with laboratory procedures, not according to their use in children's everyday contexts. The work of Saxe (1991) and Saxe and colleagues (1987) and Walkerdine (1988) are notable exceptions. Using interview/questionnaire methodology, Saxe and colleagues focused on children's everyday experiences with these components of mathematical competence. Walkerdine, using the observational data in the Tizard and Hughes (1984) study of English pre-schoolers, showed how children's home and school experiences with mathematics are very different, even when they seem to be similar. For example, she illustrated the different discourse rules associated with uses of the word *more* at home and school; *more* at home was contrasted with *not more*, as in an eating activity, and *more* at school was contrasted with *less*. Such rule differences, as well as differences in power relationships between children and adults are, for Walkerdine, responsible for class differences in mathematics. While extant research provides rich descriptions of everyday mathematical competence of older children (e.g., Carraher *et al.*, 1985), children from other nations (e.g., Saxe, 1991; Walkerdine, 1988) and adults (e.g., Lave, 1988), it provides little guidance as to the actual locations, materials, social processes and participants which typify young American children's encounters with these components of mathematical competence outside of school.

In this chapter we will apply the developmental niche (Super and Harkness, 1986) to LSES American black and white children. Our basic premise, following Ginsburg and Russell (1981), Lave (1988), and Saxe *et al.* (1987), is that LSES black and white children fail in school because of a mismatch between the mathematical experiences of their niches and the niche of school mathematics, not because of basic differences in 'cognitive processing capability'. School mathematics tends to reflect specific, often MSES, experiences whereas the experiences of LSES children are different from the MSES. The specificity of mathematical competence can be further illustrated by the mismatch at another, more general level, between school mathematical competence and everyday mathematical competence (Lave, 1988); Heath (1989) has made a similar point regarding literacy in school and the work place.

They, like some students of the sociology of knowledge (e.g., Shapin, 1992), suggest that the ways in which subjects are taught in school, or idealized by some of its practitioners, does not match with the demands for that same subject in the work place or with the ways in which scholars in various disciplines conduct their work. Specifically, Heath (1989) and Shapin (1992) have noted that the successful solution of problems in various work places, such as fast food restaurants and scientific laboratories, respectively, involve social collaboration among workers; this practice is noticeably absent from most school curricula. The developmental niche helps to locate and explicate such differences.

The developmental niche

At the most general level, the developmental niche (Super and Harkness, 1986), like other conceptualizations of development in context (Bronfenbrenner, 1979; Lave, 1988; Saxe, 1991), represents an attempt to describe the macro- and micro-level processes that characterize children's development. While the components are listed separately, they are conceptualized as interacting with each other. Further, individual children's development is described in terms of their gradual assumption of task responsibility. Thus, children's contributions to the processes makes it a transactive system.

The physical setting

The first dimension of the developmental niche is a micro-level variable: the physical and social setting (Super and Harkness, 1986). At this level, the materials (e.g., sticks, Sesame Street's counting and number programmes, board games, flash cards), people (e.g., siblings, mother, father, grandmother, baby sitters) and processes (e.g., direct instruction by mother, solitary interaction with materials) that compose children's

mathematical experiences are described. Many researchers have documented the importance of the social and physical environments in
children's development (e.g., Bradley and Caldwell, 1977). Two literatures are particularly important in this regard. The first is the ethological
literature which suggests that cognition evolved in the context of individuals coordinating social relationships (e.g., Humphrey, 1976; Jolly,
1966; Strayer, 1989). For example, sophisticated cognitions are required
for children to coordinate their roles in relation to a large number of
familiar participants. Further, scholars in this tradition view physical
dimensions of the niche as 'instruments' which facilitate social interaction among participants (Strayer, 1989). Children and adults typically
use objects in their immediate environment as a locus of communication.
Co-constructed representations of those situations are the bases of
cognitive development.

A second relevant literature here is the social network literature (e.g.,
Cochran and Riley, 1988; Gottlieb, 1981). This literature, too, sees a varied social context as supportive of individuals' development and emotional
well being. We know from this literature that different segments of society
systematically construct different physical and social settings. For example,
the social networks of LSES black, compared to LSES white, children are
characterized by greater interaction with kin children, such as siblings and
cousins; MSES, compared to LSES, black children interact with a larger
number of non-kin children and adults (Cochran and Riley, 1988). We
know that these different social settings affect children's primary school
achievement (Cochran and Riley, 1988), but we do not know about the
specific kinds of mathematical experiences of black and white children
from LSES and MSES backgrounds. We still need to determine the specific
types of materials and social settings that best describe each group's mathematical experiences however. Rather than following a functional model of
social and physical settings determining cognition, it seems important to
describe the ways in which different groups construct mathematical relations in varied social and physical settings. Construction of mathematical
competence in these settings, varies in turn, as a function of customs of
child care.

Customs of child care

The second dimension of the developmental niche, customs of child care,
is a macro-level variable and mediates the physical and social setting (Super
and Harkness, 1986). That is, child-care arrangements influence the materials and people that children have available. People and materials, in turn,
have an effect on children's cognitive status. Children in stable and familiar child-care arrangements have the opportunity to form relationships with

other participants in those arrangements. Following relationship theory, stable and familiar relationships, such as attachment relationships, are necessary if children are to enter into the types of reciprocal social interactions which characterize effective learning environments (Hinde, 1983). For example, significant relations between attachment status and cognitive development (Slade, 1987) have been documented. Current attachment theorists suggest that children construct attachment-based representational models of social relationships which become used in subsequent social cognitive development (Main et al., 1985). However, relationships other than mother–child relationships and the extent to which these relationships typify different aspects of the society, must be described. We, like Strayer (1989) and Trivers (1972), propose that the primary attachment system is embedded in a larger social network. Representations between children, other participants, such as older siblings and pre-school teachers, can be co-constructed.

It follows, then, that variation in child-care arrangements among different segments of the populace, and the relation of such arrangements to mathematical competence, must be described. While we know that LSES children, compared to MSES children, have limited access to institutional child care (Rogoff, 1991), we do not know much about the specifics of these arrangements; for example, children who go to organized, after-school programmes probably interact with numerous non-kin children and adults, often around varied and sometimes school-like tasks. Parents' ability to pay for safe and organized after-school care, then, determines to a great extent children's opportunities to explore different aspects of, and take different roles in, physical and social settings. The positive relation between child-care experience and cognitive status, even when SES is controlled, (e.g., Berieter, 1985; Strayer, 1989), suggests the social arrangements themselves do indeed have an effect. We need to know, however, the specific processes that typify these different child-care arrangements and the specific ways in which they affect children's mathematical competence.

These different child-care configurations should, according to our model, affect children's school achievement to the extent that children with more varied experiences, i.e., children with a variety of social networks which are characterized by a variety of school-like mathematics materials and processes, should be more successful in school mathematics than children with less varied experiences. Children who spend time in child-care arrangements in which they interact with adults (kin or non-kin) or with younger children (kin or non-kin) around varied mathematics materials should perform better on mathematical tasks than children with less varied social and material experiences. The reasoning here is that adults teach children when they interact with them; further, older children typically teach younger children, with both groups accruing benefits from these experiences. The research of Strayer (1989) supports this claim to the extent that children attending day care, compared to other, similar children not in day care, have higher levels of representational thought, as defined by Sigel's (1982) distancing model.

In short, experience in varied areas with familiar others should result in higher school achievement because the social interaction around objects in such settings facilitates children's concept development. We further posit that school-like activities are more likely to be found in these settings than in cases of less varied experience. Like Snow (1992), we propose that more varied experiences relate to more varied mathematical competence, some of which are likely to include specific, school-like experience. Specifically, children who have repeated experiences in a variety of niches should also be more likely to perceive similarities across niches; similarities may exist in terms of social roles, motivations and materials. An important, though often ignored, issue involves children who participate in social interaction patterns which are 'test-like'. For example, Cazden (1972) has shown teacher–child interaction patterns in 'structured' pre-school programmes resemble the structure of test questions. Thus, congruence in social interaction patterns is partially responsible for achievement scores.

Psychology of the caretakers

Child-care customs are related to the third dimension of the developmental niche: the psychology of the caretakers (Super and Harkness, 1986). The psychology of the caretakers includes their beliefs about the ways in which children learn; their aspirations for children; and their attitudes towards school, in general, and school mathematics, in particular. These beliefs, aspirations and attitudes, according to McGillicuddy-DeLisi (1982), are reflected in parents' and other caretakers' interactions with children. The importance of caretakers' psychological orientation for children's mathematics learning has recently been advanced by Stevenson and Lee (1990), who found that differences among American, Chinese and Japanese parents' achievement orientations played an important role in their children's differential school mathematics achievement. Consequently, an important aspect of studying parental beliefs and attitudes is that they provide a point of origin within the family for looking at the actual processes by which children are exposed to and taught mathematical concepts. Examining these aspects of the psychology of caretakers enables us to begin to move beyond the mere labelling of SES, as a proxy variable, to actually explicating the social processes and expectations that typify different groups. Clearly, parents' beliefs and expectations affect the ways in which they interact with their children and, in turn, their children's development (Bandura, 1989). Thus, if parents have low expectations for their children, children will probably meet those expectations.

The extant child development literature demonstrates both systematic variation in parental beliefs among different segments of American society and a relation among parental beliefs, parent and child behaviour, and various child outcome measures (McGillicuddy-DeLisi, 1982; Sigel *et al.*, 1983). These descriptions, however, are generally limited to LSES blacks and whites and MSES whites, not MSES blacks. For example, LSES parents, more so than MSES parents, believe in direct instruction of their children (McGillicuddy-DeLisi, 1982); within the LSES group, black parents, compared to white parents, have a more behaviouristic orientation (Sutherland, 1983). Furthermore, LSES whites are more fatalistic than their LSES black counterparts to the extent that they believe that children are limited by their innate capabilities (Sutherland, 1983). MSES parents, compared to LSES parents, are more stage-like and school-readiness oriented in their beliefs; MSES parents also believe that they can use dimensions of their everyday environment to help children develop (McGillicuddy-DeLisi, 1982). Finally, MSES parents, compared to LSES parents, demonstrate more self-efficacy, or confidence, in the correctness of their beliefs (McGillicuddy-DeLisi, 1982).

Development in the niche

Following Sigel (1982), Strayer (1989) and others (e.g., Humphrey, 1976), we propose that interaction with physical objects is made meaningful by the social participants in those events. That is, the cognitions that children have of events are based on their social interactions around materials. Further, 'familiar social partners', from which social relationships expand, include not only mothers, but also fathers, siblings, grandparents, child-minders, peers and teachers, to name a few. It is important, we think, to move beyond the mother–child dyad as the basic unit of socially mediated models of cognition. Importantly, it has also been shown that some social partners, such as older siblings, are more effective teachers in certain areas than are mothers (Dunn, 1988).

Like more traditional models of adult–child interaction, such as Vygotksy's zone of proximal development (1978), the proposed model also stresses children's gradual appropriation of responsibility from their tutors. That is, as children interact with various social partners in different physical settings, development is defined as their gradual assumption of task responsibility in varied, specific settings. Using standardized counting and number reproduction tasks, this social appropriation process has been examined and supported, by Saxe and colleagues, for both LSES and MSES mother–child dyads. As suggested above, researchers should now examine other, and probably more common, social settings, for example, grandparents or siblings, with indigenous materials rather than standardized materials.

It is this process of social co-construction (Sigel, 1982; Strayer, 1989) that spurs children's cognitive development. By social co-construction we mean the process by which children represent their interactions with people and objects. Developmentally, these representations become less situation specific and more varied.

Development, first, can be defined as the extent to which children appropriate task responsibility from their tutors. The ability to transfer competence to different contexts resides in the ability of participants to find similarities in the activity rules governing mathematics in different contexts (Brown *et al.*, 1983; Leont'ev, 1978; Scribner and Cole, 1973; Snow, 1992). Competence begins with repeated experiences in individual settings, and expands by interacting with different people and different materials. Explication by participants of between-task rule similarities should result in transfer as the 'new' problems are treated as extensions of a class of problems, not as isolated problems (Brown *et al.*, 1983; Scribner and Cole, 1973). As Saxe (1991) has noted, repeated experiences in different contexts is necessary for transfer. Transfer, from this perspective, first involves the ability to perceive cross-situation similarities. Perception of cross-situation 'affordances', or what situations offer, will determine the extent to which children use specific strategies. If they perceive familiar social and physical arrangements, they will transfer a related strategy. Thus, transfer involves the recognition of cross-situation affordances and using strategies that match the new situations. An assumption here is that different situations have very different rules and that repeated and varied experiences in different situations increase the likelihood of perceiving cross-situational affordances.

Differences in developmental niches

Extant research on children and families can be drawn on as we begin to study children's experiences with number. These different experiences should result in different levels of mathematical competence to the extent that they are characterized by different social and physical rule systems. In extreme cases, it may be that children's mathematical competence minimally resembles the components of mathematical competence that we have outlined above, just as Saxe's (1991) Brazilian candy sellers used a different representational system for numbers. The developmental niche, in such cases, should help us explicate the ways in which mathematical competence is defined in different groups. This is accomplished by documenting differences in aspects of the niches for different cultural groups. For example, because of income differences, LSES, compared to MSES, families have fewer and less varied toys, such as number puzzles and toy clocks; this limited physical setting is particularly true of LSES black families (Rogoff, 1991). Further, the toys in LSES homes are often different from those of

MSES children and from those used in elicitation tasks which typify child development research (Rubin *et al.*, 1983). These physical differences may be responsible for some of the observed SES differences in laboratory studies of children's counting and adding among children whose levels of performance are similar in more familiar tasks (Stigler and Baranes, 1988). Indeed, the social and physical arrangements in many LSES homes is varied and rich but happens to differ from the arrangements in schools (Stigler and Baranes, 1988).

The social settings of the niche, as noted above, probably interacts with the physical dimension. For example, MSES, compared to LSES, children have fewer siblings and, therefore, greater access to parents as teachers (Blake, 1989). Within the LSES group, black families are more often characterized by single parents and children are more often cared for by grandparents (Rogoff, 1991); this difference in the social setting leads to different interactions with the material setting and may be responsible for some differences in mathematical competence.

Access to child-care programmes demonstrates an overlap between the social setting and the second dimension of the developmental niche, customs of child care. Such differences in child-care probably have implications for the development of mathematical competence. For example, MSES children, compared to LSES children, more frequently attend preschool and after-school child-care programmes (Rogoff, 1991). These programmes typically utilize materials similar to those of school-based mathematics events. These similarities could be responsible for observed differences in school mathematics.

Available evidence about the third element of the developmental niche, the psychology of the caretakers, also points to possible effects on mathematical competence. It may be, for example, that the differences in parental self-efficacy described above may result in gender differences in exposure to mathematical experiences within a particular group, but not in all groups.

Describing children's mathematical competence in the developmental niche

One should be able to identify both continuous and discontinuous developmental paths of mathematical competence within and across contexts (Kagan, 1971; Lave, 1988; Laboratory of Comparative Human Cognition, 1983; Saxe, 1991). Descriptions of the school and everyday niches should provide specific examples of continuity and/or discontinuity. Specific aspects of their developmental niches of school and home may vary by year; these differences, in turn, may result in different school related trajectories. Consequently, the developmental niche (Super and Harkness, 1986) informs us of the ways in which children and their environments interact.

It should be stressed that the rich description generated by application of the developmental niche to different segments of society are necessary first steps that must be taken before we can talk about transfer to school contexts. We do not suggest, however, that the aim of any research programme should be to transfer everyday competence to school mathematics as it is currently conceptualized. Indeed, we argue that the current state of school mathematics can best be improved by studying the ways in which children learn mathematics in different contexts, both in and out of school. In this way we can better understand development. Descriptions of match-mismatch between home and current school practices documented by this model are necessary to understand children in schools in that mismatches often result in school failure.

There are a number of questions associated with each dimension of the developmental niche which this type of analysis will allow us to pose. As noted above, the descriptions provided by the developmental niche framework are necessary before issues of transfer of competence from everyday to school contexts are addressed. For example, regarding participants in the social setting, do children in different groups have different social configurations during mathematics events. Next, do children who participate in mathematics events with a variety of other children and adults, that is, a varied social network, perform better in school mathematics compared to children with a less varied social network? This level of analysis might also provide developmental insight into the later gender stereotyping of school mathematics. More specifically, it has been suggested (Maccoby and Jacklin, 1987) that gender segregation around specific activities is an important basis for subsequent gender-role stereotyping. It may be that the social groupings of young boys and girls around mathematics events predicts the male preference for and superior performance in mathematics which appears during adolescence. Relatedly, specific customs of child care (and the related physical and social settings) should also be important to children's experiences with number. For example, does participation in early childhood education programmes (Rogoff, 1991) forecast cognitive developmental status (Strayer, 1989) and school achievement (Bereiter, 1985). This form of child care often may be associated with particular materials (e.g., flash cards, flannel board numbers, other commercially developed mathematics materials) and associated social processes (e.g., teachers asking particular kinds of questions) that have design features almost identical to those of school. It is important to determine whether it is indeed the particular type of materials or processes or simply the variety of materials and processes that enhances subsequent school task performance. Alternatively, it may be the case that pre-school experience predicts cognitive development simply because children in such settings interact with more diverse social partners than children who stay at home (Strayer, 1989; Strayer and Moss, 1989). Theories (e.g., Humphrey, 1976; Jolly,

1966) on origins of primate intelligence suggest that intelligence evolved as a result of having to coordinate social relationships in large and diverse groups. If this were the case, social diversity, not similarity in materials between contexts, should predict school mathematics.

The above examples of research questions highlight the power of the developmental niche in identifying elements of children's lives that determine their mathematical competence in school and the larger community. The developmental niche provides a heuristic whereby we can flesh out the actual processes which typify the experience of children from different segments of society and the specific ways in which these processes forecast development. This construct is particularly useful in describing the ways in which different children experience mathematics at home and at school. Only after we have these descriptions in hand can we begin to address the transfer of mathematical competence from one situation to another.

From everyday to school: building networks

The developmental niche is certainly useful in understanding children in their communities and in their schools. Simultaneous descriptions of children at school, home and work settings is necessary to describe the different ways in which mathematics is constructed. Only after we have such thorough descriptions can we begin to understand the development of mathematical competence. Then we can address the question of improving school mathematics curricula. Descriptions of home and school niches would begin to address ways in which the everyday experiences of children from different segments of society lead to differential success in school mathematics. Why is it, for example, that an individual's mathematical competence in one situation, such as grocery shopping, is unrelated to their school mathematical competence? Descriptions of children in and out of school, like those provided by Lave (1988) for her adult shoppers and dieters, are crucial to our understanding of the meaning of mathematical competence. Studying the school as part of the developmental niche is both difficult and important, for schooling probably means different things for children from different groups. Even particular schools or classrooms probably exhibit different physical and social settings (e.g., a certain group may have limited access to classroom materials and the teacher), different childcare customs (e.g., a certain group may receive more rewards or reprimands for particular behaviour) and different caretaker beliefs and attitudes (e.g., a teacher may hold higher expectations for a certain group) for different children. It seems to us that we must understand the competence that children come to school with if they are to learn school mathematics.

The issue of the adequacy of the school mathematics curriculum is beyond the limits of this chapter, but the reported disconcordance between everyday and school mathematical competence, noted by Lave (1988), and the consistent SES differences in school mathematics achievement reported above, suggest problems exist. A reasonable place to start may be for educators to ask themselves what function school mathematics should serve. It may be, for example, that the mathematics of different occupations could be the bases of school curriculum. Heath (1989) suggests the design features of literacy events in various work places, such as group problem definition and solution, could be used to redesign school literacy events. Similarly, Shapin (1992) suggests that scientists, too, work collectively on problems and that they often revise or correct previous judgements. These features of the work place, it seems to us, are often inconsistent with much current pedagogy, where individuals, not groups, often work toward one correct answer. Certainly the use of standardized tests as measures of mathematical competence is congruent with this view. If use in the work place is a rationale for teaching mathematics in schools, perhaps educators should compare the various dimensions of target occupations. Again, the developmental niche would be a useful heuristic for such an exercise.

Our proposed model of curriculum and instruction, consistent with the attempt to bridge everyday and school mathematics experiences, includes non-school personnel, such as kin and non-kin adults and peers. Generally, children who are embedded in a large and varied social network do better in school than children in less varied networks (Cochran and Riley, 1988). Thus, the first order of business should be to facilitate network formation. A necessary aspect of this process is parent empowerment (Cochran and Woolever, 1983). By empowerment we mean enabling parents and other caretakers to realize their strengths as teachers of their children and to build upon these strengths with new skills specific to children's mathematics performance in school. That is, first parents and other caretakers should be reminded of the effective teaching skills they possess, such as teaching children to read measuring cups while cooking. This step is based on the non-deficit premise that parents and teachers have some very effective strategies in their repertoire for teaching their children. Adverse social and economic conditions may lead some parents to doubt their own abilities. This first step, then, will re-establish caretakers' self-efficacy as teachers of children. We certainly know that self-efficacy plays an important role in children's and adults' social and cognitive development (Bandura, 1989). Similarly, it is important for children to recognize their own competence. This can be done by pointing out to them the ways in which they already use mathematics in their everyday worlds. This process not only builds confidence but it also serves to make explicit similarities between seemingly different contexts; such explication, as noted above, is crucial for transfer.

The second step in the process of building social networks involves reducing isolation (Cochran and Woolever, 1983). Isolation has been exacerbated by the growth of non-traditional family forms. Although all sectors of contemporary industrial society have witnessed changes in family structure, certain segments of society have been more profoundly affected than others, and they generally tend to be poor; for example, American black children are now most likely to live in single-parent families; 51 per cent of black children, 27 per cent of Hispanic children and 16 per cent of white children live with their mothers only (Rogoff, 1991). The issue is how to help children and parents who are forced by economic conditions to live in non-traditional arrangements.

Reducing isolation is best accomplished by encouraging parents to attend meetings of other parents with similar concerns. In earlier work on non-mainstream-culture literacy (Pellegrini *et al.*, 1990), this step enabled parents to recognize that they were not alone in their situation and that other like-minded and like-situated parents were available to help. Meetings involved sharing lists of names, phone numbers and addresses of community resources, such as reciprocal after-school-care arrangements, child minders, free housing materials and tutors. Parents' self-efficacy was enhanced in these sessions to the extent that they were sharing their effective coping strategies with others. The information and the resources gained from such exchanges became a valued reason for attending meetings.

These two steps result in the reformulation of children's developmental niches. At the level of physical and social setting, children should be embedded in larger and more varied groups. Similarly, child-care arrangements should be more varied to the extent that parents have more options. Lastly, at the level of caretakers' beliefs, parents should become more aware of their own beliefs and the implications of those beliefs through their interactions with other parents about child rearing. This self-awareness is just one step in considering those alternative beliefs that may facilitate children's achievement (Sigel *et al.*, 1983). When provided with some level of support, parents usually will adopt those beliefs that maximize their children's well being and success.

Conclusion

The knowledge gained from applying the concept of developmental niche to children's mathematical competence would be useful to the educational community on a number of levels. First, identification of children's mathematical competence in their everyday lives provides important information for the design of curriculum materials and instructional techniques. In order to attain the long-term goal of maximizing children's achievement in school mathematics, we must begin by designing materials and instructional strategies which have activity structures (Leont'ev, 1978) similar to those of children's everyday tasks. Construction of such bridges to school mathematics maximizes the likelihood of transfer (Laboratory of Comparative Human Cognition, 1983). The information generated from the developmental niche (Super and Harkness, 1986) perspective will allow us to begin to design a school mathematics programme appropriate for non-mainstream-culture children. Such a venture should result, in turn, in improved school mathematics achievement of these children.

Another important contribution to the field of education relates to the empowerment of the parents and other caretakers of LSES children. By designing programmes that increase the social networks of caretakers, we will be simultaneously increasing their self-efficacy as teachers of their children and providing them with opportunities to gain access to resources in their communities. The extant research is replete with examples documenting the positive effect on children's education of parental involvement and increasing social networks. A clear educational benefit of the proposed research agenda would be the broadening of children's educational setting to include not just school, but also home and community. Of course, a more political, and less psychological, perspective should also be considered: that LSES children are simply treated badly in schools (Kozol, 1991), and if we change educational practice, this SES differences in achievement would be minimized. While the model presented here can clearly address this issue, possibly in terms of beliefs that teachers have of certain groups, educators may want to confront this specific issue directly.

11 Teacher expectations

As we saw in Chapter 8, there has been an enormous amount of research on classroom interaction and teacher–pupil interactions in particular. In the next two chapters we concentrate on two specific topics, involving teacher–pupil interactions, that have been the subject of much debate and research. In this chapter we look at teachers' expectations and then, in the next chapter, sex differences in classroom interaction. We have chosen these two areas because they are educationally important, involve lively debate and controversy, are informed by psychological perspectives and are centrally connected to classroom interactions.

Teacher expectancies

Historically, one main aspect of research on teaching is that on teachers' 'expectations' and in particular the possible effects they have on pupils' educational progress. Research and debate in this area has been conducted for some time. As Wineburg (1987) noted, the 'self-fulfilling prophecy', as the expectancy effect is often called, has a long history, but it reached a mass audience and seeming support with the publication of the *Pygmalion in the Classroom* book (Rosenthal and Jacobson, 1968). We look more closely at this study below, but here we just summarize the basic argument: when teachers expect children not to do well academically, even when this is not based on accurate information on their abilities, there is a tendency for such children not to do well. As we shall see, this notion, and Rosenthal and Jacobson's findings, remain controversial (Wineburg, 1987; Rosenthal, 1987), but the topic continues to be a very important one for several reasons.

First, teacher expectations have been assigned a leading role in explanations of educational failure. It is commonplace to hear pupils' educational underachievement attributed to low teacher expectations. This has been a feature of political rhetoric in the UK from Conservative and more recently Labour administrations. Wineburg shows how in the US the self-fulfilling prophecy has been seen as a main mechanism through which social inequalities and poverty are perpetuated: 'Behind the failure of minority children lurked the bigotry of teachers' (1987, p. 32). Weinstein (1998) has pointed to the wide disparities in expectations (beyond those predicted by actual achievements and motivation toward school) and argues that these can be expected to increase with rising levels of poverty and diversity between students. In the UK, a main claim of the Swann Report (1985) was that low expectations were a main factor in the relatively poor educational progress of ethnic minority children.

Expectations also have a main role in recent conceptualizations of school effectiveness and improvement, except the emphasis in this work is on *high* expectations. As Rogers (1998) points out, many of the recent models of school effectiveness (e.g. Mortimore *et al.*, 1988; Stoll and Mortimore, 1995), as well as case studies of successful schools (National Commission on Education, 1996), have high expectations as a leading attribute of successful schools.

A second main reason for the importance of teacher expectations is that it is an example of an educational process to which social psychological theory has been systematically applied, and which, in contrast to much other research on teacher–pupil relations, has been insightful and to a degree successful in explaining links with student outcomes. Much research on teaching has been criticized for being atheoretical and heavily descriptive (Shulman, 1986). In contrast, research on teacher expectations and their effects has been much more informed by psychological concepts, research and theory on topics such as motivation, attributions, self concept, prejudice, stereotypes, labelling, impression formation and person perception (e.g. Dusek, 1985). Rogers (1982) used the expectancy process as the central notion in a book that sought to offer a wider social psychology of schooling.

An allied point to make is that research on teacher expectations serves to highlight some important issues and dilemmas in any attempt to understand relationships between teaching and student outcomes. Important questions are raised about the certainty with which claims for causality can be made, the extent to which mediating variables can be identified and the limitations and appropriateness of alternative research approaches.

Expectations can be considered developmentally. There is evidence that they are most influential in the early years of schooling – the Pygmalion study in fact only found effects in the first two grades of school. As we shall see below, the study by Rist (1970) has been influential in the implicit acceptance of a developmental conception of expectations – that is, the teacher's expectation of children at the point of entry to school can set in train powerful processes that profoundly shape children's subsequent school careers. The effect of expectations later in children's school careers may not be so profound. This is especially likely once children have left primary school, and have not one teacher for most of the time, but many different teachers for different subjects. Moreover, with age children are not so dependent on adults for their self-view – as we see elsewhere in this book, friendship and peer groups can be alternative frames of reference and influence.

In this chapter we look critically at the literature on teachers' expectations in four ways. First, what is the nature of expectations, and how can they be defined? Second, do expectations affect student academic outcomes? Third, what classroom processes mediate the effect of expectations on outcomes? Fourth, what factors influence expectations? The chapter will not seek to be comprehensive but will rather highlight what we feel are main issues, review some main research studies and refer to research (involving one of the authors) at the Institute of Education.

What are expectations?

Although the term 'teacher expectations' is widely used and its effects often cited, its exact meaning is often implicit and there is surprisingly little attention paid to its actual nature and definition. What exactly are 'expectations'? In an everyday sense they might refer to expectations about a student's current academic performance, expectations about the future, say by the end of the school year, or expectations about behaviour or effort in class. Prescriptions about the need for high expectations are less convincing if the actual reference is not clear. It is difficult for teachers to know how to raise expectations if the nature of expectations is vague.

Rogers (1982, 1998) has drawn a useful distinction between probabilistic and prescriptive expectations. Probabilistic expectations are what teachers feel is likely to happen, while prescriptive expectations refer to levels a student ought to attain. It is the second of these two types of expectations which are, albeit implicitly, central to notions of effectiveness. Expectations will be connected to assumptions teachers have about factors influencing students' success at school, their ability and motivation, as well as beliefs about their own ability to change students' progress. A similar distinction is between expectations as descriptive and expectations as the basis for action. If teachers have low expectations, and little belief they can change things, the prognosis for students is gloomy. However if they have low expectations (which may be realistic, perhaps on the basis of past performance), but a strong belief in the ability to change things, then the improvements in students' achievements may be high.

Cooper (1985) sought to clarify the different definitions of expectations that have been used. He categorized these into four groups: first, ability or achievement measures (which usually involve a rating of a student's current ability or achievement and, although used extensively in the expectation literature, are really not expectation measures at all); second, expected improvement (how much progress is expected over a given time period – the most obvious measure of what is usually understood as 'expectation'); third, manipulated expectations (as in the Rosenthal and Jacobson study, expectations are created by false information); and, fourth, natural discrepancy measures (how much a teacher over- or underestimates a student's performance, usually calculated on the basis of the degree of mismatch between teacher estimates of a child's ability or achievement and test scores or some other objective measure).

At an even more general level, there are two ways of looking at expectations. On the one hand there is the view that expectations are relatively broadbrush. Some researchers have seen teachers' conceptions of their pupils in terms of relatively general, static categories, sometimes applied to whole classes, so that they are perceived and dealt with in terms of stereotypes (Keddie, 1971). In a sociological study, Sharp and Green (1975) categorized teacher perceptions of their pupils into those where pupils were known to the teachers ('consociates') and those where pupils were not known so well ('contempory'). This general classification appeared to have implications for teacher–pupil relations. The suggestion is that if a child has a 'contemporary' relationship with the teacher, and initial impressions lead a teacher to think a child is difficult, then the expectancy effect can begin and is then difficult to change. This and other work is consistent with the view that negative impressions are more salient and long lasting than positive impressions.

The first view is then relatively comfortable with a conceptualization of teachers' expectations in terms of broad, relatively static categories. An alternative view, expressed by, for example, Hargreaves, Hestor and Mellor (1986) is that expectations are more complex, dynamic and open to change. Drawing on labelling theory, they document the development of expectations over time in terms of 'typifications'. This process, whereby individual pupils gradually become known to teachers, is seen to go through several stages, that is, an initial stage of 'speculation' (little confidence), to 'evaluation' (ideal matching, still tentative and relatively simplistic), 'elaboration', and, finally, 'stabilization' (by which time knowledge of pupils is more complex). Hargreaves *et al.* argue that the processes involved can be generalized to apply to social perception more generally:

> there is also in our theory an implicit general theory about how any person comes to type any other person. What teachers are doing with respect to children is not a phenomenon confined to schools; it is a phenomenon common to all people in all places at all times.
>
> (p. 182)

The notion of elaboration over time in expectations is also seen in Jussim's (1986) distinction between 'flexible' and 'rigid' expectations.

Expectations, if anything, are a psychological phenomenon. Schmuck and Schmuck (1983) have shown how integral expectations are to everyday life: 'Expectations are such a natural part of interpersonal relations that for our own security and cognitive clarity, we normally make subconscious predictions about how an interpersonal interchange will transpire' (p.70). As

Schmuck and Schmuck argue, expectations as interpersonal predictions are communicated in a multitude of direct and indirect ways. Research has not been concerned with expectations in terms of hopes or aspirations, but more in terms of working predictions that are used in relating to others in the classroom (Schmuck and Schmuck, 1983). As Jussim (1986) has shown, a good deal of research in social and cognitive psychology has addressed the nature and accuracy of intuitive prediction processes, of which expectations are presumably one. There have been a number of attempts to describe the nature of expectations using psychological theory (e.g. Braun, 1987; Jussim, 1986; Peterson and Barger, 1985).

Expectations can be seen as one aspect of person perception, and inaccuracies have been examined in terms of stereotyping and prejudice. More particularly, attribution theory has been used to explain teacher expectations; for example, Peterson and Barger (1985) draw on Weiner's theory to show how teachers use information about a student's past performance to make attributions for the causes of their present performance, for instance by forming attributions that maintain a 'consistent' picture of the causes of performance. So, in the case of a high ability student, an expected outcome such as success in school work is attributed to a stable factor like the student's ability, while an unexpected outcome, such as success on the same task by a low ability student, is likely to be attributed to an 'unstable' factor such as luck or the nature of the task. An early and more common sense version of this idea was advanced by Finn (1972, in Schmuck and Schmuck, 1983) who defined expectations as evaluations that one person forms of another which lead the evaluator to treat the person being evaluated as though the assessment were valid. The evaluator then tends to predict that the other will act in a manner consistent with the assessment.

Attribution theorists have also distinguished attributions of actors or participants in a situation from those of onlookers uninvolved in the social interaction. The basic notion here is that the participants – in this case teachers – have a vested interest, and so engage in self serving (sometimes called 'ego enhancing') attributions, the most widely cited being that they will accept responsibility for student success but blame the student if they fail. This is similar to Snyder's (in Rogers, 1998) notion that expectations have an ego-defence function, for example, a failing student may reflect badly on a teacher, so holding low expectations of the student will serve to reduce the possibility of perceived lack of success on the teacher's part. However, one of the problems with attribution theory has been the plausibility of quite opposing trends. Peterson and Barger (1985) review studies that show teachers blame themselves for student failure and credit students for their own successes. The adaptability, but also the imprecision, of attribution theory is reflected in yet another term from this literature – teachers' 'humility bias' has been used to describe the reluctance of teachers to attribute pupils' performance to their own influence. The literature is therefore complex – Jussim's (1986) review remains one of the most thorough accounts.

Rogers (1998) has helpfully integrated the connections between motivational theories and expectations in terms of three different models. The first (following Atkinson) sees motivation as a function of personality, the second (following Weiner – see above) sees motivation as a function of information processing, and the third (following Dweck (1986) and many others) sees motivation as a function of learning goals (especially ego or performance v. learning or mastery goals). As Rogers points out, these three models could be seen to represent the chronological development of motivational theory more generally as it has moved from stable personality characteristics through to less stable and changeable features like learning goals. It is the more recent theories, such as those concerning learning goals, which give most room to teacher influences, in that learning goals may be affected by what the teacher does in class in terms of feedback, face to face teaching, etc.

Do expectations causally affect pupils' achievements?

The concern about teachers' expectations has been that if they are not accurate and not open to corrective feedback – if they are based perhaps on stereotypes, children's social status, or personal appearance – they may then serve to affect adversely the learning opportunities and attainments of pupils. To what extent has research supported this concern? At the outset it is important to distinguish between two main types of effects. Although a number of different and sometimes confusing terms have been used, the essential distinction is between, first, judgements of pupils that are accurate and, second, those which are biased and causally and adversely affect pupils. To take an example: one way to look at the association between expectations and pupil achievement would be to collect expectations at the beginning of the school year, by, say, getting teachers to rank the children in terms of their academic potential, and to then correlate this with pupils' achievement, measured at the end of the school year. Research has shown this correlation to be high (Blatchford *et al.*, 1989). But this finding is not remarkable – it just means that teachers are generally good judges of how well children in their class will do. What is of concern is the possibility that the judgement of teachers actually *brings about* a change in children's performance rather than just reflecting it. Rogers (1982) used the notion of the tipster and the racehorse to help explain this distinction. The success of the tipster might be measured in terms of the accuracy of his/her predictions about runners in a race, but we would be seriously worried if it was felt the tipster actually caused the success or not of a horse.

Brophy (1983) uses the terms 'expectancy' and 'bias' to describe these two types of effects, and claims there is much evidence for an expectancy, but less for a bias, effect. Cooper (1985) uses the terms 'maintaining' and 'enhancing' to describe the same distinction. There is nothing remarkable about maintaining differential treatment of students, if this relates to real differences between children – indeed taking account of pupil differences is an essential part of teaching – but there is little evidence for teachers 'enhancing' these differences.

How can we discover whether expectations have an effect? What kind of research design would help settle the issue? A review of different approaches to this is informative about more general difficulties facing educational and psychological research when addressing issues of causality.

Experimental designs

The traditional way of establishing causality is by use of an experimental design – that is, a design in which the variable of interest, in this case teacher expectations, is manipulated or controlled in such a way that any change in outcomes can be reliably attributed to it. The study by Rosenthal and Jacobson is the most famous example of an experimental approach to the expectancy effect. The basic components of the research were the testing of children at the beginning of the school year, the feeding to teachers of information on the 20 per cent expected to 'bloom' (though in fact these children were chosen at random) and the examination of whether these high expectation children fared any better by the end of the school year. The logic of the experiment was that, because of random selection, any differences between high expectation and other children *must* be attributable to the inculcation of high (though false) expectations, and not because of any other factor such as the characteristics of the children.

There has been enormous controversy over the validity of the results, which cannot be described in full here (see Rogers, 1982). Criticisms have included worries about the validity and reliability of the tests used, and the fact that results were in the expected direction for only some of the age groups studied. There has also been a noticeable lack of replications of the study (Brophy, 1985; Rogers, 1982), though this might not necessarily mean the effect was not real – it could even be, for example, that the publicity generated by the original experiment served to alter the behaviour of participants in future experiments. In a more recent forum on the expectancy effect, Wineberg (1987) criticizes the experiment and the way the expectancy idea, supported by the study, has, in his view, quite unfairly taken on a degree of certainty in the US, even to the point of being used as evidence in court cases.

But over and above these arguments about the credibility of this one study, there is a general difficulty with the research approach used. Even if in the Pygmalion experiment the independent variable really did causally affect the outcome, and thus in this sense the expectancy effect was proven, the problem remains that expectations generated by the feeding of information (whether fictitious or not) are not the same as expectations and judgements of children built up naturally over the early days after entry to a class. There is, in other words, a question about the validity of findings from experimental research.

Naturalistic quantitative studies

This point reflects a central problem with evidence in educational research that we feel deserves more attention. If there are problems with the validity of findings of experimental research in education, how, without experiments, can one establish causality? The usual position adopted here is to assume that experiments are the 'gold standard' in any test of causality and that, because experiments are difficult to do in education, other designs are adopted reluctantly and as a kind of second best. But another way to view this is to say that experiments in education have a number of difficulties of interpretation that render them *less* able to answer questions about causality, and that more naturalistic designs are actually more valid. This argument is developed with regard to research on class size differences by Goldstein and Blatchford (1998) – see also Chapter 7.

One such alternative approach has been used in research on teacher expectations, and we review this here in order to examine its strengths and limitations. As we have said, simply finding a correlation between start of year teacher expectations and end of year pupil attainments is not necessarily evidence of an expectation effect, because it may simply reflect the accurate judgements made by teachers of a child's abilities and attainments. One way to overcome this problem, at least partially, is to conduct longitudinal studies, and then control for, or partial out, the child's start of year attainments when calculating the association between start of year expectations and end of year attainments. The logic of this is that the aspect of expectations, which overlaps with initial attainment, that is, which reflects accurate matching to attainment, is thereby controlled, and any remaining effect presumably reflects an independent expectation effect. This method can begin to approach the strength of experimental research without the attendant validity problems. It should allow us to distinguish between expectancy and bias effects.

The logic of this approach is shown in Figure 11.1. There may well be a correlation between T Exp1 and Ach2, and there is likely to be a correlation between Ach1 and Ach2, but some of the correlation between T Exp1 and Ach2 may be explained by that between Ach1 and Ach2 (teachers will hold expectations in line with pupils' initial achievements). If we control for the overlap between T Exp1 and Ach1 (the shaded area in Figure 11.1) and there is still an association between T Exp1 and Ach2 then this should be evidence for an independent effect of T Exp1 on Ach2.

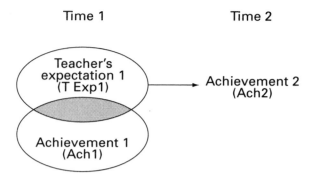

Figure 11.1 Relationships between teachers' expectations and children's achievement

Brophy (1985), in a comprehensive review, found that the size of effect found in studies of this sort was not great, but educationally significant. He suggests 5 to 10 per cent of the variance on average. Smith (in Brophy, 1985) found on the basis of meta analysis an effect size of 0.38 standard deviations for expectations on student achievement. This means that on a standardized reading test, teachers' expectations are likely to make a difference of about 5 points either way to a child's progress. This is about the same effect size as that commonly reported for sex and ethnic differences (Tizard et al., 1988).

As far as we know this non-experimental longitudinal approach has only been used systematically in one UK study. In the Institute of Education longitudinal study (Blatchford et al., 1989) over 300 children in 33 inner London infant schools were followed from entry over the first three years of school. Teacher expectations were assessed by asking teachers on average three weeks after the beginning of each school year to judge the academic potential of each child in terms of whether they were above average, average or below average. In the first year (the reception year) teachers were asked about academic work in general, and in the second and third year they were asked the questions separately for maths and reading. The pupils' attainments in maths and reading were assessed at the beginning and at the end of each school year. It was therefore possible to, first, find out whether expectations were associated with end of year attainments (see Table 11.1). Results showed they were. But the question of most interest, as we have just seen, is whether this association still holds when start of year attainments were controlled for. Table 11.2 shows that they were. The size of effects – 0.4 to 0.8 of a standard deviation – is substantial, especially when compared to effects noted in Brophy's review. In fact this association still held when a range of other factors were examined in relation to pupils' progress (see Tizard et al., 1988). Teacher expectations were one of two main school variables related to progress (the other was curriculum coverage, which we come to below).

Table 11.1 Associations between teacher expectations and attainment

	Range of Effects (SD units)[1]	P
RECEPTION (N = 238)		
Mathematics	0.9	<0.001
Reading and Writing[2]	1.5	<0.01
MIDDLE (N = 420)[3]		
Mathematics	1.4	<0.001
Reading	1.5	<0.001
TOP (N = 353)[3]		
Mathematics	1.7	<0.001
Reading	1.9	<0.001

Source: Blatchford *et al.*, 1989
Notes: 1. i.e., from above average to below average on the teacher expectation scale.
2. See note 2 to Table 11.2.
3. Numbers of children had increased by middle infants because the sample now included all children who had entered in September, 1982, and not just those from the nursery class. By top infants some children were lost, because, for example, they had moved or gone into the junior school.

Table 11.2 Associations between teacher expectations and progress

	Range of Effects (SD units)[1]	P
RECEPTION (N = 238)		
Mathematics	0.4	<0.01
Reading and Writing[2]	0.6	<0.001
MIDDLE (N = 407)[3]		
Mathematics	0.7	<0.001
Reading	0.4	<0.01
TOP (N = 326)[3]		
Mathematics	0.5	<0.001
Reading	0.8	<0.001

Source: Blatchford *et al.*, 1989
Notes: 1. i.e., from above average to below average on the teacher expectation scale.
2. Reading and writing were combined for the reception year because of their conceptual and actual association. Writing was not assessed at the end of middle infants so progress measures for both middle and top infants were restricted to reading.
3. See note 3 to Table 11.1. Numbers of children are slightly lower than in Table 11.1 because analyses on progress were only possible on those children for whom there were test data at both the beginning and end of each school year.

Have we therefore shown that teacher expectations causally affect attainment? Probably. But the problem, as is often said, is that correlation does not prove causality. Longitudinal research and multiple regression, if used properly, can go a long way in controlling for possibly connected variables but can still not entirely rule out the possibility that another variable may be causing the association. For example, it may be that teachers, even after the short time they have children before giving the expectation rating, draw on a wider range of information about a child than that provided by an initial assessment of their attainments. They may, for instance, have formed an impression of the child's *rate* of learning and it may be this which relates to expectations at time one and which overlaps with expectation judgements. In this sense the association between teacher expectations and later attainment may still reflect accurate judgements of the child by the teacher. The association, in other words, could still be child-driven rather than teacher-driven.

Case studies

A very different approach to research has provided perhaps the most compelling but controversial evidence for the negative effects of an expectation effect. Once again it is important to evaluate critically the claims made, particularly with regard to the validity of the evidence and interpretation of results.

Perhaps the most widely cited study in this tradition is that by Ray Rist (1970). This is an account of how one kindergarten teacher in an all black school grouped her children after only eight days, ostensibly on academic criteria, but, according to Rist, actually on the basis of physical appearance, cleanliness and the newness of clothes, whether they spoke Standard American, their parents' income, education and the size of the family – all of which were known to the teacher beforehand. Rist argues that the teacher had an ideal type of pupil in mind – middle class and well educated – and it was this rather than the pupils' ability that was the basis for her initial grouping. The consequence of this early grouping was profound. The teacher concentrated on the first table and more often penalized and ignored the children at the second and third tables. The children at the first table identified with the teacher and ridiculed the other children. The second and third tables were forced to discuss amongst themselves what they should be doing (secondary learning), and came to insult each other. In a depressing finding, Rist argues that the children at the third table could not even see the blackboard properly, as if they were not disadvantaged enough! Rist's argument has a convincing logic to it:

1. teacher has an ideal type – that is, characteristics necessary for success – and this is related to social class;
2. students on entry are subjectively evaluated in terms of the presence of these characteristics and put into groups expected to succeed (fast learners) or fail (slow learners);
3. the groups are differentially treated by the teacher – the fast learners receiving most teacher time. Slow learners are taught infrequently, receive more control and receive little support from the teacher;

4. interactional patterns become rigid and caste-like with the completion of academic material widening over the year;
5. the process continues into later years but is now no longer based on sub-jective judgements but on objective performance information (which the judgements originally served to cause).

This is a coherent argument and a vivid description of how the self-fulfilling prophecy might work. However, there is in this case an inverse relationship between the clarity of the conclusions and the strength of the data on which the conclusions are based. There are a number of difficulties of interpretation. It could be for example that the teacher did base her judgements on academic criteria and that Rist was actually wrong. In this case it may be that later differences were more the result of teacher responses to initial child differences. Perhaps most importantly, even if Rist's description is valid, it relates only to one teacher. It may be that Rist chanced upon a truly awful teacher – a teacher who behaved in a profes-sionally and ethically unacceptable way. As Brophy (1985) has argued, what may underlie an average teacher expectation effect is the possibility that it may be found in only a minority of teachers, and not at all in the majority. In other words, most teachers base their teaching and curriculum on appropriate and accurate judgements about the children in their care, but some are biased in their expectations and allow this to affect their class-room interactions and ultimately the pupils' educational achievements.

What processes mediate the connection between expectations and achievement?

Even if an expectation effect on pupils' educational attainments is found this still leaves open questions about just how it works. There must be some mechanism or process by which the expectation works, that is, which medi-ates the expectation effect. Unfortunately the Rosenthal and Jacobson study had little to offer in terms of explaining why there was an expectation effect.

There are likely to be many varied and subtle ways that expectations are conveyed and received by students. Expectations may be reflected in the opportunities afforded a student in class, in terms of the tone and nature of interactions and feedback, but also the work they are set, written comments on work, facial and non-verbal expressions, allocation to groups and classes, and registration for examinations. Expectations may be detected by pupils in terms of everyday encounters but also through one critical inter-change or behaviour. One of the authors has few memories of his interac-tions with teachers in his secondary school days but does remember well a brief encounter with an older technical drawing teacher who, in a kindly and interested voice (not common in that school!), showed his expectation for a future career not previously considered by the pupil. Just a few sentences opened up a different possible future, and perhaps laid the seed of a wish to succeed.

There have been many models that attempt to describe the processes that might operate (Braun, 1987; Cooper, 1979, 1985; Darley and Fazio, 1980; Jussim, 1986). Harris (in Dusek 1985) suggested four social psychological mechanisms by which expectations are communicated: climate (e.g. teachers' warmth toward high expectation children); input (teaching of increasingly difficult material to children of whom they have high expectations); verbal output (teacher's persistence in and frequency of academic interactions; greater opportunities for high expectation children to respond); and feedback (increasingly differentiated and positive information to children of whom they have high expectations). Weinstein (1998) used children's reports, rather than observers', and drew up a model of expectancy communication in the classroom, which elaborates Rosenthal's four-factor model. Elements are:

1. ways in which students are grouped for instruction (if grouped by ability, ability comparisons are heightened),
2. the tasks through which the curriculum is enacted (a differential curriculum lessens opportunities for low expectation children),
3. the motivational strategies that teachers use to engage learning (competitive reward systems heighten ability comparisons, decrease intrinsic motivation),
4. the role that students are asked to play in directing their own learning (differential opportunities for responsibility – limited pupil agency diminishes pupil motivation),
5. evaluation (teacher ability beliefs affect provision of performance opportunities for evaluation),
6. differential allocation of warmth, trust, humour and concern,
7. different parent–class relations for high and lows.

There is not space to fully review all the possible mediating processes. Here we discuss three main possibilities – teacher–pupil interactions, pupil self-perceptions, and curriculum coverage.

Teacher–pupil interaction

Common sense might suggest that a teacher's expectations would be mediated, or realized, through the nature of the interactions a teacher has with pupils. This would be consistent with what Rogers has called 'interactional behavioural effects'. This was seen in Rist's descriptions of the teacher concentrating her teaching on the high expectancy group, reflected in more and qualitatively different interactions. But we need to look at other systematic studies, involving more classrooms, to examine the connection between expectations and interactions. Perhaps the most widely cited is the study by Brophy and Good (1986b). Structured observations were conducted during the Spring term in four first grade classes. There were three boys and three girls classified on the basis of teacher rankings as 'highs' and three boys and three girls classified as 'lows'. Brophy and Good were surprised to find that highs received more praise by teachers and more work-related contacts. There was none of the expected teacher 'compensation' for lows, who might have been expected to receive more attention and feedback in order to help them catch up.

Brophy and Good recognized that these differences between expectation groups might be due to differences between the children themselves, in the sense that teachers were merely responding to differences between children. The effect may therefore be child-driven. To deal with this they calculated further measures that took account of absolute differences in frequencies of behaviour, and to thus allow comparisons of teachers' behaviour to groups in equivalent situations. So these measures were not the number of correct child answers (which would represent child differences) or the amount of teacher praise, but, for example, the percentage of correct answers followed by praise. Using this method they found that highs received a higher percentage of correct answers followed by praise, more repetition/rephrasing following wrong answers, more giving of clues following reading problems, and lows received more criticisms following wrong answers, and more answers not followed by any feedback from teachers. In short, teachers appeared to favour highs by 'demanding and reinforcing quality performance'.

The calculation of these ratio variables is a useful addition to the more common use of basic frequencies of occurrence of individual categories. The clarity of the study, and perhaps the way results were consistent with a negative expectation effect, may help to explain its frequent citation. But once again, what at first appear to be convincing results, on closer inspection and testing prove less so. One problem is the small number of classes and teachers. The timing of the collection of 'expectation' ratings makes claims that this is a study of expectations problematic. Had teachers' interactions already changed by the Spring? Perhaps at the beginning of the year there were no differences? Brophy and Good, to their credit, sought to replicate their findings in a follow-up study of nine first grade classes, and with expectation ratings given at the beginning of the school year. This time they found that, overall, teachers were not treating lows differently, though three of the nine teachers did, suggesting again that only *some* teachers show a bias affect.

The link between teacher expectations and classroom interactions is by no means clear-cut (Hall and Merkel, 1985). Weinstein (1976), in a study of teacher–pupil interaction in three first grade classes, did not find consistent differences between high, medium and low expectancy groups. In the

Institute of Education study (Blatchford *et al.*, 1989) the connection between teachers' expectations and teacher–pupil interactions and child behaviours in class was examined. In line with Brophy and Good and other studies, it was hypothesized that children rated above average would have higher mean frequencies of teacher praise, teacher instruction, teacher feedback on work and initiations to the teacher, and lower mean frequencies of criticism from teachers and 'task avoidance' behaviour. Whilst mean frequencies for the expectation groups were sometimes in the expected direction for some of the three years, there were no strong or consistent relationships over the three years.

One possible way that expectations may be linked to interactions in classrooms is that teachers are more concerned about the control of low expectation pupils, so interactions with them are not so much concerned with performance as with controlling behaviour (Cooper, 1985, 1979, in Schmuck and Schmuck, 1983). Accordingly, they receive less praise for performance, they decrease performance initiations, and this in turn increases the teacher's attempted control. Eccles and Wigfield (1985) support this idea and suggest this may make low expectancy students less likely to seek out the teacher. The explanation here is therefore in terms of ways the teacher controls opportunities for interaction (which Eccles and Wigfield prefer to an attribution explanation). Weinstein (1998) reminds us that the Harris and Rosenthal (in Dusek, 1985) meta analysis found less support for teacher feedback than the other three factors (see above for these), and points out that it is then ironic that much current intervention work has focused on teacher feedback, for example, by attempting to equalize praise and criticism to highs and lows.

Pupil self-perceptions

A second possible mediating process, involved in the expectancy process, is through pupil self-perceptions. Teachers may differ in their behaviour toward expectation groups and this may affect the educational experience of pupils, but, presumably, pupils have also to take on in some way a teacher's expectation for it to have an effect. There has been an enormous body of work on pupils' self-perceptions in educational settings which are relevant to the expectation effect, but which can only be touched on here. Relevant areas of interest include motivation, self concept and ability perceptions, attributions for success and failure, self efficacy (see Anderman and Maehr, 1994; Eccles and Wigfield, 1985; Jussim, 1986; Pintrich and Schunk, 1996; Rogers, 1982; Weinstein, 1985). A difficulty with this literature is the plethora of convincing possibilities, often overlapping and difficult to review or synthesize effectively. Here we look at just a few of the more closely examined processes.

Jussim (1986) points out that one of the most important links between expectations and pupil perceptions concerns effort–outcome covariation. If it is the case that high expectation pupils differ in terms of teacher feedback – an example would be getting more praise for strong efforts – then highs, but not lows, will come to feel their efforts will lead to success. Once again attribution analysis has been used. In general terms, an attribution account would see pupil's explanations of their own success or failure at school tasks affecting their future efforts. One attribution version of processes connected to success and failure at school work runs something like this: if pupils do not do well or fail and they see this as attributable to internal and uncontrollable factors such as their ability, this will undermine their confidence and they may be more likely to give up. If, on the other hand, failure is seen as surmountable and due to something changeable like lack of effort or knowledge then the student will be less likely to give up and will believe that increased effort will improve future results (see e.g. Jussim, 1986).

The effect teachers have on these processes is more speculative but, conceptually, if teachers' low expectations are expressed through explanations of pupils' poor performance in terms of low ability, then pupils' own explanations will be reinforced. On the other hand, if teachers do not have a fixed view of the child, and see performance as changeable and uncontrollable, then the pupil may come to see their own attainments as changeable. Much hinges on the degree to which teachers' interpretations of a child's performance and behaviour are fixed. More specifically, if teachers provide non-contingent and less favourable feedback to low expectation children they may lead such children to believe performance is not contingent on effort. Consequently such children will try less hard, and ultimately their attainments will suffer. A child's belief that their own actions do not affect outcomes is central to the attribution approach to 'learned helplessness'. In a well-known extension of this account, Dweck (e.g. Dweck *et al.*, 1978) (in Eccles and Wigfield, 1985) suggests that differences in teacher feedback patterns might predispose boys and girls to develop different attribution patterns for themselves.

Logical though this account may appear, Eccles and Wigfield (1985) question the findings related to sex differences. In contrast to Dweck (see next chapter) they found that teachers gave more work-related criticism to boys, there were no differences in criticism about non-intellectual aspects of their work, and there were no sex differences in pupil attributions – almost all attributions were to lack of effort (a finding replicated by Blatchford, 1996). Furthermore, they argue that children's everyday experiences of teacher affective feedback and teacher attributions are *not* powerful determinants of their classroom motivation. This is partly because these are not common in the course of classroom life. Eccles and Wigfield argue that

teachers' influences on student motivation are mediated by teachers' confidence to teach *all* students (teachers' sense of personal efficacy) and by teachers' knowledge of effective teaching practices for children of different ability levels. Low teacher expectancies have a debilitating effect on children's motivation when the teacher believes that low expectancy children can't improve their performance and when the teacher doesn't know effective teaching practices for low skill-level children – that is, when teachers believe that they can not succeed at teaching low skill-level children.

(p. 188)

Pupils' perceptions of their own ability may also be affected by expectations. There is an enormous body of research which has examined the links between ability perceptions and achievement in school (e.g. Eccles and Wigfield, 1985; Pintrich and Schunk, 1996). Some research indicates that in classrooms where children perceive high differential treatment, children's own academic expectations more closely matched the teachers' expectations than was the case in classrooms with more equal treatment of students. Other studies using observer (rather than student) information supports this link between highly differentiated classrooms and greater stratification of pupil ability perceptions. By fifth grade (the equivalent, in Britain, of Year 5), children in classes where teachers held low expectations reported more negative-ability perceptions, whether in high or low differentiated classrooms (c.f. Weinstein, 1998). Weinstein makes the point that children's expectations about their ability come from differential access to learning (see below) but also their awareness of differential treatment by teachers.

Curriculum coverage

In Chapter 8 we looked at research that showed that, as a proportion of a pupils' time in school, interactions between teachers and pupils occurred relatively infrequently and often when the child was a part of a larger group or the whole class. Most time was spent on individual work. It is possible that recent curriculum and other reforms, e.g. the literacy hour, may have increased the amount of interaction (this is suggested by the follow-up to the ORACLE study – Galton, 1998), but individual children will still rarely be the focus of a teacher's attention. If it is the case that expectation effects are not obviously mediated through interactions between teachers and pupils, this raises the possibility that expectations may be reflected in the level and difficulty of the work they are set. In the UK there can be considerable variation between pupils in their curriculum experiences (Tizard et al., 1988).

In an early experimental study (Beez, 1968), 60 graduate students were taught the meaning of a series of pictorial signs. Each of these 'teachers' then worked with one 5–6 year old. The teachers were provided with a faked psychological report on the child and the extent to which they were expected to benefit from education (the children were involved in the US Head Start programme). The children were categorized as either of normal intelligence or of low average intelligence and school adjustment was expected to be difficult, though in reality the reports were allocated at random. It was found that the teachers of 'higher ability' children attempted to teach nearly twice as many signs as teachers of 'low ability' pupils. Also, 'higher ability' children learned more signs – 77 per cent of them learned 5 or more signs, compared to only 13 per cent of 'low ability' pupils. They also received higher ratings in terms of, for example, intelligence. The study seems to show that the curriculum provided to pupils, and in turn their attainments, are affected by the expectations held by teachers. Once again, though, there is a problem with the validity of an experimental study. These were not real teachers, the 'curriculum' was artificial, and there is no guarantee that results would be replicated in the real world of the classroom and in the way teachers actually form expectations and judgements of children.

In the Institute of Education longitudinal study (Blatchford *et al.*, 1989) it was possible to examine, using a naturalistic longitudinal design, the possibility that teachers' expectations were mediated through curriculum experiences. In order to provide a measure of the range and depth of children's curriculum experiences, teachers completed checklists of activities in mathematics and written language to which children had been introduced. We have already seen that in this study expectations were related to attainment and to progress. It was also found that teachers' expectations were related to curriculum coverage in the second and third years (the analysis could not be done for the first year). Teachers' expectations and curriculum coverage were still related to each other, even after controlling for initial attainment, indicating that the association was more than just accurate matching of curriculum to entry skills. Further regression analyses also showed that when teacher expectations, curriculum coverage and entry skills were regressed on end of year school attainments, teacher expectations and curriculum coverage were independently related to end of year attainments. This indicates that, although there was overlap between expectations and curriculum coverage, this did not fully account for the effect of expectations on progress.

If it is possible that we overrate the influence of interaction factors on pupils' progress and, as a mediator of expectation effects, it may be that we underestimate the way in which the curriculum presented to children is informed by teachers' expectations. The curriculum may affect pupils' academic progress by setting limits on children's academic experiences. This is not to suggest that curriculum experiences will need to be the same for every child, but these results indicate that differences will need to be well founded. As Braun (1987) has said, the teacher expectation cycle is 'maintained more than anything by the intellectual and affective constraints characteristic of the curriculum of the failing child . . . Curricular constraints frequently restrict the failing child to sterile, irrelevant, artificially contrived learning experiences' (p. 604).

What factors affect expectations?

Finally, in order to complete this account of teacher expectations, we turn to factors that might influence expectations – what Braun (1987) calls 'input factors'. One of the main concerns about teachers' expectations is that they may be based on a feature such as the child's ethnic group or gender, they may be inaccurate and stereotypical with respect to pupils' academic potential, and this may in turn have a deleterious effect on the child's educational progress. A meta-analysis of North American research suggests that teacher expectations are to some extent influenced by social class and race, but less often by sex (Dusek and Joseph, 1985).

It was possible in the Institute of Education longitudinal study to test the extent to which expectations were affected by gender and ethnic origin (see Tizard *et al.*, 1988). In order to research these connections it is important to control for children's abilities and school achievements. Three sources of knowledge were collected: first, information on child characteristics including gender and ethnic origin; second, children's academic achievement; and, third, teachers' expectations. As part of the study, a novel method was used to assess the match or mismatch between expectation and children's attainment. Each child was given an expectation rating by the teacher in terms of above average, average and below average (as described above). Children were then ranked from high to low on the basis of their test scores and put into three groups – above average, average, and below average – the same size as the three expectation groups. A mismatch or misclassification was said to have occurred when the teacher expectation rating was not the same as the test rating. Results were calculated separately for maths and reading and for the four groups in the study – black boys and girls and white boys and girls.

For reading there was no evidence of mismatch or misclassification in relation to gender or ethnic group but there was in the case of maths. As can be seen in Table 11.3, teachers' expectations for black boys during Year 2 (top infants) were high relative to their test scores, that is, more were put in the top group by their teachers, and fewer in the bottom group, than would have been expected from their test results. On the other hand, expectations for white girls were low, in the sense that more were put into the average group when on the basis of their test results we would have expected them to be in the top group. The black boys were therefore over estimated and the white girls underestimated.

These are complex results that require careful and cautious interpretation. Overall the white girls in comparison to the other three ethnic/gender groups

Table 11.3 Mismatch between teacher expectations and test results for maths, by ethnic group and sex (top infants)

Teacher Expectations	White Boys (n=95)		White Girls (n=82)		Black Boys (n=50)		Black Girls (n=49)	
	Expect. %	Test %	Expect. %	Test %	Expect. %	Test %	Expect. %	Test %
Above Average	38	39	24	38	46	26	39	33
Average	39	42	56	39	30	44	43	51
Below Average	23	19	20	23	23	30	18	16

appeared to be more 'invisible' to teachers (Tizard *et al.*, 1988). As a group, they received less disapproval and criticism from the teachers than did the other children, but also less praise. They were less often said to have behaviour problems. They were less likely to say they found school interesting (see Tizard *et al.*, 1988). All this may indicate that the teacher's perception of white (mostly working class) girls is less well developed than that of other groups and, accordingly, their expectations, at least in maths, are less accurate.

The results concerning white girls are worrying when set alongside other results from the same study concerning the girls' self-assessments of academic attainment. The white girls were the least likely of the four groups at 11 years to consider themselves better than others at reading, and at 7 and 11 years were more likely to underestimate themselves in both reading and mathematics. At 16 years the white girls still underestimated themselves in English (Blatchford, 1997). Other self report data at 11 years also showed that white girls were more likely to say they did not like maths because it was not interesting to them, and were more likely to say they were not pleased with their work because of their ability (Blatchford, 1997). Whilst the causal connections involved are difficult to disentangle, it is interesting that long term underestimation by this group of children appears to be preceded in the early school years by lower teacher expectations. It might also be worth noting that the long-term attainments of these girls at 16 years were poor in terms of GCSEs. There has been much comment on the tendency of girls to have less confidence in schoolwork than boys (Meece and Courtney, 1992). Here this trend seems true of just the white girls, not the black girls. These results on London children indicate that gender and ethnic origin need to be considered together.

Teachers' expectations may be based on other factors than ethnic group and sex. There is some evidence that teachers tend to have lower expectations of children with non-standard English and lower verbal skills (Brophy and Good, 1986b; Rist, 1970). It has also been found that expectations can be affected by children's social class background (e.g. Baron *et al.*, 1985; Dusek and Joseph, 1985). There is some indication from early research that placement of children into ability groups in school is affected by socioeconomic status (Barker Lunn, 1970). Brophy (1983) and Cooper (1979) conclude that teachers are more likely to have lower expectations of children with problem behaviour, particularly when it threatens control of the class. There are also a number of suggestions that teachers tend to have higher expectations of children who are more physically attractive. Studies have found that attractive children are seen as possessing a higher IQ, greater educational potential and more interested parents than less attractive children (Clifford and Worstyer, 1973, in Braun, 1987). Crano and Mellon (1978) found that teachers had higher expectations of children who they thought were a pleasure to have in the class.

Once again it is important to assess the influence of these 'input' characteristics on teacher expectations, while controlling for student achievement. In the longitudinal study, just described, the mismatch between teacher expectations and tested performance was examined in relation to four factors:

1. children's verbal skills, as measured by the Wechsler Pre-school and Primary Scale of Intelligence (WPPSI) Vocabulary sub-test scores, assessed at the point of school entry;
2. parental income (a measure of home circumstances);
3. whether children were seen by teachers as having a behaviour problem that interfered with their learning;
4. whether children were seen as a pleasure to teach.

Of these four, two were found to be connected: first, children who had higher verbal skills were misclassified upwards (that is, expectations were higher than would be expected from test scores) and, second, children who had worse verbal skills and were not seen as a pleasure to teach were misclassified downwards (that is, expectations were too low relative to tested attainment). These results suggest that the personal relationships between teacher and child, as well as attributes of the child, can affect judgements about a child's academic potential and that this can be over and above the child's actual attainment.

Conclusions

So how strong is the evidence of a teacher expectancy effect? Evidence from experimental, naturalistic quantitative studies, and case studies indicates that there is an average expectation effect over and above what might have been expected when considering the judgements based on pupils' existing achievements. However, research indicates that the effect is likely to be found in some teachers more than others (Brophy, 1985).

This chapter has been concerned with ways in which expectations are formed and what effects they have. As Rogers (1998) has pointed out, the literature has been less clear on *why* these things happen. Some insights come from psychological theory, as we saw above, for example, with regard to explanations such as ego defence (teachers have low expectations of pupils in order to protect themselves from the possibility of being seen as failing). But this raises important questions about the broader context of expectations in schools. If we are to take an active as well as an analytical view of expectations we need to be concerned with how expectations work in the context of schools today and how psychological theories and explanations can be used to help students. Weinstein (1998) widens this point. She argues that 'the important task lies in the identification of the conditions under which expectancy effects are magnified or diminished – for example, the qualities of the teachers, schools and students that predict susceptibility to such prophecy effects'(p. 84). There are a number of background factors here, for example, concerning the culture and ethos of schools, and the effect on individual teachers' expectations, as well as the belief systems of teachers and the social background of pupils. Given the concern with school success, and the renewed recognition of the insights psychology can provide about learning and the learner, there is a clear need for a wider and more applied analysis of expectations.

12 Sex differences in classroom interaction

In this chapter we are interested in sex differences in classroom interactions between children and their teachers, and connections with academic performance. Consistent with the theme of this part of the book, we will not discuss sex differences in peer interactions in this chapter. We examine these in the first half of the book.

One of the most important and topical debates at present in education concerns the relatively recent advance of girls over boys in academic performance, at least in the UK. From the point of view of classroom interaction, there is something of a central puzzle, that serves as a theme running through this chapter. We shall see below that boys get more attention from teachers and engage in more interactions with them, in comparison to girls, and yet seem overall to be doing less well academically. The debate about sex differences in classroom interaction has shifted relatively recently from a concern with the possible disadvantages suffered by female students to a concern with, and something of a mystery about, the failing male student.

Better understanding of influences on the relative performance of boys and girls is a main challenge for educational research, with important theoretical and practical implications. There is a need to examine closely the research literature and the sometimes competing explanations for differences. In line with the overall concern of this book with interactions in school, this chapter will focus on the role of teaching and classroom interactions, but we also look at ways in which other within-child factors such as self perceptions, self concept and motivational processes help inform gender differences in interaction and achievement.

Exploration of the links between sex differences, classroom interaction and academic achievement is also important because it is one way of assessing the extent to which interactions in educational settings impact on learning and educational progress. It can therefore contribute in a broader way to understanding the effects of teaching. We will be asking whether the interactions between teachers and boys and girls are different and, if they are, what implications these differences have for the academic progress of boys and girls. The strategy will be to review research evidence selectively by concentrating on studies that have affected debate and understanding.

So in this chapter we are concerned with two main questions:

1. Are there differences between girls and boys in their academic interactions with teachers?
2. What is the role of such interactions in the educational achievement and progress of boys and girls?

The educational attainments of girls and boys

In order to provide a background to the discussion of classroom interactions we need, first, to review information on the relative performance of boys and girls during the school years. International comparisons of school achievement data are notoriously difficult to interpret (Powney, 1996). Given that much of the literature on classroom interaction that we will be reviewing stems from the UK, here we concentrate on school achievements in England and Wales. In recent years there has been set in place a National Curriculum and accompanying assessment arrangements, which means that students are now faced with assessments at the end of each of the first three 'Key Stages', that is, at 7, 11 and 14 years, and at the end of Key Stage 4, at 16 years, they will take GCSE exams. All of these assessments are nationally implemented and results broken down by gender, and so we have a relatively clear idea about the attainments of boys and girls. Statistics related to these assessments are published on an annual basis by the Department for Education and Employment (DFEE). Assessments at the end of the first three Key Stages are in the areas of reading and English, mathematics and science and are presented in terms of 'levels'. The levels are organized in terms of a 10 point scale, with pupils expected to reach certain levels at the end of each Key Stage (Levels 2, 4 and 6 at the end of Key Stages 1, 2 and 3 respectively). Results for 1995 have been helpfully summarized by Arnot *et al.* (1998) and are shown in Tables 12.1 and 12.2.

It can be seen that in reading and English girls are much more likely to reach the higher levels and much less likely to only reach the lower levels at each Key Stage. As an example, at Key Stage 1, 39 per cent of the girls reached Level 3 – higher than would have been expected at this age – compared to 28 per cent of boys, while only 16 per cent of girls reached Level 1 – lower than would be expected, in comparison to 24 per cent of boys. Test results for maths and science are broadly similar for boys and girls for all three ages.

Results for examinations at the end of compulsory schooling – at 16 years – are given in Figure 12.1, again helpfully summarized by Arnot *et al.* (1998). Differences between boys and girls are presented in terms of the number of boys per 100 girls securing five or more A*–C grades. It can be seen that up to about 1985, achievements of boys and girls were much the same, but that from this point through to the early 1990s a gap opened up

Table 12.1 Performance in English, mathematics and·science National Assessments (1995) at Key Stages 1, 2 and 3: reading and English

Level	KS1 Boys (%)	Reading Girls (%)	KS2 Boys (%)	English Girls (%)	KS3 Boys (%)	English Girls (%)
10					0	0
9					0	0
8					0	1
7					2	4
6			0	0	12	21
5			5	10	31	38
4	0	0	37	46	32	24
3	28	39	43	35	13	6
2	45	44	9	4	3	1
1	24	16	2	1	1	0
Other	3	1	4	4	6	5

Table 12.2 Performance in English, mathematics and science National Assessments (1995) at Key Stages 1, 2 and 3: mathematics

Level	KS1 Boys (%)	KS1 Girls (%)	KS2 Boys (%)	KS2 Girls (%)	KS3 Boys (%)	KS3 Girls (%)
10					0	0
9					0	0
8					2	1
7					9	9
6			0	0	23	23
5			13	12	23	25
4	0	0	31	33	21	21
3	21	18	36	37	12	11
2	56	63	7	6	2	2
1	19	17	2	1	0	0
Other	4	2	10	9	8	8

in favour of girls – a gap that has continued through to the time of writing. In 1995/6 very nearly half of girls achieved five or more grades A*–C, while for boys the figure was 40 per cent. It is not always easy to compare boys and girls in individual school subjects, because of differences in numbers entering examinations, for example, but in the core subjects, where numbers of entries are much the same, girls are far ahead of boys in English (in 1995/6, in English Language, 64.3 per cent of girls but only 47 per cent of boys got grade A*–C) and had similar scores overall in maths and science.

This review indicates a shift over time in the achievements of boys and girls. The picture is now one where girls do very much better in areas in which they have traditionally done better than boys; in areas where they have traditionally done less well (at least up to GCSE) they are now roughly comparable. So overall, as Croll and Moses (1990) conclude, it is very difficult to argue that girls overall are academically disadvantaged at school.

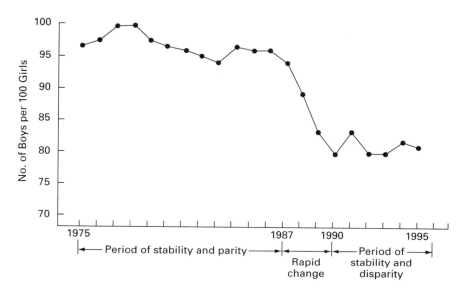

Figure 12.1 Changing levels of performance at GCE/CSE or GCSE (1975–1995): number of boys per 100 girls securing 5+ A*–C grades

Gender differences in classroom interaction

In this section we look at the evidence for gender differences in classroom interaction. Are girls and boys treated differently? Do they have different educational experiences? If so, what implications do these have for later development and educational achievements?

Much of the early interest in gender differences in teacher–pupil interactions was generated by a concern with the supposed underachievement of girls and an attempt to show ways in which they are disadvantaged at school through the quality and quantity of interactions with their teachers. A number of writers have argued that the education system is in various ways implicated in the disadvantages females suffer later in life. As Croll and Moses (1990) show, the view has been that schools not only reflect the different sex roles in society but also emphasize traditional female roles and discriminate further against girls. Dale Spender has often been quoted in this regard. She argued that boys receive much more attention from teachers than girls and that gender imbalances are routine and so deeply ingrained that they occur even when teachers try to equalize attention (see Croll and Moses, 1990). However compelling this argument, we need to question whether it is supported by convincing evidence.

Here we describe one study in this tradition of research and argument. Michelle Stanworth (1981) was interested in the extent to which gender was a salient factor in teachers' perceptions of their pupils. Her study was based on interviews with teachers about their attitudes to particular pupils – which would appear to be a more reliable method than asking about attitudes to boys and girls as a whole. One technique she used was to present to teachers of sixth form pupils (aged 16–18 years) a number of sets of cards bearing the names of two boys and one girl or two girls and one boy and then to ask teachers to chose children who were alike in some educationally important way. The number of times teachers paired pupils of the same sex was then calculated. It was found that male teachers were more likely to select same sex pairs, and this is explained in terms of male teachers being much more likely to view the sexes as discrete groups. Stanworth also found that teachers were more attached to, and concerned for, boys and were more likely to reject girls. This applied to teachers of both sexes, but was more pronounced for male teachers.

One of the teacher interview transcripts used to illustrate this argument is as follows:

> *Question*: What were your first impressions of Emma?
> *(Male) teacher*: Nothing really. I can only remember first impressions of a few who stood out right away: Adrian, of course; and Phillip; and David Levick; and Marion, too, because among the girls she was the earliest to say something in class. In fact, it was quite some time before I could tell some of the girls apart.
> *Question*: Who was that?
> *(Male) teacher*: Well, Angie, and her friends Leonore and Helen. They seemed rather silent at first, and they were friends, I think, and there was no way – that's how it seemed at the time – of telling one from the other. In fact, they are very different in appearance, I can see that now. One's fair and one's dark, for a start. But in the beginning they were just three quiet girls.
>
> (Stanworth, 1981, p. 27)

Stanworth argues that girls are more invisible than boys, particularly if they are quiet. She also documents differences in teachers' views about the future careers of boys and girls. Teachers were not so confident that girls would complete their 'A' levels, and had stereotypical job expectations for girls, for example, that they would become a nurse, secretary or teacher. These careers did not match the girls' own aspirations. Marriage was often mentioned in the case of girls but never boys. Stanworth, like others, argued that it is only when a girl contradicts this pattern of behaviour that she is looked at differently by teachers, and noticed.

A similar picture emerges in other feminist research (Walkerdine, 1990). This early work is interesting but there is uncertainty about the validity of results. Moreover, in the case of the Stanworth paper it is rather dated, and the world of work and education, and teacher attitudes, have changed. It is also unclear whether teachers' perceptions and attitudes are reflected in actual classroom interactions.

French and French (1984) used a more systematic methodology based on direct observation of primary-aged children. They obtained verbatim descriptions of a fourth year junior class (10–11 years) lesson. There were 16 boys and 13 girls and a male teacher. Observations were of a class discussion on 'What I do on Mondays and what I would like to do on Mondays'. French and French found that boys had more turns than girls (50 v. 16), but report that the gender difference was due to a small group of four boys who tended to dominate classroom interactions with the teacher. French and French feel this dominance is not due to a bias on the teacher's part so much as due to interactional methods used by these pupils to get attention, and to the newsworthiness of their comments. These behaviours can be largely invisible to teachers who may be powerless to stop the dominance of classroom talk by some boys. Gender differences in classroom participation are therefore related to classroom management and control.

This suggests that teachers find it hard to avoid giving boy's more attention. A kind of 'collaboration' between teachers and boys is also seen in the work of Swann and Graddol (1988), who show how teachers, in monitoring boys' behaviour for signs of potential trouble, and in the strategic positioning of children in places where they can be seen, can look at boys more (more 'gaze attention') and so bring about their greater involvement. The reason, therefore, that boys get more attention is because the teacher finds it difficult not to respond to certain children in the class, despite efforts to distribute attention evenly. The differences become apparent when interaction is analysed in fine detail, and teachers are probably not aware of any preference for boys.

One problem with the research so far considered is that sample sizes can be small (in the case of French and French, only one lesson), and the reliability of data are not often examined. It is possible that unusual cases, for example, where there is very much more attention paid to either boys or girls, can be seen as typical. For this reason it is important to also look at studies of sex differences which have used systematic observation methods, with larger and more carefully chosen samples, predetermined categories, systematic sampling of behaviour, and numerical analysis. This is not to say that such methods do not have limitations (see McIntyre and MacLeod, 1986), but they are well suited to provide quite precise estimates of the frequencies of main types of teacher interaction with boys and girls.

Given limitations of space, it is helpful to provide an overview of these studies, and Kelly (1988) has provided one of the best reviews. She conducted a meta-analysis of 81 studies, mostly American, which had employed systematic observation techniques and where quantitative results were available. The main results are presented in Table 12.3.

This shows that on average girls received 44 per cent of all interactions with their teachers, while boys received 56 per cent. Boys in fact received more of almost all main categories of behaviour. They received more praise,

Table 12.3 Average percentage amount of teacher interaction with boys and girls

	Girls %	Boys %
Total teacher–pupil interaction	44	56
Total teacher initiated	44	56
Total pupil initiated	46	54
Total praise	48	52
Total criticism	35	65
Pupil volunteering, hands up	52	48
Pupil call outs	41	59
Process of abstract questions	43	57
Total response opportunites	44	56
Total questions	44	56
Criticism for behaviour	32	68

Source: adapted from Kelly, 1988
Notes: Ratio variables
% correct answers praised
% wrong answers criticized
% response not followed by feedback   } no difference
% praise for academic work
% wrong answers followed by second chance g > b
% criticism for behaviour b > g

more criticism overall and criticism for behaviour, more total questions and abstract or process questions, and more opportunities to respond. Much of this may be because boys also initiated more to teachers (though teachers also initiated more contacts to boys) and called out more. Interestingly, the one category where girls exceeded boys was volunteering and hands up – indicating that girls were actually keen to be involved. Kelly found that these differences applied to different countries, to different social class and ethnic groups, across different curriculum subjects and with both male and female teachers (though more so with male teachers).

With regard to age differences, she found a marked concentration of studies of younger children, particularly in US studies, over half of which involved children under 9 years of age. She detected some noticeable patterns with age. Girls at nursery school received only 41 per cent of the teacher's attention, while slightly older girls of infant school age received almost their fair share of praise and also criticism. Infant boys, however, were taught more than girls. Girls in the 6 to 9 year age group received almost as much instruction as boys, but thereafter the amount of instruction declined markedly (Kelly, 1988).

Another helpful review of studies using systematic observation methods has been conducted by Croll and Moses (1990). In contrast to Kelly, they review UK studies – choosing five studies, only one of which was included in the Kelly meta-analysis. In three of these studies – the ORACLE research (Galton et al., 1980), 'One in Five' (Croll and Moses, 1990), and the ILEA junior school study (Mortimore et al., 1988) – differences very similar to those reported in the Kelly meta-analysis were found. The percentage of individual teacher attention received by boys was 54 per cent in the ORACLE study, 54 per cent in the One in Five study, and 54 per cent and 58 per cent in the ILEA study (for the second and third-year juniors respectively). However, it is worth stating that in the ORACLE study, when all interactions were added (including whole class contacts that dominate), boys and girls received very much the same amount of attention (51 per cent and 49 per cent).

One of the studies reviewed by Croll and Moses is a detailed systematic observation study of London infant schools, based at the Institute of Education. In this study, no systematic differences were found in the total amount of academic interactions teachers had with boys and girls, or black and white children (Blatchford *et al.*, 1987; Tizard *et al.*, 1988). However, in line with other research, boys received more criticism/disapproval (boys 55 per cent, girls 45 per cent) and more praise (56 per cent, girls 44 per cent). In this study of multicultural schools, the importance of examining ethnic and gender groups together was highlighted. White boys had the most academic interactions with their teachers, black boys least. Black boys engaged more in some 'task avoidant ' behaviours: they showed more 'fooling around' with other children when the expectation was that they should be working (these differences were statistically significant), and also more inappropriate off-task behaviour to teachers, and aggression toward other children, though these behaviours were infrequent and differences were not statistically significant. Interestingly, in view of results concerning the relatively low self- and teacher-assessments of white girls and the suggestion that they were more invisible to teachers (see below), they also received the least disapproval/criticism *and* the least praise from teachers, though again low frequencies meant these differences were not statistically significant. In contrast they engaged in more 'procedural' matters, like getting materials or sharpening pencils when on their own (these results were statistically significant); behaviour that can be a sign of avoiding work (without overtly avoiding the task) and also the teacher. We return to other connections between gender and ethnicity below.

There is some suggestion from Kelly's meta-analysis that sex differences in classroom interaction are more pronounced in the case of male than female teachers. This was deliberately tested by Merritt and Wheldall (1992) who also compared primary and secondary schools. In the primary sample there were 22 women teachers and 10 men, and in the secondary sample there were 21 men and 17 women. In contrast to other research their results indicate that there were no differences at primary level. However, at secondary level boys received more total positive, total negative and more total teacher responses overall than girls. Interesting differences were found for male and female teachers at secondary level. Male teachers were more likely to respond positively to boys' academic behaviour, while female teachers were more likely to respond negatively to boys' social behaviour. The authors interpret these results in terms of female teachers experiencing, and reacting more to, disruptive behaviours from boys, and that boys work harder for male teachers. However there appeared to be no differences overall in on-task behaviour.

So, to sum up, the evidence from studies that have used systematic observation methods and numerical analysis shows a clear tendency for girls to receive slightly less interaction than boys, though this is not true of all studies or classrooms. There is a suggestion that after the age of 9 girls receive progressively less instruction from teachers. These differences between boys and girls are not huge, and some of the claims made in the past about gender differences in teacher–child interaction do seem exaggerated. However, as Kelly (1988) reminds us, if these differences are added up over a child's school career – say 15 000 hours – this would mean something like 1 800 more hours will have been spent with boys than girls. She estimates that the average girl will end up with 30 hours less individual attention than the average boy.

One profitable line of enquiry is likely to come from closer attention to the teacher–pupil contacts in different situations and school subjects within classrooms. In a recent review Howe (1997) looks at research on small group work and around computers, though this is more concerned with group interaction than interactions between pupils and teachers. She concludes that this research shows that in structured group work girls ask for more help than boys, and both girls and boys prefer to ask boys. Boys can also monopolize apparatus. Webb (1984, in Howe, 1997) studied groups of four in secondary mathematics, and found that girls asked for help more than boys and made more requests for general strategic explanations (e.g., what kind of sum is this?), while boys focused on specific procedural information (e.g., which column do you add first?). Girl requests were more than twice as likely to be ignored, so boys got more explanations overall. Although this closer attention to dialogue and sensitivity to learning context looks profitable, relationships between these differences and educational outcomes are not clear.

Study of conversations around computer use, show that they are more extended in same-sex than mixed-sex groups. In girl/boy groups, children are less likely to negotiate, and claims are asserted rather than discussed. Girls and boys then withdraw, reducing turn taking still further. So in same-sex groups the more they disagreed the more they discussed, while in mixed-sex groups the more they disagreed the more they inclined toward silence. There are also differences in dialogue around computer work. In boy pairs there is more interest in whether an answer is right or wrong. In girl pairs the interest is in the structure of the problem being solved. Dialogue is less important in mixed pairs, indicating that they were uncomfortable and not learning from each other. Boys tend to dominate the equipment (see review in Howe, 1997).

By way of summing up research on gender differences in classroom inter-action, Howe (1997) has provided a cogent summary:

> Probably the most striking point to emerge from the research is that contributions from boys predominate during classroom interaction. In whole class sessions where the decisions about who contributes are usually made by teachers, boys make more contributions than girls, and their contributions are usually more elaborate. They achieve their higher levels of contribution partly through activities within discus-sion sessions, for example, hand raising and restlessness, and partly through reputations for misbehaviour which led to greater monitoring by teachers. In small group work where rights to contribute are resolved between pupils, boys usually have the upper hand. They dominate the physical context, volunteering for practical demonstra-tions in science and controlling the mouse and keyboard in comput-ing. They do the same where the emphasis is on talk. Research into oral assessment suggests that boys interrupt girls more than the reverse. Although interruption has not been studied in other contexts, the assertive rather than the negotiating style reported for mixed-sex work with computers suggests a similar pattern. In addition, boys ensure their dominance by establishing themselves as sources of help, for the research shows that boys are asked for help more than girls are.
>
> (Howe, 1997, p. 42–43)

The question that we now need to return to is what the implications of these differences in classroom interaction might be for educational progress and learning. On the face of things the situation is puzzling. Although boys receive more attention than girls overall, they seem at least in a general way to be doing less well academically. This raises questions about the educa-tional significance of the contacts children have with teachers. It does seem to cast doubt on the rather simplistic assumption of many so-called process-product studies (see Dunkin and Biddle, 1974; Shulman, 1986) that educational attainment is linked in a linear fashion to the quantity of instruction. As Arnot *et al.* (1998) conclude, 'Gender differences in class-room *processes* are therefore present but their significance for educational *performance* is not self-evident' (p. 26). One possibility is that the role of teacher–pupil interaction in educational progress is easily over exaggerated. Children learn in a number of ways and the experience of more teacher contact may not be significant.

Other within-child factors related to gender differences

We now consider other processes that might help understanding of differ-ences in classroom interaction and educational attainment. There is a host of possible factors, many of which have been recently reviewed by Arnot *et al.* (1998), Howe (1997), and Powney (1996). They include curriculum content, the way subjects are taught, changes to assessment arrangements, school organization changes, biological and school peer cultural influences, school subject choices, and home influences. There is not space to review these here. Instead we will concentrate on within-child factors such as self-perceptions and attitudes, self concept and motivational processes because recent research has provided insights into connections between gender and academic interactions and performance. The choice of within-child factors reflects our conceptualization of context: children and their surroundings influence each other. By examining individual differences we sharpen understanding of the effects that children have on their environments.

Different ways of learning and 'knowing'

One possibility is that girls develop alternative and compensatory strategies that aid their learning and their measured attainments. So although boys may get more of a teacher's attention, girls find other ways to get information and learn. In the classroom context, for example, it may be that girls approach teachers individually in order to have their questions answered.

Arnot *et al.* (1998) review studies that give some indication that girls and boys may have different 'ways of knowing'. They cite a study by Boaler (1997) of a year group of pupils in each of two schools over the period Year 9 to Year 11. The schools were in similar areas and had similar scores on tests of cognitive ability at the beginning of Year 9. However, the schools had different approaches, with one more traditional and textbook-led and the other more open and project based, with an emphasis on process. Boys and girls had similar achievements in maths in terms of grades A–C in the more open school but girls significantly underachieved in the school with the traditional approach, particularly the girls in the top set. Interviews with pupils indicated that these girls were disaffected by the pace and competitiveness and wanted to understand and discuss things more. This is a study of only two schools but it seems consistent with the view that boys and girls prefer different ways of knowing, with girls preferring 'connected knowing' which builds on personal experience and integrates a wide range of understandings, while boys favour 'separate knowing' which is based more on impersonal procedures to establish truths. Arnot *et al.* conclude that

> Boys show greater adaptability to more traditional approaches to learning which require memorising abstract, unambiguous facts and rules that have to be acquired quickly. They also appear to be more willing to sacrifice deep understanding, which requires sustained effort, for correct answers achieved at speed.
>
> (p. 28)

Powney (1996) wonders whether students learn that only some kinds of responses are likely to succeed in achievement and assessment situations and that these favour conformity, being 'good' pupils, and not taking risks. Although alternative strategies may in other circumstances be more a sign of creativity, in school they can disadvantage children in achievement situations, and this may be more likely in the case of boys.

However, the research evidence base for these claims appears rather slight, and the possibility of differences between boys and girls in terms of different strategies and learning styles could benefit from more research. As Powney (1996) has said, we need more understanding about how boys and girls learn and the kind of peer pressure and supports that influence their approaches to learning. Psychologists have been studying for many years possible differences in a number of relevant areas. One topic has been cognitive style, with perhaps the most well known distinction being between field dependent and independent (Witkin *et al.*, 1962), and impulsive/reflective styles, but the link between cognitive style and gender is not clear cut. Moreover it seems likely that research will need to examine pupil strategies more widely than cognitive style and will need to attend more to everyday classroom interactions and attitudes.

In a long-standing line of research, Fennema and her colleagues (e.g., Fennema, 1996) have argued that males and females learn differently and perform differently in mathematics. She characterizes much research on general gender differences as 'positivist' and concludes that gender differences in the amount and type of interaction are not a major driving force so much as symptoms of existing and more fundamental gender differences. She concludes that classroom organization and instruction favour boys in maths. Competitive activities are more common in maths classes than cooperative activities, but the former encourages boys' learning while the latter encourages girls'. Fennema takes the view that 'autonomous learning behaviour' is important to success in maths but girls are less likely to be encouraged in this, partly because of their own preferences and partly because of social and teacher influences.

In suggestions that are similar to the findings of Stanworth, Fennema argues that teachers' knowledge about boys who are successful is more accurate than girls who are successful, and that teachers think more about boys during instruction because they pressure teachers more. She also argues that girls and boys engage in different mental activities during cooperative problem-solving. So in the same situation there are different processes at work. She also argues that not much is known, for example, about the development of male and female confidence levels in maths. Fennema's research is consistent with other research and comment (e.g., Walkerdine, 1990) in addressing difficulties faced by girls in maths, though it is less clear how reliable the findings are and whether they will need to be revised with the seeming advances of girls in mathematics attainment.

Pupil attentiveness

In one Australian study, Hill *et al.* (1993, in Arnot *et al.*, 1998) found that girls were rated as more attentive in class and this was positively related to achievement and progress. So attention and concentration are a likely explanation for differences in achievement. This is tied to changes to the curriculum in Australia which now demands high levels of attentiveness in response to portfolios, extended prose and research projects.

Preliminary results from a large scale study of pupils' progress in Key Stage 1 in England (part of the Class Size project, described in Chapter 7), it was found that girls in the first, reception year, were rated by teachers as more likely to concentrate in class, and, in findings which support the Australian research, this was highly related to attainment at the end of the reception year, and progress over it (Blatchford unpublished). This research suggests one reason why achievement levels may differ, but it is less clear why differences have become more marked recently and it is not clear if differences in the reception year will continue as the children get older (this is being studied at present).

Pupil self perceptions and attitudes to school

Research on self concept and motivation has made a number of advances recently. It is widely recognized that more general measures such as self concept and self-esteem are too global to be helpful. Hattie and McInman (1991, in Bracken), in a meta-analysis, found few differences in average self concept scores for males and females. However, specific dimensions on which males scored higher were mathematics and physical ability self concepts, and for females, verbal self concept. The weak and inconsistent results from earlier studies on general self concept measures may well have been because of differences on sub scales within self concept. Marsh and colleagues found that pre-adolescent boys (grades 2–5) have higher self concepts than girls in the areas of maths, general self, physical appearance and physical abilities, while girls have higher self concepts in areas of reading and general school (see Crain, 1991, in Bracken). During adolescence (grades 6–10) girls tend to have higher verbal, honesty–truthworthiness and same sex relations, while boys have higher scores on physical abilities, physical appearance and maths. Hattie and Marsh (in Bracken, 1991) argue that males tend to be more inclined to be 'self-enhancers', while females are more likely to attribute negative concerns to themselves (they are 'self-verifiers'), though these differences may not be particularly evident until adulthood. Crain (1991, in Bracken) reminds us that these differences should not be overstated. Gender effects are actually quite small and account for little of the variation. She also concludes that it would not be warranted to intervene in educational settings in order to affect boys' and girls' self concept, for example, to improve adolescent girls' physical appearance and ability self concepts. By and large, boys and girls are more similar than different with regard to self concept.

In the TCRU longitudinal study (Tizard *et al.*, 1988) pupil self perceptions and attitudes to school were studied and the importance of considering gender and ethnicity together was indicated. In this study a main concern was with pupils' perceptions of their own attainments, which can be considered one part of academic self concept. Four groups were studied – black boys and girls whose parents were of Afro-Caribbean origin, and white boys and girls whose parents were white indigenous. There were differences between the two girl groups. To take the black girls first: at 11 years in English/reading they had by far the highest self ratings of their own attainments and at 16 years showed a continued confidence in their attainments (Blatchford, 1997). These results supported interviewers' accounts of black girls at 16 years being more articulate, confident and motivated, and were reinforced by interview results when the children were 16 years. Black girls had the highest Marsh SDQ11 general self-esteem scores, and also tended to have higher SDQ11 verbal self concepts. More detailed analyses of individual items from the SDQ11 showed that black girls were also less likely than the other groups to say that nothing that they did turned out well, less likely to say that they were not good at reading, more likely to agree that things they did turned out well, more likely to disagree that nothing they did turned out well, and more likely to agree that they did most things well. They were also more likely to say their parents came to parents' evenings. So although there were important main effects for ethnic groups (Blatchford, 1997), results concerning some items reinforces the view that the black girls were the most confident group, and most positive about their performance in schoolwork.

These results are consistent with those from ethnographic research in the UK. In a well-known study of a small group of black girls in a London secondary school (Fuller, 1984), they were found to be strongly committed to doing well at school, despite appearing disaffected from school in some respects. This anti-school but pro-education attitude has been reported in other studies (see Woods, 1990, for a review). Mirza (1992) argues that there has been a failure to document the relative success of black girls in schools and therefore to misunderstand the nature of ethnic differences in educational attainment. Mirza's explanation concentrates on West Indian female orientations toward the labour market and a belief, unlike their white female peers, in the relative independence of female and male roles and hence the feasibility of upward occupational mobility. There is some consensus that black girls are motivated to gain academic qualifications as an expression of self worth in the face of feeling undervalued in comparison to males.

The results concerning white girls were quite different (Blatchford,

1997). At 7 and 11 years they were the least likely of the four groups to consider themselves better than the others in reading. White girls at both 7 and 11 years were likely to underestimate themselves in both reading and maths. At 16 years white girls still underestimated their attainments in English. These results are further supported by other self-report data at 11 years. They were more likely to say that they were not looking forward to secondary school because of the work there, that they did not like maths because it was not interesting to them and that they were not pleased with their work because of their ability (Blatchford, 1997). These kinds of results have been reported for girls generally (see Meece and Courtney, 1992); here we find them only for the white girls.

The conclusion, therefore, seems to be that white girls show a long standing tendency to underestimate and show little confidence in their own attainments. Analysis of GCSE results showed that white girls were now performing at a lower level than black girls and were now similar to the two male groups. Whilst causal direction is difficult to establish with certainty, one question concerns to what extent the long term underestimation of attainments by white girls, even in areas in which they performed better than boys, has by the end of the secondary school stage had a negative effect on their progress at school.

These results indicate that one line of enquiry would be further exploration of reasons for pupil ability assessments in relation to gender and ethnic group differences. The white sample in the TCRU study were also predominantly working class and relatively disadvantaged and so social class may be a factor as well. It may be that underestimation by white girls is a form of defensive strategy used to preserve self-regulation. Further research could be directed at the links between group differences in underestimation and other motivational measures (see Blatchford, 1997).

More generally, these results on pupil self perceptions indicate the complexity of attempts to explain gender differences in achievement in school. Recent reviews have pointed to the complex interconnections of gender, race and achievement (Powney, 1996); the present discussion indicates the value of an accompanying and more fine-grained analysis of self perceptions.

Motivational process

Motivational processes have been linked to gender differences in classroom processes and academic achievement. One view is that motivational styles can be seen as differing in main ways. One well-used distinction is between 'mastery' and 'performance' orientation. The argument is that students differ in the extent to which failure and success in academic work is attributed to external causes (e.g., teachers' explanations or classroom equipment) and internal factors such as their own effort. Girls are thought more likely to attribute success to external causes and failure to their own efforts.

Dweck's research has been influential in showing ways that teachers' feedback can affect pupils' feelings of 'learned helplessness'. Dweck *et al.* (1978) analyzed types of feedback to girls and boys from teachers in elementary school. Negative and positive feedback to boys focused on conduct rather than academic aspects of their work. In contrast girls received little criticism for their conduct and so most of the criticism was on the intellectual quality of their work. When teachers criticized children for the quality of work they were eight times more likely to attribute boys' problems to lack of effort – typically not making any overt attribution for girls' performance. Dweck *et al.* suggest that these differences in feedback might mean boys and girls develop different attributional patterns. If boys receive criticism focusing on their behaviour they may see negative feedback as about them rather than their academic ability. In addition, the emphasis on lack of effort in teachers' feedback may encourage boys to blame their academic failures on lack of effort. In contrast, if girls are criticized less they may be less likely to attribute their failures to lack of effort and may come to attribute failures to lack of ability. Dweck *et al.* (1978) manipulated teacher feedback in a laboratory situation and found as expected that children who received a boy-type feedback had higher expectations for success and attributed failures to external factors and lack of effort than did children who received a girl-type pattern.

These results are described at length because of the wide currency they have in debates on gender differences. However, serious questions have been raised about the findings and interpretation. One factor concerns the often low frequencies of overt teacher attributions about quality of work. More fundamentally, as we alluded to in the last chapter, Eccles and her colleagues, as well as others, have not found that girls are more prone to learned helpless behaviours than boys (see Eccles and Wigfield, in Dusek, 1985). Also, observational studies have found that teachers give more work-related criticism to boys, rather than girls, and that the proportion of criticism given to work versus conduct is the same for boys and girls (Parsons *et al.*, 1982, in Eccles and Wigfield, 1985). Kelly's meta-analysis of observation studies also showed that boys receive higher criticism for work and behaviour, and that boys did not get a higher proportion of praise for academic work than girls. These studies indicate that teacher feedback does not vary as would be predicted by Dweck, and that learned helplessness may not be gender specific. Eccles and Wigfield (1985) conclude that 'we now believe that the typical experiences that children have with affective feedback and teacher attributions are not powerful determinants of their classroom motivation.'

Peer pressure

Although we have called the processes considered in this section 'within-child' factors, the attitudes that children have toward school work, and their self perceptions, will develop in social and educational contexts. One significant context will be the peer group, and this is likely to become more influential in the secondary years. There is not space to review this topic in depth. It is often said that within the schools there is peer pressure against seeming to be too good at schoolwork. Terms like 'boff' have replaced 'swot' as a term of ridicule, and it can be difficult to persuade particularly boys that it is cool to want to learn at school.

An interesting distinction was made in Harris *et al.* (1993) between boys' and girls' perceptions of what schoolwork meant in terms of freedom and autonomy during lesson time. More girls than boys were found to interpret 'freedom' as an opportunity for self expression and developing confidence in managing their work, while boys tended to see freedom as an opportunity to talk about things unrelated to work. There also appeared to be differences in perceptions of peer pressures. Girls tended to refer to the ability to ignore peers when they wanted to get on with their work and were more likely to do as the teacher wanted. It is likely that boys' attitudes, supported by peer group pressure, will be hard to change. If it is the case that they are implicated in male underachievement at school then a main challenge of school improvement efforts will be to find ways of understanding and affecting peer group pressures. There is a danger of oversimplifying effects of peer pressure by considering boys and girls as groups; it would be helpful to have more information on individual differences in the susceptibility to peer pressure, for example by considering a connection to temperament.

Homework

The peer group context may be related to one out of school activity that is likely to impact in a direct way on school progress. It has often been said that girls are more likely to engage in more homework and do this more conscientiously than boys. One recent study (Harris *et al.*, 1993) looked at female and male student attitudes in three schools in traditional working class areas. There appeared to be differences with regard to homework, and these appeared to be connected to attitudes in the wider community. There was a strong sense of men upholding a traditional distinction between work and time off work, and this was reflected in the attitudes of boys at school who maintained a similar distinction, spending time out of school with larger groups of friends, on sport, etc. Women were more likely to be seen as organizers, and even when holding a job as well were still likely to have a domestic role, and in this sense 'work', at home. Girls were also more likely to be with one other friend, do homework together and work at homework every night and at weekends.

Wider social and cultural influences

We have hinted in this section at the wider social and cultural influences that will condition pupil attitudes and self perceptions. We have seen that it is necessary to explain what appear to be fairly recent changes in gender differences in school attainments. We end this section by looking briefly at accompanying wider changes in employment which have been associated recently with problems faced by males. Whereas boys in traditional working-class areas in particular would once have moved as a matter of course into traditional manual employment when they left school at 16 years, these jobs may not now be available. They are then forced to compete for alternative employment, for example in the public sector, where they can be less successful than girls, who may be more attractive as employees. So the collapse of manufacturing industry may be one factor which has conspired to make working-class boys feel useless and unwanted.

This line of reasoning is consistent with early sociological research (e.g., Hargreaves, 1967; Willis, 1977) which showed that children grouped in lower groups or sets could respond by reacting negatively to school and adopting anti-school activities. But while the older account accommodated employment patterns, more recent sociological research suggests a worrying isolation of male culture from wider society. Connell (1989, in Arnot *et al.*, 1998) and Mac an Ghaill (1994, in Arnot *et al.*, 1998), for example, reach similar conclusions about the way that male working-class boys who have been denied traditional male employment and forms of power reacted by adopting a kind of heightened masculinity and challenging of authority. In an attempt to regain control of their situation they took pride in sporting prowess, physical aggression and sexual conquest.

To make matters worse for boys, it may also be that girls are changing their attitudes to future careers and becoming more confident and less inclined to a domestic role and marriage, though differences may well vary between girls (Arnot *et al.*, 1998). Though plausible, these descriptions are difficult to weight in terms of how widespread the behaviours and attitudes are (samples are typically small). It is also difficult to know to what extent they are related to educational interactions and school progress. We have clearly come a long way from pupil self perceptions and concentration in class. But enough has been said though to indicate that such self perceptions are likely to be supported by powerful and entrenched social, cultural and structural factors, and this is why simplistic solutions will be unlikely.

Conclusions

In this chapter we have looked at two main questions. In the first place we asked if there were differences in academic interactions at school involving boys and girls and their teachers. In general, the research evidence supports the view that boys get more of a teacher's attention across most classroom behaviours and participate more in classroom discussions, though the quality of some research and its consistency can be questioned. Through the discussion so far we have touched on reasons why these gender differences in classroom behaviour are found. One main possibility is that the effect is essentially child-driven, in that teachers are merely responding to existing differences in children's behaviour. If boys get more of a teacher's attention this is because teachers are responding appropriately to their greater demands. This is similar to the literature on teachers' expectancies, in which, as we saw in Chapter 11, at least some of the expectancy effect is actually better considered as accurate teacher judgements about children. When it comes to sex differences, though, this argument has to accommodate findings such as those in Kelly's meta-analysis that show that girls were as willing as boys to volunteer in class. Another possible explanation is that it is not boys in general who get more of a teacher's attention so much as a small group of boys. Differences between boys and girls may be more a matter of classroom management than a bias toward one gender *per se*. Another explanation, as we have seen, is that there is a kind of implicit, possibly subconscious, interactional preference for boys.

If the interaction results are relatively clear, answers to the second main question addressed in this chapter are less so. This concerns what effect these differences have on educational progress. We have seen that there does not appear to be a direct link between gender differences in classroom interaction and gender differences in school progress. Indeed there is something of a puzzle. If the bias in favour of males in classroom interactions were mirrored in educational progress, we would expect girls to be at a disadvantage. This was indeed the background for much early research on this issue. But we have seen that recent changes make this linkage much more problematical. At very least, it does seem to cast doubt on any simple linear connection between educational attainment and quantity of instruction.

However, this is not to say that differences in classroom interactions are insignificant. Given the pace of change and lack of understanding, they may be significant in ways that are not yet clear. There may also be an indirect link. It is possible that differences in classroom interaction between boys and girls are more likely to affect pupil attitudes, for example in the science laboratory and when using computers the physical control by boys of apparatus and equipment may still disadvantage girls by putting them off and affecting their school subject choices and involvement in class lessons (Powney, 1996; Howe, 1997). It is also possible, though more speculative, that the different contributions of boys and girls to classroom conversations may have long term implications for future careers. If it is true that boys are more likely to take part in classroom talk, are responded to more in public and have more experience of public speaking and claiming turns in classroom discourse, and that girls are more likely to listen, and to talk in more private contexts, then this might create the pattern for similar gender differences in the work place and possibly have a negative effect on career advancement.

With apologies for the predictability of the conclusion it is clear that much more research is needed on a wide range of topics connected to gender differences in school interactions. Given the wide recognition of the scale of the problem of male underachievement in schools, there is some urgency to this task. A limitation of research in this area has been that different approaches, for example, psychological and sociological, have been quite separate from each other. There is much potential in combining approaches from different disciplines, for example, to link psychological research on self perceptions and motivation, research on classroom interaction and classroom discourse, sociolinguistic research and sociological research on peer cultures and employment patterns. There is perhaps a particular role for social psychological research (Howe, 1997). It is likely that research will be successful in affecting and informing policy on underachievement, to the extent that it illuminates linkages between classroom interactions, pupil attitudes and perceptions, and wider social, cultural and structural factors.

It is worth reiterating that this chapter has been concerned with only some aspects relevant to a full coverage of sex differences in school progress. To add to the list above, there are a number of external factors such as changes to the nature of examination and course work. The increasing emphasis on course work is believed to favour girls (though not as much as is often thought (Arnot *et al.*, 1998; Elwood, 1994)). Boys are thought to do better on multiple choice questions and traditional exams where they can cram at the last minute. It is also worth remembering that a theme of this chapter has been the need to attend to relatively recent changes in measured school progress. A number of results on sex differences are interesting but are not always clear about recent changes in sex differences. Some traditional explanations for gender differences, for example biological explanations, are therefore insufficient.

A last point to make is that there are a number of clues that gender differences will vary between schools. This was shown in Boaler's research, described above, in which two schools had different approaches to maths. Girls underachieved in the more traditional school, and interviews suggested that girls there became disaffected by the pace, competitiveness, and closed approach. An allied question arises out of Kelly's review: why are gender differences more marked in some classes than others? She reports that in 31 per cent of classrooms studied, girls received less than 45 per cent of interactions, yet in 4 per cent of classrooms girls received more than 55 per cent. There are also big differences between LEAs in differences between boys and girls in measured attainments; for example, in 1998 there was a 15 point gap in the percentage of boys and girls getting five A*–C at GCSE in some authorities (e.g., Croydon and North Somerset), but little difference in other authorities (e.g., Barking and Dagenham and Sutton). Interestingly, these differences occurred within both relatively poor and relatively affluent areas. The conclusion then is that although there is a 'natural' or genetic component to sex differences, there is also a sense in which sex differences are not 'natural'; rather they arise in context and are subject to historical and cultural shifts.

13 A concluding note

Writing this book about children's social lives in school has been an interesting scholarly task. It enabled us to think about and present much of what we've been studying and teaching for a number of years. The topic also has implications for public policy: children in schools are the concern of all levels of the populace. In this concluding note, we address these two general themes, beginning with the more traditional.

The developmental and social world of children in school

Writing a book of this sort has been productive because it affords opportunities to re-think what may have become familiar. These sorts of efforts are especially productive when they involve a collaboration between two scholars. As we have argued throughout the book, when peers interact with each other around an interesting task, both learn a great deal. The conflicts and resolutions that are the inevitable product of these interactions lead to deeper and broader understanding.

Our joint efforts in this volume, as we outlined in the first chapter, were guided by a common orientation. Basically, we took a developmental perspective towards our study of children in schools. Correspondingly, we considered children's social and cognitive lives in schools to be inextricably linked. We have spelt out the implications of this position for schools. Most basically, schools for young children should be different places to schools for adolescents. What gets taught and how it gets evaluated should vary.

The importance of children's social lives has been our central focus, and what we think is unique about our discussion of children in schools. One instance of this was framing children's social worlds in terms of a broader construct, social competence, and noting the differing demands and hallmarks of social competence as children develop from infancy to adolescence. Most broadly, social competence is expressed as children's adaptation to an environment. In schools, this includes interacting with peers (both friends and non-friends alike), teachers and the demands of the school curriculum. These social factors affect and are affected by more traditional measures of school performance, such as achievement. That we included separate chapters on social competence and peer interaction, friendships, teacher expectations, and teacher–student interaction highlights the depth and breadth of the issues involved here. A couple of examples of the inter-relations between these social processes and achievement will highlight our argument.

Take the case of friendships. Friendships are relationships that provide mutual support and challenges for youngsters. Friends are very important to children, as they, and their parents, will readily tell us, yet they are typically not considered in traditional discussions of schooling. Not only do friendships relate (both positively and negatively) to children's adjustment, but they also provide an effective context in which academic subjects get learnt. As we noted in the chapter on friendship, when children interact with friends, compared to acquaintances, learning goes on. This typically happens by friends interacting around a subject, disagreeing about their interpretation and resolving the disagreement. This process enables youngsters to reflect upon the processes constitutive of the subject matter at hand.

Social relationships are also affected by academic aspects. As we noted in the discussion of aggression, youngsters who are having trouble academically, often affiliate with others like them, as do children who do well academically. Affiliation with low achievers often leads to an anti-school orientation, further academic decline and affiliation with anti-social youngsters. This process often ends with these youngsters dropping out of school.

We are, of course, aware that not all peer relationships and interactions are positive. The occurrence of bullying in schools is a testament to this problem. Indeed, the occurrence of bullying is one frequently cited reason for the marginalizing of breaktime in schools in both the UK and the USA. We suggest, however, that a *lack* of opportunities for peer interaction may actually be contributing to the problem. By this we mean that children learn the social skills necessary to get along with each other, and the consequences of anti-social behaviour, by having repeated and sustained opportunities to interact with peers relatively free from adult control. Consequently, breaktime should be viewed as an important venue in which children learn social skills. The current practice, at least in many American schools, of implementing 'character education programs' seems to miss the point. Children, as Piaget noted, develop social understanding and morality through peer interaction. We do not mean to imply that breaktime should be a time when children are unsupervised and allowed to interact in any way they please. It needs to be supervised in such a way that real aggression is not tolerated and cooperative interaction is encouraged.

Implications

A second consequence of writing this book was the clearer recognition that it has real implications for public and educational policy. Schools, after all, are public places which are typically supported by the public through rates or taxes. Further, the end result of schooling – young adults taking their places in society – has an important societal impact, as the American philosopher John Dewey noted 100 years ago.

This line of reasoning can be considered consistent with the current political Zeitgeist in both Britain and America. League tables of school exam results and accountability are the most visible consequences of this. Our concern in this book may appear at odds with some aspects of current education policy. But this may be looked at a different way. Specifically, psychologists and educational researchers have reasonably good knowledge about what works in schools and what does not. Ratepayers, parents and children deserve those educational programmes and policies which have withstood the rigours of empirical testing. These stakeholders in the educational process should demand no less, and they should hold educational policy makers and politicians accountable for their choice of programmes and policies. The case of breaktime is a good example of educational policy not being guided by data. Other aspects of children's educational experiences, such as the practice of discouraging peer or friendship interaction during academic lessons, is another practice not rooted in theory or data.

In conclusion, the study of children in schools is a complex enterprise. Scientifically, we must integrate many aspects of children's lives in order to understand their development and performance in schools. These findings, in turn, are very important for the vitality and soundness of our education and social policies.

Bibliography

ADAMS, M.J. 1990: *Beginning to rea: Thinking and learning about print.* Cambridge, MA: MIT Press.

ADAMS, R.S. and BIDDLE, B.J. 1970: *The realities of teaching: exploration with videotape.* New York: Holt, Rinehart and Winston.

ALDIS, O. 1975: *Play fighting.* New York: Academic.

ALEXANDER, R., ROSE, J. and WOODHEAD, C. 1992: *Curriculum organisation and classroom practice in primary schools: a discussion paper.* London: DES.

AMES, C. 1992: Classrooms: goals, structures and student motivation. *Journal of Educational Psychology, 84,* 3, 261–71.

ANDERMAN, E.M. and MAEHR, M.L. 1994: Motivation and schooling in the middle grades, *Review of Educational Research, 64,* 2, 287–309.

ANDERSON, S. and MESSICK, S. 1974: Social competency in your children. *Developmental Psychology, 10,* 282–93.

APPLEBEE, A. 1978: *The child's concept of story.* Chicago: University of Chicago Press.

ARENDS, R.I. 1994: *Learning to teach* (Third Edition). New York: McGraw-Hill.

ARNOT, M., GRAY, J., JAMES, M. and RUDDOCK, J. 1998: Recent research on gender and educational performance. *Office for Standards in Education (OFSTED) Reviews of Research.* London: The Stationery Office.

AXELROD *et al.* 1979: Comparison of two common classroom seating arrangements. *Academic Therapy, 15,* 29–36.

BAINES, E. 1996: Discourse topic management and discussion skills of 4-, 6- and 9-year-olds. Unpublished PhD thesis. University of Strathclyde.

BAKEMAN, R. and GOTTMAN, J M. 1986: *Observing interaction: An introduction to sequential analysis.* Cambridge: Cambridge University Press.

BANDURA, A. 1973: *Aggression: a social learning analysis.* Engelwood Cliffs, NJ: Prentice-Hall.

—— 1989: Regulation of cognitive processes through perceived self-efficacy. *Developmental Psychology, 25,* 729–35.

BARKER, R. 1968: *Ecological psychology.* Stanford, CA: Stanford University Press.

BARKER LUNN, J.C. 1970: *Streaming in the primary school.* Windsor: NFER.

BARON, R.M., TOM, D.Y.H. and COOPER, H.M. 1985: Social class, race and teacher expectations. In Dusek, J. B. (ed.) *Teacher expectancies* (pp. 251–69). London: Erlbaum.

BARROW, S.G. 1984: The logic of systematic classroom research: the case of ORACLE. *Durham and Newcastle Research Review, 53,* 182–8.

BATESON, P.P.G. 1978: How does behavior develop? In Bateson, P.P.G. and Klopfer, P.H. (eds) *Growing points in ethology* (Vol. 3, pp. 55–66). New York: Cambridge University Press.

—— 1981: Discontinuities in development and changes in the organization of play in cats. In Immelmann, K., Barlow, G., Petrinovich, L. and Main, M.

(eds) *Behavioral development* (pp. 281–95). New York: Cambridge University Press.

BAUMRIND, D. 1967: Child care practices anteceding 3 patterns of preschool behavior. *Genetic Psychology Monographs, 75,* 43–88.

——1971: Current patterns of parental authority. *Developmental Psychology Monographs, 4,* (1 Pt 2).

——1989: Rearing competent children. In Damon, W. (ed.) *Child development today and tomorrow* (pp. 349–78). San Francisco: Jossey-Bass.

BEEZ, W. V. 1968: Influence of biased psychological reports on teacher behaviour and pupil performance. *Proceedings of the 76th Annual Convention of the American Psychological Association, 3,* 605–6.

BELSKY, J. and MOST, R.K. 1981: From exploration to play. *Developmental Psychology, 17,* 630–9.

BENNETT, S.N. 1987: Architecture. In Dunkin, M. (ed.) *International Encyclopedia of Teaching and Teacher Education.* Pergamon, 530–7.

——1996: Class size in primary schools: perceptions of headteachers, chairs of governors, teachers and parents. *British Educational Research Journal, 22,* 33–55.

BENNETT, N. and BLUNDELL, D. 1983: Quantity and quality of work in rows and classroom groups. *Educational Psychology, 3,* 93–105.

BENNETT, N. and DUNNE, E. 1992: *Managing groups.* Hemel Hempstead: Simon and Schuster Education.

BENNETT, N., DESFORGES, C., COCKBURN, A. and WILKINSON, B. 1984: *The quality of pupil learning experiences.* London: Erlbaum.

BENNETT, N., JORDAN, J., LONG, G. and WADE, B. 1976: *Teaching styles and pupil progress.* London: Open Books Publishing Ltd.

BEREITER, C. 1985: The changing face of educational disadvantage. *Phi Delta Kappan, 66,* 538–41.

BERLYNE, D. 1966: Curiousity and exploration. *Science, 153,* 25–33.

BERNDT, T. J. 1989: Obtaining support from friends during childhood and adolescence. In Belle, D. (ed.) *Children's social networks and social supports.* New York: Wiley, 308–31.

——1996: Exploring the effects of friendship quality on social development. In Bukowski, W. M., Newcomb, A. F. and Hartup, W. W. (eds) *The company they keep: friendships in childhood and adolescence.* Cambridge: Cambridge University Press.

BERNDT, T. J. and KEEFE, K. 1992: Friends' influence on adolescents' perceptions of themselves at school. In Schunk, D. H. and Meece, J. L. (eds) *Student perceptions in the classroom.* Hillsdale, New Jersey: Lawrence Erlbaum Associates.

BERNDT, T. J., HAWKINS, J. A. and HOYLE, S. G. 1986: Changes in friendship during a school year: effects on children's and adolescents' impressions of friendship and sharing with friends. *Child Development, 57,* 1284–97.

BERNSTEIN, B. 1960: Language and social class. *British Journal of Sociology, 1,* 217–27.

——1971: *Class codes and control* (Vol. 1) London: Routledge and Kegan Paul.

——1972: Social class, language, and socialization. In Giglioli, P. (ed.) *Language and social context* (pp. 157–78). Harmondsworth: Penguin.

BIGGS, J. B. and MOORE, P. J. 1993: *The process of learning* (Third Edition). Englewood Cliffs NJ: Prentice-Hall.

BIRNS, B., and STERNGLANZ, S. 1983: Sex-role socialization. In Liss, M. (ed.) *Social and cognitive skills* (pp. 235–51). New York: Academic.

BJORKLUND, D. F. and GREEN, B. L. 1992: The adaptive nature of cognitive immaturity. *American Psychology, 47,* 46–54.

BLAKE, J. 1989: Number of siblings and educational attainment. *Science, 245* (July), 32–6.

BLATCHFORD, P. 1979: The development of social interaction between infants. Unpublished PhD, University of Surrey.

——1989: *Playtime in the primary school: problems and improvements.* Windsor: NFER-Nelson. Now London: Routledge.

——1996: Pupils' views on school and school work from 7 to 16 years. *Research Papers in Education, 11,* 3, 263–88.

——1997: Pupils' perceived academic attainment at 7, 11 and 16 years: effects of sex and ethnic group. *British Journal of Educational Psychology, 67,* 169–84.

——1998: *Social life in school: pupils' experience of breaktime and recess from 7 to 16 years.* London: Falmer Press.

——1999: Friendships at school; the role of breaktimes, *Education 3–13, 27,* 1, 60–5.

BLATCHFORD, P. and MARTIN, C. 1998: The effects of class size on classroom processes: 'It's a bit like a treadmill - working hard and getting nowhere fast!' *British Journal of Educational Studies, 46,* 2 (June), 118–37.

BLATCHFORD, P. and MORTIMORE, P. 1994: The issue of class size for young children in schools: what can we learn from research? *Oxford Review of Education, 20,* 411–28.

BLATCHFORD, P. and SUMPNER, C. 1998: What do we know about break-time?: results from a national survey of breaktime and lunchtime in primary and secondary schools. *British Educational Research Journal, 24,* 1, 79–94.

BLATCHFORD, P. , BAINES, E. and KUTNICK, P. 1999a: *Grouping practices within primary classrooms: the effect of class size on within-class grouping practices.* Paper to British Educational Research Association Annual Conference, Sussex University.

BLATCHFORD, P. , BATTLE, S. and MAYS, J. 1982: *The First Transition: Home to Pre-school.* Windsor: NFER-Nelson.

BLATCHFORD, P. , BURKE, J., FARQUHAR, C., PLEWIS, I. and TIZARD, B. 1987: An observational study of children's behaviour at infant school. *Research Papers in Education, 2,* 1 (Reprinted in Woodhead, M. and McGrath, A. (eds) 1998: *Family, School and Society.* Open University/Hodder and Stoughton).

——1989: Teachers' expectations in infant school: associations with attainment and progress, curriculum coverage and classroom interaction. *British Journal of Educational Psychology, 59,* 19–30.

BLATCHFORD, P. , CREESER, R. and MOONEY, A. 1990. Preschool reading related skills and later reading achievement: further evidence. *British Educational Research Journal, 32,* 3, 163–74.

BLATCHFORD, P. , GOLDSTEIN, H. and MORTIMORE, P. 1998: Research of class size effects: a critique of methods and a way forward. *International Journal of Education Research, 29,* 691–710.

BLATCHFORD, P. , KUTNICK, P. and BAINES, E. 1999b: *The nature and use of classroom groups in primary schools.* ESRC Project Ref: R000237255, Final Report.

BLOCK, J. 1987: School play: a review. In J. Block and N. King (eds) *School play* (pp. 253–76). New York: Garland.

BLUMENFELD, P. C., HAMILTON, V. L., BOSSERT, S. T., WESSELS, K. and MEECE, J. 1983: Teacher talk and student thought: socialization into the student role. In Levine, J. and Wang, M. (eds) *Teacher and student perceptions: implications for learning.* Hillsdale, NJ: Erlbaum Associates.

BLURTON JONES, N. 1972a: Characteristics of ethological studies of human behavior. In Blurton Jones, N. (ed.) *Ethological studies of child behavior* (pp. 3–33). London: Cambridge University Press.

—1972b: Categories of child–child interaction. In N. Blurton Jones (ed.) *Ethological studies of child behavior* (pp. 97–129). London: Cambridge University Press.

—1976: Rough-and-tumble play among nursery school children. In Bruner, J., Jolly, A. and Sylva, K. (eds) *Play – its role in development and evolution* (pp. 352–63). New York: Basic Books.

BOALER, J. 1997: *Experiencing school mathematics: teaching styles, sex and setting.* Milton Keynes: Open Uversity Press.

BOLDIZAR, J., PERRY, D. and PERRY, L. 1989: Outcome values and aggression. *Child Development, 60,* 571–9.

BOSKER, R., BLATCHFORD, P. and MEIJNEN, W. 1999: The oncoming class size initiative. In Creemers, B., Stringfield, S. and Bosker, R. (eds) *Enhancing Educational Excellence, Equity and Efficiency* (pp. 89–112). Dordrecht, NL: Kluwer Academic Publishers.

BOSSERT, S. 1979: *Tasks and social relationships in classrooms.* New York: Cambridge University Press.

BOWERS, L., SMITH, P. and BINNEY, V. 1994: Perceived family relationships of bullies, victims, and bully/victims in middle childhood. *Journal of Social and Personal Relationships, 11,* 215–32.

BOWLBY, J. 1969: *Attachment and loss, Vol. 1: Attachment.* New York: Basic Books.

BRACKEN, B. A. 1991: *Handbook of self concept: developmental, social and clinical considerations.* New York and Chichester: Wiley.

BRADLEY, R. and CALDWELL, B. 1977: Home environment, social status, and mental test performance. *Journal of Educational Psychology, 69,* 697–701.

BRAUN, C. 1987: Teachers' expectations. In Dunkin, M. (ed.) *International encyclopedia of teaching and teacher education,* 598–605.

BRONFENBRENNER, U. 1979: *The ecology of human development.* Cambridge, MA: Harvard University Press.

BROPHY, J. 1983: Research on the self-fulfilling prophecy and teacher expectations. *Journal of Educational Psychology, 75,* 631–61.

— 1985: Teacher–student interaction. In Dusak, J. B. (ed.) *Teacher expectancies.* London: Erlbaum.

— 1986: Teacher influences on student behaviour. *American Psychologist, 41,*10, 1069–77.

— 1989a: Research on teacher effects: uses and abuses. *The Elementary School Journal, 9,* 1, 3–21.

— 1989b: Introduction to advances in education. In Brophy, J. (ed.) *Advances in research on teaching,* Vol 1. London: JAI Press.

BROPHY, J. and GOOD, T. 1986a: Teacher behavior and student achievement. In Wittrock, M. (ed.) *Handbook of research on teaching.* New York: Macmillan.

— 1986b: Naturalistic studies of teacher expectation effects. Reprinted in Hammersley, M. (ed.) *Case studies in classroom research.* Milton Keynes: Open University.

BROWN, A., BRANSFORD, J., FERRARA, R. and CAMPIONE, J. 1983: Learning, remembering, and understanding. In Flavell, J. and Markman, E. (eds) *Handbook of child psychology,* Vol. 3: *Cognitive development* (pp. 77–166). New York: Wiley.

BROWN, B. B. 1989: The role of peer groups in adolescents' adjustment to secondary school. In T. J. Berndt and G. W. Ladd (eds) *Peer relationships in child development.* New York; Chichester: Wiley.

—— 1990: Peer groups and cultures. In Feldman, S. S. and Elliott, G. R. (eds) *At the threshold: the developing adolescent.* Cambridge, MA: Harvard University Press.

BRUNER, J. S. 1972: The nature and uses of immaturity. *American Psychologist, 27,* 687–708.

BUKOWSKI, W. M. and HOZA, B. 1989: Popularity and friendship: issues in theory, measurement and outcome. In Berndt, T. J. and Ladd, G. W. (eds) *Peer relationships in child development.* New York: Wiley.

BUKOWSKI, W. M., NEWCOMB, A. F. and HARTUP, W. W. (eds) 1996: *The company they keep: friendships in childhood and adolescence.* Cambridge: Cambridge University Press.

BURGHARDT, G. 1988: Precocity, play, and the ectotherm–endotherm transition. In Blass, E. (ed.) *Handbook of behavioral neurobiology,* Vol. 9 (pp. 107–48). New York: Plenum.

BUS, A. G. and VAN IJZENDOORN, M. 1988: Mother–child interaction, attachment, and emergent literacy. *Child Development, 59,* 1262–72.

CAIRNS, R., CAIRNS, B., NECKERMAN, H., GEST, S. and GARIEPY, J-L. 1988: Social networks and aggressive behavior: peer support or peer rejection? *Developmental Psychology, 24,* 815–23.

CAMPOS, J. J., BARRETT, K. C., LAMB, M., GOLDSMITH, H. and STERNBERG, C. 1983: Socioemotional development. In Haith, M. and Campos, J. (eds) *Handbook of child psychology,* Vol. 2 (pp. 783–916). New York: Wiley.

CARPENTER, T. P. , BROWN, C., KOUBA, V., LINDQUIST, M. M., SILVER, E. A. and SWAFFORD, J. O. 1987: *Results from the fourth mathematical assessment of the National Assessment of Educational Progress.* Reston, VA: National Council of Teachers of Mathematics.

CARRAHER, T., CARRAHER, D. and SCHLIEMANN, A. 1985: Mathematics in the streets and in schools. *British Journal of Developmental Psychology, 3,* 21–9.

CAZDEN, C. 1972: The issue of structure. In Cazden, C. (ed.) *Language in early childhood education* (pp. 23–34). Washington, DC: National Association for Young Children.

—— 1986: Classrom discourse. In Wittrock, M. C. (ed.) *Handbook of research on teaching* (Third Edition), 432–63. New York: Macmillan.

CHAUVET, M-J. and BLATCHFORD, P. 1993: Group composition and National Curriculum assessment at 7 years. *Educational Research, 35,* 2, 189–96.

CHOMSKY, N. 1965: *Aspects of a theory of syntax.* Cambridge, MA: MIT Press.

CHRISTIE, J. (ed.). 1991: *Play and early literacy development.* Albany: State University of NY Press.

CHRISTIE, J. and JOHNSEN, P. 1983: The role of play in social–intellectual development. *Review of Educational Research, 53,* 93–115.

—— 1987: Preschool play. In Block, J. and King, N. (eds) *School play* (pp. 109–42). New York: Garland.

CIRCUS 1975: *A comprehensive program of assessment services for primary children.* Princeton: Educational Testing Service.

CLARK, M. 1976. *Young fluent readers.* London: Heinemann.

CLARKE-STEWART, K. A. 1973: Interactions between mothers and their young children: characteristics and consequences. *Monongraphs of the Society for Research in Child Development,* Serial No. 153, Vol. 38, Nos 6–7, December.

CLEAVE, S., JOWETT, S. and BATE, M. 1982: *. . . And so to school: a study of continuity from pre-school to infant school.* Windsor: NFER-Nelson.

COCHRAN, M. and RILEY, D. 1988: Mother reports of children's personal networks. In Salzinger, S., Antrobus, J. and Hammer, M. (eds) *Social networks of children, adolescents, and college students* (pp. 113–47). Hillsdale, NJ: Erlbaum.

COCHRAN, M. and WOOLEVER, F. 1983: Beyond the deficit model: The empowerment of parents with information and informal supports. In Sigel, I. and Laosa, L. (eds), *Changing families* (pp. 225–46). New York: Plenum.

COIE, J.D. and DODGE, K.A. 1998: Aggression and antisocial behaviour. In Eisenberg, N. (ed.) *Handbook of child psychology*, Vol. 3 (pp. 779–862). New York: Wiley.

COLE, M. and BRUNER, J. 1971: Cultural differences and inferences about psychological processes. *American Psychologist, 26,* 866–76.

COOK-GUMPERZ, J. 1977: Situated instructions: language socialization of school age children. In Ervin-Tripp, S. and Mitchell-Kernan, K. (eds) *Child discourse* (pp. 103–24). New York: Academic Press.

COOPER, H. M. 1979: Pygmalion grows up: a model for teacher expectation communication and performance influence. *Review of Educational Research, 49,* 389–410.

—— 1985: Models of teacher expectation communication. In Dusek, J. B. (ed.) *Teacher Expectancies,* 135–58. London: Erlbaum.

—— 1989: Does reducing student-to-instructor ratios affect achievement? *Educational Psychologist, 24,* 1, 79–98.

COOPER, P. and MCINTYRE, D. 1996: *Effective teaching and learning: teachers' and students' perspectives.* Milton Keynes: Open University Press.

COSTAS, M. A. 1998: The changing nature of educational research and critique of postmodernism. *Educational Researcher, 27,* 2, 26–33.

CRANO, W. D. and MELLON, D. M. 1978: Causal influence of teachers' expectations on children's academic performance: a crossed lagged panel analysis, *Journal of Educational Psychology, 70,* 39–49.

CRICK, N. R. 1996: The role of overt, relational aggression, and prosocial behavior in the prediction of children's future social adjustment. *Child Development, 67,* 2317–27.

CRICK, N. R., and GROPETER, J. K. 1995: Relational aggression, gender, and social-psychological adjustment. *Child Development, 54,* 1386–99.

CREEMERS, B. 1994: *The effective classroom.* London: Cassell.

CROLL, P. 1986: *Systematic classroom observation.* London: Falmer.

CROLL, P. and MOSES, D. 1990: Sex roles in the primary classroom. In Rogers, C. and Kutnick, P. (eds) *Social psychology of the primary school.* London: Routledge.

DARLEY, J .M. and FAZIO, R. H. 1980: Expectancy confirmation processes arising in the social interaction sequence. *American Psychologist, 35,* 867–81.

DAUNCEY, M. and JAMES, W. 1979: Assessment of heart rate method for determining energy expenditure in man, using a whole body calimeter. *British Journal of Nutrition, 42,* 1–13.

DAVIES, B, 1982: *Life in the classroom and the playground: the accounts of primary school children.* London: Routledge and Kegan Paul.

DE WAAL, F. B. M. 1985: The integration of dominance and social bonding in primates. *Quarterly Review of Biology, 61,* 459–79.

DELAMONT, S. 1983: *Interaction in the classroom* (Second Edition). London: Routledge.

DELAMONT, S. and HAMILTON, D. 1986: Revisiting classroom research: a continuing cautionary tale. In Hammersley, M. (ed.) *Controversies in classroom research.* Milton Keynes: Open University Press.

DEVRIES, R. 1997: Piaget's social theory. *Educational Researcher,* March, 4–17.

DODGE, K. 1991: The function and structure of reactive and proactive aggression. In Pepler, D. and Rubin, K.H. (eds) *The development and treatment of childhood aggression.* Hillsdale, NJ: Erlbaum.

DODGE, K. and COIE, J. 1989, April: *Bully–victim relationships in boys' play groups.* Paper presented at the biennial meetings of the Society for Research in Child Development, Kansas City.

DODGE, K., PETTIT, G., MCCLASKEY and BROWN, M. 1986: Social competence in children. *Monographs of the Society for Research in Child Development, 51, 2.*

DOISE, W. and MUGNY, G. 1984: *The social development of the intellect.* Oxford: Pergamon.

DOYLE, W. 1986: Classroom organization and management. In Wittrock, M. C. (ed.) *Handbook of research on teaching* (Third Edition). New York: Macmillan.

DOYLE, W. and CARTER, K. 1984: Academic tasks in the classroom. *Curriculum Inquiry, 14, 2,* 129–49.

DREEBEN, R. 1973: The school as a workplace. In Travers, R. M. W. (ed.) *Second handbook of research on teaching* (pp. 450–73). Chicago: Rand McNally.

—— 1984: First-grade reading groups: their formation and change. In Peterson, P., Wilkinson, L. and Hallinan, M. (eds) *The social context of instruction.* Orlando, Fla: Academic Press.

DUNBAR, R. 1988: *Primate social systems.* Ithaca, NY: Cornell.

—— 1993: Coevolution of neocortex size, group size, and language in humans. *Behavioral and Brain Sciences, 16,* 681–735.

DUNKIN, M. J. and BIDDLE, B. J. 1974: *The study of teaching.* Holt, Rinehart and Winston. Lanham, MD.

DUNN, J. 1988: *The beginning of social understanding.* Cambridge: Harvard University Press.

—— 1993: *Young children's close relationships: beyond attachment.* Newbury Park, CA: Sage.

DUNN, J. and SLOMKOWSKI, C. 1992: Conflict and the development of social understanding. In Shantz, C. U. and Hartup, W. W. (eds) *Conflict in child and adolescent development* (pp. 70–92). Cambridge: Cambridge University Press.

DURKIN, D. 1966: *Children who read early.* New York: Teachers College.

DUSEK, J. B. (ed.) 1985: Teacher expectancies. London: Erlbaum.

DUSEK, J. B and JOSEPH, G. 1985: The bases of teacher expectancies. In Dusek, J. B (ed.) *Teacher expectancies* (pp. 229–50). London: Erlbaum.

DWECK, C. 1986: Motivational processes affecting learning. *American Psychologist, 41,* 1040–8.

DWECK, C. S., DAVIDSON, W., NELSON, S. and ENNA, B. 1978: Sex differences in learned helplessness 11. The contingencies of evaluative feedback in the classroom: an experimental analysis. *Developmental Psychology, 124,* 268–76.

EATON, W. and ENNS, L. 1986: Sex differences in human motor activity level. *Psychological Bulletin, 100,* 19–28.

EATON, W. and YU, A. 1989: Are sex differences in child motor activity level a function of sex differences in maturational status? *Child Development, 60,* 1005–11.

EATON, W., ENNS, L. and PRESSE, M. 1987: Scheme for observing activity. *Journal of Psychoeducational Assessment, 3,* 273–80.

ECCLES, J. and WIGFIELD, A. 1985: Teacher expectations and student motivation. In Dusek, J. B. (ed.) *Teacher expectancies,* (pp. 185–226). London: Erlbaum.

ECCLES, J., MIDGLEY, C. and ADLER, T. F. 1984: Grade-related changes in the school environment: effects on achievement motivation. In *Advances in Motivation and Achievement,* Vol. 3 (pp. 283–331).

EGELAND, B., and SROUFE, L. 1981: Attachment and early maltreatment. *Child Development, 52,* 44–52.

EIFERMANN, R. 1970: Cooperativeness and egalitarianism in kibbutz children's games. *Human relations, 23,* 579–87.

—— 1971: Social play in childhood. In Herron, R. and Sutton-Smith, B. (eds) *Child's play* (pp. 270–97). New York: Wiley.

—— 1978: Games of physical activity. In Landry, F. and Orban, W. (eds) *Physical activity and human well being* (pp. 741–51). Miami: Symposium Specialists.

—— 1979: It's child's play. In Shears, L. and Bower, E. (eds) *Games in education and development* (pp. 75–102). Springfield, Il: Thomas.

ELARDO, R., BRADLEY, R. and CALDWELL, B. 1975: The relation of infants' home environments and mental test performance from six to thirty-six months: a longitudinal analysis. *Child Development, 46*, 71–6.

ELWOOD, J. 1994: Equity issues in performance assessment: undermining gender stereotypes: examination performance in the UK at 16. Paper to American Educational Research Association Annual Meeting, New Orleans.

EPSTEIN, J. L. 1989: The selection of friends: changes across the grades and the different school environments. In Berndt, T. J. and Ladd, G. W. (eds) *Peer Relationships in Child Development*. New York: Wiley.

ERICKSON, F. 1986: Qualitative methods in research on teaching. In Wittrock, M. (ed.) *Handbook of research on teaching* (Third Edition). New York: Macmillan.

ERWIN, P. 1993: *Friendship and peer relations in children*. Chichester: Wiley.

EVANS, J. 1989: *Children at play. Life in the school playground*. Geelong, Australia: Deakin University Press.

EVANS, J. and PELLEGRINI, A. D. 1997: Surplus energy theory: an endearing but inadequate justification for break time. *Educational Review, 49*, 229–36.

FAGEN, R. 1981: *Animal play behavior*. New York: Oxford University Press.

FANTUZZO, J.W., SUTTON-SMITH, B., COOLAHAN, K. C., MANZ, P., CANNING, S. and DEBNAM, D. 1995: Assessment of play interaction behaviors in low income children: Penn Interactive Play Scale. *Early Childhood Research Quarterly, 10*, 105–20.

FENNEMA, E. 1996: Scholarship, gender and mathematics. In Murphy, P. F. and Gipps, C. G. (eds) *Equity in the classroom: towards effective pedagogy for girls and boys*. London: Falmer and UNESCO.

FIELD, T. 1979: Games parents play with normal and high-risk infants. *Child Psychiatry and Human Development, 10*, 41–8.

FINN, J. D. 1996: Class size and students at risk: What is known? What next? Report prepared for The National Institute in the Education of At-Risk Students, Office of Educational Research and Improvement. U.S. Department of Education.

FINN, J. D. and VOELKL, K. E. 1992: Class size: an overview of research. Department of Counselling and Educational Psychology, Occasional Paper No. 92–1, State University of New York at Buffalo.

FINNAN, C. 1982: The ethnography of children's spontaneous play. In Spindler, G. (ed.) *Doing the ethnography of schooling* (pp. 355–81). New York: Holt, Rinehart and Winston.

FLANDERS, N. 1970: *Analyzing Teacher Behavior*. Reading, MA: Addison-Wesley.

FRENCH, J. and FRENCH, P. 1984: Gender imbalances in the primary classroom: an interactional account. *Educational Research, 26*, 2, 127–36.

FREUD, A. and DANN, S. 1951: An experiment in group upbringing. In Eissler, R., Freud, A., Hartmann, H. and Kris, E. (eds) *The psychoanalytic study of the child*, Vol. 6. New York: International Universities Press.

FULLER, M. 1984: Black girls in a London comprehensive school. In Hammersley, M. and Woods, P. (eds) *Life in school*. Milton Keynes: Open University.

FURMAN, W. 1989: The development of children's networks. In Belle, D. (ed.) *Children's social networks and social supports*. New York: Wiley.

GAGE, N. L. 1978: *The scientific basis of the art of teaching.* New York: Teachers College Press.

—— 1985: Hard gains in the soft sciences: The case of pedagogy. *A CEDR monograph for phi delta kappan.* Bloomington: Indiana.

—— 1989: The paradigm wars and their aftermath: a historical sketch of research on teaching since 1989. *Educational Researcher, 18,* 7, 4–10.

GALDA, L., PELLEGRINI, A. D. and COX, S. 1989: A short-term longitudinal study of preschoolers' emergent literacy. *Research in the Teaching of English, 23,* 292–309.

GALTON, M. (ed.) 1978: *British mirrors: a collection of classroom observation instruments.* Leicester University, School of Education.

—— 1987: Structured observation. In Dunkin, M. (ed.) *International encyclopaedia of teaching and teacher observation.* London: Pergamon.

—— 1990: Grouping and group-work. In Rogers, C. and Kutnick, P. (eds) *Social psychology of the primary school.* London: Routledge.

—— 1998: Back to consulting the ORACLE, *TES* 3 July.

GALTON, M. and SIMON, B. 1980: *Progress and performance in the primary school.* London: Routledge and Kegan Paul.

GALTON, M. and WILLIAMSON, J. 1992: *Group-work in the primary school.* London: Routledge.

GALTON, M., HARGREAVES, L. and PELL, A. 1996: *Class size, teaching and pupil achievement.* Leicester University/ NUT.

GALTON, M., SIMON, B. and CROLL, B. 1980: *Inside the Primary Classroom.* London: Routledge and Kegan Paul.

GARDNER, H. 1985: *Frames of mind.* New York: Basic Books.

GARVEY, C. 1977: *Play.* Cambridge: Harvard.

GELMAN, R. and GALLISTEL, C. R. 1978: *The child's understanding of number.* Cambridge: Harvard University Press.

GINSBURG, H. and RUSSELL, R. 1981: Social class and racial influences on early mathematical thinking. *Monographs for the society of child development* (Serial No. 193), *46,* 6.

GLASS, G., CAHEN, L., SMITH, M. L. and FILBY, N. 1982: *School class size.* Beverley Hills, CA: Sage.

GOLDSTEIN, H. 1995: *Multilevel statistical models.* London: Edward Arnold.

GOLDSTEIN, H. and BLATCHFORD, P. 1998: Class size and educational achievement: a review of methodology with particular reference to study design. *British Educational Research Journal, 24,* 3.

GOTTLIEB, B. (ed.) 1981: *Social networks and social support.* Beverly Hills: Sage.

GROOS, K. 1901: *The play of man.* New York: Appleton.

GUMP, P. 1967: *The classroom behavior setting: its nature and relation to student behavior.* (Final Report) Washington DC: US Office of Education, Bureau of Research. (ERIC Document Reproduction Service No. ED 015 515).

—— 1974: Operating environments in schools of open and traditional design. *School Review, 82,* 4, 575–93.

GUMPERZ, J. 1986: Interactional sociolinguistics in the study of schooling. In J. University Press.

HALL, V. C. and MERKEL, S. P. 1985: Teacher expectancy effects and educational psychology. In Dusek, J. B. (ed.) *Teacher Expectancies.* London: Erlbaum.

HALLIDAY, M. and HASAN, R. 1976: *Cohesion in English.* London: Longmans.

HALLINAN, M. 1981: Recent advances in sociometry. In Asher, S. and Gottman, J. (eds) *The development of children's friendships* (pp. 91–115). New York: Cambridge University Press.

HARGREAVES, D. H. 1967: *Social relations in a secondary school*. London: Routledge.

HARGREAVES, D. H., HESTOR, S. K. and MELLOR, F. J. 1986: A theory of typing. In Hammersley, M. (ed.) *Case studies in classroom research* (pp. 180–209). Milton Keynes: Open University.

—— 1975: *Deviance in classrooms*. Boston: Routledge and Kegan Paul.

HARLOW, H. 1962: The heterosexual affection system in monkeys. *American Psychologist, 17,* 1–9.

—— 1965: Age-mate or peer effection a system. In Lehrman, D. S. (ed.) *Advances in the Study of Behaviour,* Vol. 2. New York: Academic Press.

—— 1969: Age-mate or peer affectional system. In Lehrman, D. S. (ed.) *Advances in the study of Behaviour,* Vol. 2. New York: Academic Press.

HARLOW, H. and HARLOW, M. 1962: Social deprivation in monkeys. *Scientific American, 207,* 5, 136.

—— 1965: Effects of various mother–infant relationships on Rhesus monkey behaviours. In Foss, B. M. (ed.) *Determinants of infant behaviour IV*. London: Methuen.

HARMAN, D. 1970: Illiteracy: an overview. *Harvard Educational Review, 40,* 226–43.

HARPER, L. and SANDERS, K. 1975: Preschool children's use of space: sex differences in outdoor play. *Developmental Psychology, 11,* 119.

HARRIS, S., NIXON, J. and RUDDOCK, J. 1993: Schoolwork, homework and gender. *Gender and Education, 3,* 3–14.

HARTUP, W. 1983: Peer relations. In E. M. Hetherington (ed.) *Handbook of child psychology,* Vol. 4. New York: Wiley.

—— 1989: Behavioral manifestations of children's friendships. In Berndt, T. J. and Ladd, G. W. (eds) *Peer relationships in child development*. New York: Wiley.

—— 1992: Friendships and their developmental significance. In McGurk, H. (ed.) *Childhood social development: contemporary perspectives*. Hove: Lawrence Erlbaum Associates.

—— 1996: The company they keep: friendships and their developmental significance. *Child Development, 67,* 1–13.

HEATH, S. B. 1982: Questioning at home and at school: a comparative study. In Spindler, G. (ed.) *Doing the ethnography of schooling: educational anthroplogy in action*. New York: Holt, Rinehart and Winston.

—— 1983: *Ways with words*. New York: Cambridge University Press.

—— 1989: Oral and literate traditions of black Americans living in poverty. *American Psychologist, 44,* 376–3.

HESS, R. D. and SHIPMAN, V. C. 1965: Early experience and the socialization of cognitive modes in children. *Child Development, 36,* 869–86.

HETHERINGTON, E. and PARKE, R. 1979: *Child psychology*. New York: McGraw-Hill.

HINDE, R. 1976: On describing relationships. *Journal of Child Psychology and Psychiatry, 17,* 1–19.

—— 1983: Ethology and child development. In Campos, J. and Haith, M. (eds) *Handbook of child psychology*. Vol. 1 (pp. 27–94). New York: Wiley.

HOVELL, M., BURSICK, J., SHARKEY, R. and MCCLURE, J. 1978: An evaluation of elementary students' voluntary physical activity during recess. *Research Quarterly for Exercise and Sport, 69,* 460–74.

HOWE, C. J. 1997: *Gender and classroom interaction: a research review*. Edinburgh: The Scottish Council for Research in Education.

HOWE, C. J., TOLMIE, A. and RODGERS, C. 1992: The acquisition of conceptual knowledge in science by primary school children: group interaction and the understanding of motion down an inclined plane. *British Journal of Developmental Psychology, 10,* 113–30.

HUMPHREY, N. 1976: The social function of intellect. In Bateson, P. and Hinde, R. (eds) *Growing points in ethology* (pp. 303–17). Cambridge: Cambridge University Press.

HUMPHREYS, A. and SMITH, P. K. 1984: Rough-and-tumble in preschool on a playground. In Smith, P. K. (ed.) *Play in animals and humans* (pp. 291–370). London: Blackwell.

—— 1987: Rough-and-tumble play, friendship and dominance in school children: evidence for continuity and change with age. *Child Development, 58,* 201–12.

HUTT, S. J. and HUTT, C. 1970: *Direct observation and measurement of behaviour.* Springfield, Illinois: Charles C. Thomas.

HYMES, D. 1967: Models of the interaction of language and social setting. *Journal of Social Issues, 23,* 8–28.

JACKSON, P. 1968: *Life in classrooms.* New York: Holt, Rinehart and Winston.

JOHNSON, D. and JOHNSON, R. 1987: *Learning together and alone.* Englewood Cliffs: Prentice-Hall.

JOHNSON, M. 1935: The effect on behavior of variation in the amount of play equipment. *Child Development, 6,* 56–68.

JOLLY, A. 1966: Lemur social behavior and primate intelligence. *Science, 153,* 501–6.

JONES, I. and PELLEGRINI, A. 1996: First graders' computer assisted writing: Metacogntive and linguistic effects. *American Educational Research Journal, 33,* 691–718.

JUSSIM, L. 1986: Self-fulfilling prophecies: a theoretical and integrative review. *Psychological Review, 93,* 4, 429–45.

KAGAN, J. 1971: *Change and continuity in infancy.* New York: Wiley.

—— 1980. Perspectives on continuity. In Brim, O. and Kagan, J. (eds) *Constancy and change across the life span* (pp. 26–74). Cambridge, MA: Harvard University Press.

KEDDIE, N. 1971: Classroom knowledge. In Young, M. F. D. (ed.) *Knowledge and control.* London: Collier Macmillan.

KELLY, A. 1988: Gender differences in teacher–pupil interactions: a meta-analytic review. *Research in Education, 39,* 1–23.

KING, N. 1979: Play: The kindergartners' perspective. *Elementary School Journal, 80,* 81–7.

—— 1987: Elementary school play: theory and research. In Block, J. and King, N. (eds) *School play* (pp. 143–66). New York: Garland.

KLEIN, A. and STARKLEY, P. 1988: Universals in the development of early arithmetic cognition. In Saxe, G. and Gearhart, M. (eds) *Children's mathematics* (pp. 5–26). San Francisco: Jossey-Bass.

KLEIN, K. 1985: The research on class size. *Phi Delta Kappan, 66,* 578–80.

KOUNIN, J. 1970: *Discipline and group management in classrooms.* New York: Holt, Rinehart and Winston.

KOZOL, J. 1991: *Savage inequalities.* New York: Crown.

KRASNOR, L. and PEPLER, D. 1980: The study of children's play: some future directions. In Rubin, K. (ed.) *Child's play* (pp. 85–96). San Francisco: Jossey-Bass.

LABORATORY OF COMPARATIVE HUMAN COGNITION. 1983: Culture and cognitive development. In Kessen, W. (ed.) *Handbook of child psychology,* Vol. 1, *History, theory, and methods* (pp. 295–356). New York: Wiley.

LADD, G. 1983: Social networks of popular, average, and rejected children in school settings. *Merrill-Palmer Quarterly, 29,* 283–307.

LADD, G. W., KOCHENDERFER, B. J. and COLEMAN, C. C. 1996: Friendship quality as a predictor of young children's early school adjustment. *Child Development*, *67*, 1103–18.

LAGERSPETZ, K. M., BJORKQUIST, K. and PELTONEN, T. 1988: Is indirect aggression more typical of females? *Aggressive Behavior*, *14*, 403–14.

LAVE, J. 1988: *Cognition in practice*. Cambridge: Cambridge University Press.

LENNEBERG, E. 1966: *The biological foundation of language*. New York: Wiley.

LEONT'EV, A. 1978: *Activity, consciousness, and personality*. Englewood Cliffs, NJ: Prentice Hall.

LEVER, J. 1976: Sex differences in the games children play. *Social Problems*, *23*, 478–87.

LISS, M. 1983: Learning gender-related skills through play. In Liss, M. (ed.) *Social and cognitive skills* (pp. 147–66). New York: Academic.

LOEBER, R. and DISHION, T.J. 1984: Boys who fight at home and school: family conditions influencing cross-setting consistency. *Journal of Consulting and Clinical Psychology*, *52*, 759–68.

MACAULAY, D. J. 1990: *Educational Psychology*, *10*, 3, 239–53.

MACCOBY, E. and JACKLIN, C. 1987: Gender segregation in childhood. In Reese, H. (ed.) *Advances in child development and behavior* (pp. 239–87). New York: Academic.

MACCOBY, E. and MARTIN, J. 1983: Socialization in the context of the family: parent–child interaction. In Hetherington, E. M. (ed.) *Handbook of child psychology*, Vol IV. New York: Wiley.

MAIN, M., KAPLAN, N. and CASSIDY, J. 1985: Security in infancy, childhood and adulthood: a move to the level of representation. In Bretherton, I. and Waters, E. (eds) Growing points of attachment theory and research. *Monographs of the Society of Research in Child Development*, *50*, 41–65.

MARTIN, P. and BATESON, P. 1988: *Measuring behaviour*. London: Cambridge University Press.

MARTIN, P. and CARO, T. 1985: On the functions of play and its role in behavioral development. In Rosenblatt, J., Beer, C., Busnel, M.C. and Slater, P. (eds) *Advances in the study of behavior*, Vol. 15 (pp. 59–103). New York: Academic.

MARTIN, R. 1988. Child temperament and educational outcomes. In Pellegrini, A.D. (ed.) *Psychological bases for early education* (pp. 185–206). Chichester: Wiley.

MAXWELL, W. 1990: The nature of friendship in the primary school. In Rogers, C. and Kutnick P. (eds) *The social psychology of the primary school*. London: Routledge.

MCGILLICUDDY-DELISI, A. 1982: The relationship between parents' beliefs about development and family constellations: Socioeconomic status and parents' teaching strategies. In Laosa, L. and Sigel, I. (eds) *Families as learning environments for children* (pp. 361–400). New York: Plenum.

MCGREW, W. 1972a: *An ethological study of children's behavior*. New York: Academic Press.

—— 1972b: Aspects of social development in nursery school children with emphasis on introduction to the group. In Blurton Jones, N. (ed.) *Ethological studies of child behavior* (pp. 129–56). London: Cambridge University Press.

MCINTYRE, D. and MACLEOD, G. 1986: The characteristics and uses of systematic observation. In Hammersley, M. (ed.) *Controversies in classroom research*. Milton Keynes: Open University Press.

MCLOYD, V. 1980: Verbally expressed modes of transformation in the fantasy and play of black preschool children. *Child Development*, *51*, 1133–9.

—— 1982: Social class differences in social dramatic play: a critique. *Developmental Review*, *2*, 1–30.

MEANEY, M., STEWART, J. and BEATTY, W. 1985: Sex differences in social play. In Rosenblatt, J., Beer, C., Bushnell, M-C. and Slater, P. (eds) *Advances in the study of behavior,* Vol. 15 (pp. 2–57). New York: Academic.

MEDLEY, D. and MITZEL, H. 1963: Measuring classroom behavior by systematic observation. In Gage, N. L. (ed.) *Handbook of research on teaching.* Chicago: Rand McNally.

MEECE, J. L. and COURTNEY, D. P. 1992: Gender differences in students' perceptions: consequences for achievement-related choices. In Schunk, D. H. and Meece, J. L. (eds) *Student perceptions in the classroom.* Hillsdale, New Jersey: Lawrence Erlbaum Associates.

MEHAN, H. 1979: *Learning lessons: social oganization in a classroom.* Cambridge, MA: Harvard University Press.

MERRITT, F. and WHELDALL, K. 1992: Teachers' use of praise and reprimands to boys and girls. *Educational Review, 44,* 1, 73–9.

MINUCHIN, P. and SHAPIRO, E. 1983: The school as a context for social development. In Hetherington, E. M. (ed.) *Manual of child psychology,* Vol. 4 (pp. 197–274). New York: Wiley.

MIRACLE, A. 1987: Anthropological and sociological perspectives on school play. In Block, J. and King, N. (eds) *School play* (pp. 39–74). New York: Garland.

MIRZA, H. 1992: *Young, female and black.* London: Routledge.

MITCHELL, D. E., BEACH, S. A. and BADURUK, G. 1991: *Modelling the relationship between achievement and class size: a re-analysis of the Tennessee project STAR data.* Riverside, CA: California Educational Research Co-operative.

MORTIMORE, P. , SAMMONS, P. , STIOLL, L. and ECOB, R. 1988: *School matters: the junior years.* Wells: Open Books.

MOSTELLER, F. 1995: The Tennessee study of class size in the early grades. *The Future of Children - Critical Issues for Children and Youths, 5,* 2, Summer/Fall, 113–27.

MUELLER, E. 1972: The maintenance of verbal exchanges between young children. *Child Development, 43,* 930–8.

MUELLER, E. and BRENNER, J. 1977: The origins of social skills and interaction among play group toddlers. *Child Development, 48,* 854–61.

MUELLER, E. and LUCAS, T. 1975: A developmental analysis of peer interaction among toddlers. In Lewis, M. and Rosenblum, L. (eds) *Friendship and peer relations.* New York: Wiley.

MUELLER, E. and RICH, A. 1976: Clustering and socially-directed behaviors in a play-group of 1 year-old boys. *Journal of Child Psychology and Psychiatry, 17,* 315–22.

NATIONAL CENTER FOR EDUCATIONAL STATISTICS 1995 (October): *Student victimization at school.* Washington, DC: US Department of Education.

NATIONAL COMMISSION ON EDUCATION 1996: *Success against the odds: effective schools in disadvantaged areas.* London: Routledge.

NEWCOMB, A. F. and BAGWELL, C. L. 1995: Children's friendship relations: a meta-analytic review. *Psychological Bulletin, 117,* 306–47.

—— 1996: The developmental significance of children's friendship relations. In Bukowski, W. M., Newcomb, A. F. and Hartup, W. W. (eds) *The company they keep: friendships in childhood and adolescence.* Cambridge: Cambridge University Press.

NINIO, A. and BRUNER, J. 1978: The achievement and antecedents of labeling. *Journal of Child Language, 5,* 1–15.

NORMAN, D. A. 1978: Notes towards a complex theory of learning. In Lesgold, A. M. (ed.) *Cognitive psychology and instruction.* New York: Plenum.

NYE, B. A., ACHILLES, C. M., ZAHARIAS, J. B., FULTON, B. D. and WAL-LENHORST, M. P. 1992: *Small is far better*. Paper presented at Mid-South Educational Research Association, Knoxville, Tennessee.

OFSTED 1995: *Class size and the quality of education*. London: HMSO.

—— 1998: The annual report of Her Majesty's Chief Inspector of Schools, standards and quality in education 1996/97. London: HMSO.

OGBU, J. 1988: Culture, development, and education. In Pellegrini, A. D. (ed.) *Psychological bases for early education* (pp. 245–74). Chichester: Wiley.

OLWEUS, D. 1978: *Aggression in schools*. Washington, DC: Hemisphere.

—— 1979: Stability and aggressive reaction patterns in males: a review. *Psychological Bulletin*, *86*, 852–75.

—— 1991: Bully–victim problems among school children: Basic facts and effects of a school based intervention program. In K. Rubin and D. Pepler (eds) *The development and treatment of childhood aggression*. Hillsdale, NJ: Erlbaum.

—— 1993a: Bullies on the playground. In C. Hart (ed.) *Children on playgrounds* (pp. 85–128). Albany, NY: SUNY Press.

—— 1993b: *Bullying at school*. Cambridge, MA: Blackwell.

OPIE, I. and OPIE, P. 1959. *The lore and language of school children*. Oxford: Oxford University Press.

—— 1969: *Children's games in street and playground*. Oxford: Oxford University Press.

—— 1985: *The singing games*. Oxford: Oxford University Press.

PARKE, R., CASSIDY, J., CARSON, J. and BOYUM, L. 1992: Familial contributions to peer competence among young children: the role of interactive and affective processes. In Parke, R. and Ladd, G. (eds) *Family–peer relationships* (pp. 107–34). Hillsdale, NJ: Erlbaum.

PARKER, J. G. and ASHER, S. R. 1987: Peer relations and later personal adjustment: are low-accepted children at risk? *Psychological Bulletin*, *102*, 3, 357–89.

PARKER, J. G. and GOTTMAN, J. M. 1989: Social and emotional development in a relational context: friendship interaction from early childhood to adolescence. In Berndt, T. J. and Ladd, G. W. (eds) *Peer relationships in child development*. New York: Wiley.

PARROTT, S. 1975: Games children play: ethnography of a second grade recess. In Spradley, J. and McCardy, D. (eds) *The cultural experience* (pp. 207–19). Palo Alto, CA: SRA.

PARTEN, M. 1932: Social participation among preschool children. *Journal of Abnormal and Social Psychology*, *27*, 243–69.

PATE-BAIN, H., ACHILLES, C. M., BOYD-ZAHARIAS, J. and MCKENNA, B. 1992: Class size makes a difference. *Phi Delta Kappan*, *74*, 3, 253–6.

PATTERSON, G., LITTMAN, R. and BRICKER, W. 1967: Assertive behavior in children: a step toward a theory of aggression. *Monographs of the Society for Research in Child Development*, *35*, 5, Serial No. 113.

PELLEGRINI, A. 1980: The relationship between preschoolers' play and achievement in prereading, language, and writing. *Psychology in the Schools*, *17*, 530–5.

—— 1984a: The social-cognitive ecology of preschool classrooms. *International Journal of Behavioral Development*, *7*, 321–32.

—— 1984b: Identifying causal elements in the thematic–fantasy play paradigm. *American Educational Research Journal*, *21*, 691–702.

—— 1985: The relations between symbolic play and literate behavior: a review of the empirical literature. *Review of Educational Research*, *55*, 207–21.

—— 1987a: The effects of play context on the development of young children's verbalized fantasy. *Semiotica*, *65*, 285–93.

—— 1987b: Rough-and-tumble play: developmental and education significance. *Educational Psychologist*, *22*, 22–43.

—— 1988: Elementary school children's rough-and-tumble play and social competence. *Developmental Psychology*, *24*, 802–6.

—— 1989a: Elementary school children's rough-and-tumble play. *Early Childhood Research Quarterly*, *4*, 245–60.

—— 1989b: What is a category? The case of rough-and-tumble play. *Ethology and Sociobiology*, *10*, 331–41.

—— 1991: A longitudinal study of popular and rejected children's rough-and-tumble play. *Early Education and Development*, *3*, 205–13.

—— 1992a: Preference for outdoor play during early adolescence. *Journal of Adolescence*, *15*, 241–54.

—— 1992b: Ethological studies of the categorization of children's social behavior: A review. *Early Education and Development*, *3*, 284–97.

—— 1995a: A longitudinal study of adolescent boys' rough-and-tumble play and dominance during early adolescence. *Journal of Applied Developmental Psychology*, *16*, 77–93.

—— 1995b: *School recess and playground behaviour: educational and developmental roles.* Albany, New York: State University of New York Press.

—— 1996: *Observing children in their natural worlds: a methodological primer.* Mahwah, NJ: Erlbaum.

PELLEGRINI, A. D. and GALDA, L. 1993. Ten years after: a re-examination of the symbolic play and literacy research. *Reading Research Quarterly*, *28*, 163–75.

PELLEGRINI, A. D. and HORVAT, M. 1995: A developmental contextual critique of attention deficit hyperactivity disorder. *Educational Researcher*, *24*, 13–19.

PELLEGRINI, A. D. and HUBERTY, P. 1993: Confinement effects on playground and classroom behavior. *British Journal of Educational Psychology*, *63*, 88–95.

PELLEGRINI, A. and PERLMUTTER, J. 1989a: Classroom contextual effects on children's play. *Developmental Psychology*, *25*, 289–96.

—— 1989b: Confinement effects on playground and classroom behavior. *British Journal of Educational Psychology*.

PELLEGRINI, A. D. and SMITH, P. K. 1993: School recess implications for education and development. *Review of Educational Research*, *63*, 2, 651–71.

—— 1998: Physical activity play: the nature and function of a neglected aspect of play. *Child Development*, *69*, 577–98.

PELLEGRINI, A. D. and STANIC, G. M. A. 1993: Locating children's mathematical competence: application of the developmental niche. *Journal of Applied Developmental Psychology*, *14*, 501–20.

PELLEGRINI, A. D., BARTINI, M. and BROOKS, F. 1999: School bullies, victims, and aggressive victims: factors relating to group affiliation and victimization. *Journal of Education Psychology*, *91*, 216–27.

PELLEGRINI, A. D., BRODY, G. and SIGEL, I. 1985: Parents' book reading habits with their child. *Journal of Educational Psychology*, *77*, 332–40.

PELLEGRINI, A. D., GALDA, L., BARTINI, M. and CHARAK, D. 1998: Oral language and literacy learning in context: the role of social relationships. *Merrill-Palmer Quarterly*, *44*, 38–54.

PELLEGRINI, A. D., GALDA, L. and FLOR, D. 1997: Relationships, individual differences, and children's use of literate language. *British Journal of Educational Psychology*, *67*, 139–52.

PELLEGRINI, A. D., GALDA, L., JONES, I. and PERLMUTTER, J.C. 1995b: Joint reading between mothers and their Head Start children: vocabulary learning in two text formats. *Discourse Processes*, *19*, 441–63.

PELLEGRINI, A. D., GALDA, L. and RUBIN, D. 1984: Context in text: the development of oral and written language in two genres. *Child Development, 55,* 1549–55.

PELLEGRINI, A. D., GALDA, L., STAHL, S. and SHOCKLEY, B. 1995c: The nexus of social and literacy experiences at home and school: implications for primary school oral language and literacy. *British Journal of Educational Psychology, 65,* 273–85.

PELLEGRINI, A. D., HUBERTY, P. D. and JONES, I. 1995a: The effects of recess timing on classroom and playground behavior. *American Educational Research Journal, 32,* 854–64.

PELLEGRINI, A. D., PERLMUTTER, J., GALDA, L. and BRODY, G. 1990: Joint reading between black Head Start children and their mothers. *Child Development, 61,* 443–53.

PELLEGRINI, D., MASTEN, A., GARMEZY, N. and FERRARESE, M. 1987: Correlations of social competence in middle childhood. *Journal of Child Psychology and Psychiatry, 28,* 699–714.

PEPLER, D. J. and CRAIG, W. M. 1995: A peek behind the fence: naturalistic observations of aggressive children with remote audiovisual recording. *Developmental Psychology, 31,* 548–53.

PEPLER, D. J., CRAIG, W. and ROBERTS, W. 1993, March: *Aggression on the playground: a normative behavior.* Paper presented at the biennial meetings of the Society for Research in Child Development, New Orleans.

PERRY, D., WILLARD, J. and PERRY, L. 1990: Peers' perceptions of the consequences that victimized children provide aggressors. *Child Development, 61,* 1289–309.

PETERSON, P. L. and BARGER, S. A. 1985: Attribution theory and teacher expectancy. In Dusek, J. B. (ed.) *Teacher Expectancies* (pp. 159–84). London: Erlbaum.

PHILLIPS, S. U. 1972: Participant structured and communicative competence: Warm Springs children in community and classrooms. In Cazden, C. B., Johns, V. P. and Hymes, D. (eds) *Functions of language in the classroom.* New York: Teachers College Press, Columbia University.

PIAGET, J. 1932: *Play, dreams, and imitation.* New York: Norton.

—— 1962: *Play, dreams, and imitation.* New York: Norton.

—— 1970: Piaget's theory. In P. Mussen (ed.) *Carmichael's manual of child psychology,* Vol. 1. New York: Wiley.

PIDGEON, D. 1970: *Expectation and pupil performance.* Slough: NFER.

PINTRICH, P. R. and SCHUNK, D. H. 1996: *Motivation in education: theory, research and applications.* Englewood Cliffs, NJ: Prentice-Hall.

POLGAR, S. 1976: The social context of games. *Sociology of Education, 49,* 265–71.

POWNEY, J. 1996: *Gender and attainment: a review.* Edinburgh: Scottish Council for Research in Education (SCRE).

PRAIS, S. J. 1996: Class size and learning: the Tennessee experiment – what follows? *Oxford Review of Education, 22,* 399–414.

RAMSEY, P. G. 1991: *Making friends in school: promoting peer relationships in early childhood.* New York: Teachers College Press.

RESNICK, L. 1989: Developing mathematical knowledge. *American Psychologist, 44,* 162–9.

REYES, L. H. and STANIC, G. M. A. 1988: Race, sex, socioeconomic status, and mathematics. *Journal for Research in Mathematics Education, 19,* 26–43.

RIST, R. 1970: Student social class and teacher expectations: the self-fulfilling prophecy in ghetto education. *Harvard Education Review, 40,* 411–51.

ROBINSON, G. E. and WITTEBOLS, J. H. 1986: *Class size research: a related cluster analysis for decision making.* Arlington: VA Educational Research Service.

ROFFEY, S., TARRANT, T. and MAJORS, K. 1994: *Young friends: schools and friendship.* London: Cassell.

ROGERS, C. 1982: *A social psychology of schooling: the expectancy process.* London: Routledge and Kegan Paul.

—— 1998: Teacher expectations: implications for school improvement. In Shorricks-Taylor, D. (ed.) *Directions in educational psychology.* London: Whurr Publishers.

ROGOFF, B. 1990: *Apprenticeship in thinking: cognitive development in social context.* New York: Oxford University Press.

—— 1991 (Winter): US children and their families: current conditions and recent trends. *SRCD Newsletter,* pp. 1–3.

ROSENFIELD, P., LAMBERT, N. and BLACK, A. 1985: Desk arrangement effects on pupil classroom behaviour. *Journal of Educational Psychology, 77,* 101–8.

ROSENTHAL, R. 1987: Pygmalion effects: existence, magnitude and social importance. *Educational Researcher* (December), 37–41.

ROSENTHAL, R. and JACOBSON, L. 1968: *Pygmalion in the classroom: teacher expectation and pupils' intellectual development.* New York: Holt, Rinehart and Winston.

ROSS, L. and NESBETT, R. E. 1991: *The person and the situation: perspectives of social psychology.* New York: MacGraw-Hill.

ROWE, K. J. 1995: Factors affecting students' progress in reading: key findings from a longitudinal study. *Literacy, Teaching and Learning, 1,* 2, 57–110.

RUBENSTEIN, J. and HOWES, C.(1976): The effects of peers on toddler interaction with mothers and toys. *Child Development, 47,* 597–605.

RUBIN, K. and DANIELS-BEIRNESS, T. 1983: Concurrent and predictive correlates of sociometric status in kindergarten and first grade. *Merrill-Palmer Quarterly, 29,* 337–51.

RUBIN, K. and MAIONI, T. 1975: Play preference and its relationship to egocentrism, popularity, and classification skills in preschoolers. *Merrill-Palmer Quarterly, 21,* 171–9.

RUBIN, K. H., FEIN, G. G. and VANDENBERG, B. 1983: Play. In E. M. Hetherington (ed.) *Handbook of child psychology.* Vol. 4. *Socialization, personality, and social development* (pp. 693–774). New York: Wiley.

RUDDOCK, J. CHAPLAIN, R. and WALLACE, G. 1996: *School improvement: what can pupils tell us?* London: Fulton.

RUSSELL, A. 1985: *An observational study of the effects of staff–child ratios on staff and child behaviour in S.A. Kindergartens.* Report to Kindergarten Union of South Australia. Adelaide: South Australian Government Printer.

SANDMAN, C. and KASTIN, A. 1977: Pituitary peptide influences on attention and memory. In Drucker-Colin, R. and McGough, J. (eds) *Neurobiology of sleep and memory* (pp. 347–60). New York: Academic.

SAVIN-WILLIAMS, R. C. and BERNDT, T. J. 1990: Friendship and peer relations. In Feldman, S. S. and Elliott, G. R. (eds) *At the threshold: the developing adolescent.* Cambridge, MA: Harvard University Press.

SAXE, G. 1991: *Culture and cognitive development: Studies in mathematical understanding.* Hillsdale, NJ: Erlbaum.

SAXE, G., GUBERMAN, S. and GEARHART, M. 1987: Social process in early number development. *Monographs of the Society for Child Development* (Serial No. 216), *52,* 2.

SCHIEFFELIN, B. and COCHRAN-SMITH, M. 1982: Learning to read culturally: Literacy before schooling. In Goelman, H., Oberg, A. and Smith, F. (eds) *Awakening to literacy* (pp. 3–23). Exeter, NH: Heinemann.

SCHMUCK, R. A. and SCHMUCK, P. A. 1983 (Fourth Edition): *Group processes in the classroom*. Dubuque, Iowa: Wm. C. Brown.

SCHWARTZ, D. 1993 (March): *Antecedents of aggression and peer victimization: a prospective study*. Paper presented at the biennial meetings of the Society for research in Child Development, New Orleans.

SCHWARTZ, D., DODGE, K.A., and COIE, J. D. 1993: The emergence of chronic peer victimization in boys' play groups. *Child Development, 64*, 1755–72 .

SCHWARTZ, D., DODGE, K. A., PETIT, G. S. and BATES, J. E. 1997: The early socialization and adjustment of aggressive victims of bullying. *Child Development, 68*, 1755–72.

SCHWARTZ, J. 1972: Effects of peer familiarity on the behavior of preschoolers in a novel situation. *Journal of Personality and Social Psychology, 24*, 1276–84.

SCHWARTZMANN, H. 1978: *Transformations: the anthropology of children's play*. New York: Plenum.

SCRIBNER, S. and COLE, M. 1973: Cognitive consequences of formal and informal education. *Science, 182*, 553–9.

—— 1978: Literacy without schooling. *Harvard Educational Review, 48*, 448–61.

SELMAN, R. 1980: *The growth of interpersonal understanding: developmental and clinical analyses*. New York: Academic Press.

SERBIN, L., ZELKOWITZ, P. , DOYLE, A. and GOLD, D. 1990: The socialization of sex-differentiated skills and academic performance. *Sex Roles, 23*, 613–28.

SHAPIN, S. 1992: A magician's cloak cast off for clarity. *The Times Higher Educational Supplement, 1006*, 14 February.

SHAPSON, S. M., WRIGHT, E. N., EASON, G. and FITZGERALD, J. 1980: An experimental study of the effects of class size. *American Educational Research Journal, 17*, 144–52.

SHARP, R. and GREEN, A. 1975: *Education and social control: a study in progressive primary education*. London: Routledge and Kegan Paul.

SHULMAN, L. S. 1986: Paradigms and research programs in the study of teaching. In Wittrock, M. C. (ed.) *Handbook of research on teaching* (Third Edition). New York: Macmillan.

SIGEL, I. 1982: The relationship between distancing strategies and children's cognitive behavior. In L. Laosa and I. Sigel (eds) *Families as learning environments for young children*. New York: Plenum.

SIGEL, I., MCGILLICUDDY-DELISI, A., FLAUGHTER, J. and ROCK, D. 1983: *Parents as teachers of their children* (Final Report). Washington, DC: US Department of Education.

SIMON, A. and BOYER, E. G. (eds) 1970: Mirrors for Behaviour II: an anthology of observational instruments. *Classroom Interaction Newsletter*, special edition.

SINCLAIR, J. McH. and COULTHARD, R. M. 1975: *Towards an analysis of discourse: the English used by teachers and pupils*. London: Oxford University Press.

SLADE, A. 1987: Quality of attachment and early symbolic play. *Developmental Psychology, 23*, 78–85.

SLAVIN, R. E. 1989: Class size and student achievement: Small effects of small classes. *Educational Psychologist, 24*, 99–110.

—— 1990a: Class size and student achievement: is smaller better? *Contemporary Education, 62*, 6–12.

—— 1990b: Co-operative Learning. In Rogers, C. and Kutnick, P (eds) *The social psychology of the primary school*. London: Routledge.

SLUCKIN, A. 1981: *Growing up in the playground*. London: Routledge.

SLUCKIN, A. and SMITH, P. K. 1977: Two approaches to the concept of dominance in preschool children. *Child Development*, 4, 917–23.

SMITH, A. B., MCMILLAN, B. W., KENNEDY, S. and RATCLIFFE, B. 1989: The effect of improving preschool teacher/child ratios: 'an experiment in nature'. *Early Child Development and Care*, 41, 123–38.

SMITH, P. K. 1982: Does play matter? Functions and evolutionary aspects of animal and human play. *The Behavioral and Brain Sciences*, 5, 139–84.

—— 1988: Children's play and its role in early development: A re-evaluation of the 'Play ethos'. In Pellegrini, A. D. (ed.) *Psychological bases for early education* (pp. 207–26). Chichester, UK: Wiley.

SMITH, P. K. and CONNOLLY, K. 1980: *The ecology of preschool behavior*. Cambridge: Cambridge University Press.

SMITH, P. K. and HAGAN, T. 1980: Effects of deprivation on exercise play in nursery school children. *Animal Behavior*, 28, 922–8.

SMITH, P. K. and SHARPE, S. 1994: The problem of school bullying. In Smith, P. K. and Sharpe, S. (eds) *School bullying* (pp. 1–19). London: Routledge.

SMITH, P. K. and THOMPSON, D. (eds) 1991: *Practical approaches to bullying*. London: David Fulton Publishers.

SMITH, P. K. and VOLLSTEDT, R. 1985: Defining play: an empirical study of the relationship between play and various play criteria. *Child Development*, 56, 1042–50.

SMITH, P. K., SMEES, R., PELLEGRINI, A. and MENESENI, E. 1993 (July): *Play fighting and serious fighting: perspectives on their relationship*. Paper presented at the biennial meetings of the International Society for the Study of Behavioral Development, Recife, Brazil.

SMITH, P. K., TAKHVAR, M., GORE, N. and VOLLSTEDT, R. 1985: Play in young children: problems of definition, categorization, and measurement. *Early Child Development and Care*, 19, 37–54.

SNOW, C. 1972: Mothers' speech to children learning language. *Child Development*, 43, 549–65.

SNOW, R. 1992: Aptitude theory. *Educational Psychologist*, 27, 5–32.

SOAR, R. S. and SOAR, R. M. 1983: Context effects in the teaching–learning process. In Smith, D. C. (ed.) *Essential knowledge for beginning educators*. Washington DC: American Association of Colleges for Teacher Education.

SPIVAK, G. and SHURE, M. B. (1974): Social adjustment of young children: a cognitive approach to solving real life problems. San Francisco, CA: Fossey-Bass.

STANWORTH, M. 1981: *Gender and schooling: a study of sexual divisions in the classroom*. London: Unwin Hyman.

STEINBERG, L., DORNBUSCH, S. M. and BROWN, B. B. 1992: Ethnic differences in adolescent achievement. *American Psychologist*, 47, 723–9.

STERNBERG, R., and POWELL, J. 1983: The development of intelligence. In Flavell, J. and Markman, E. (eds) *Handbook of child psychology*, Vol. 3 (pp. 341–419). New York: Wiley.

STEVENSON, H. and LEE, S. 1990: Concepts of achievement. *Monographs of the Society for Research in Child Development* (Serial No. 221), 55, 1–2.

STIGLER, J. and BARANES, R. 1988: Culture and mathematics learning. In Rothkorf, E. (ed.) *Review of Research in Education*, Vol. 15 (pp. 253–306). Washington, DC: American Educational Research Association.

STIPEK, D. J. and DANIELS, D. H. 1988: Declining perceptions of competence:

a consequence of changes in the child or in the educational environment. *Journal of Education Psychology*, *80*, 3, 352–6.

STOLL, L. and MORTIMORE, P. 1995: School effectiveness and school improvement. *Institute of Education Viewpoint*. London: Institute of Education.

STRAYER, F. 1989: Co-adaption within the early peer group: a psychobiological study of social competence. In Schneider, B., Nadel, J. and Weisbord, R. (eds) *Social competence in developmental perspective* (pp. 145–74). Hingham, MA: Kluwer.

STRAYER, F. and MOSS, E. 1989: The co-construction of representational activity during social interaction. In Bornstein, M. and Bruner, J. (eds) *Interaction in human development* (pp. 173–96). Hillsdale, NJ: Erlbaum.

SULLIVAN, H. S. 1953: *The Interpersonal Theory of Psychiatry*. New York: Norton.

SUOMI, S. and HARLOW, H. 1972: Social rehabilitation of isolate-reared monkeys. *Developmental Psychology*, *6*, 487–96.

SUPER, L. and HARKNESS, S. 1986: The developmental niche: a conceptualization at the interface of child and culture. *International Journal of Behavioral Development*, *9*, 545–69.

SUTHERLAND, K. 1983: Parents' beliefs about child socialization. In Sigel, I. and Laosa, L. (eds) *Changing families* (pp. 137–66). New York: Plenum.

SUTTON-SMITH, B. 1959: *The games of New Zealand children*. Berkeley: University of California Press.

—— 1971: A syntax for play and games. In Herron, R. and Sutton-Smith, B. (eds) *Child's play* (pp. 298–310). New York: Wiley.

—— 1975: The useless made useful: play as variable training. *School Review*, *83*, 197–214.

—— 1981: *A history of children's play*. Philadelphia: University of Pennsylvania Press.

—— 1982: A performance theory of peer relations. In Borman, K. (ed.) *The social life of children in a changing society* (pp. 65–77). Norwood, NJ: Ablex.

—— 1986: *Toys as culture*. New York: Garland.

—— 1987: School play: a commentary. In Block, J. and King, N. (eds) *School play* (pp. 277–90). New York: Garland.

—— 1988: War toys and childhood aggression. *Play and Culture*, *1*, 57–69.

—— 1990: School playground as festival. *Children's Environment Quarterly*, *7*, 3–7.

SWANN, J. and GRADDOL, D. 1988: Gender inequalities in classroom talk. *English in Education*, *22*, 48–65.

SWANN REPORT 1985: *Education for all*. Final report of the Committee of Inquiry in education of children from ethnic minority groups. London: HMSO.

TANN, S. 1981: Grouping and group-work. In Simon, B. and Willcocks, J. (eds) *Research and practice in the primary school*. London: Routledge and Kegan Paul.

THORNE, B. 1993: *Gender play: girls and boys in school*. Buckingham: Open University Press.

TIZARD, B. and HUGHES, M. (1984): *Young children learning*. London: Fontana.

TIZARD, B., BLATCHFORD, P., BURKE, J., FARQUHAR, C. and PLEWIS, I. 1988: *Young children at school in the inner city*. Hove: LEA.

TOMPOROWSKI, P. and ELLIS, N. 1986: Effects of exercise on cognitive processes: a review. *Psychological Bulletin*, *99*, 338–46.

TRIVERS, R. 1972: Parental investment and sexual selection. In Campbell, B. (ed.) *Sexual selection and the descent of man* (pp. 136–79). Chicago: Aldine.

VYGOTSKY, L. 1967: Play and its role in the mental development of the child. *Soviet Psychology*, *12*, 62–76.

—— 1978: *Mind in society: the development of higher mental processes*. Cambridge, Mass: Harvard University Press.

WALKERDINE. V. 1988: *The mastery of reason.* London: Routledge.

—— 1990: *Counting girls out.* London: Falmer.

WANG, M. C., HAERTEL, G. D. and WALBERG, H. J. 1993. Toward a knowledge base for school learning. *Review of Educational Research, 63,* 3, 249–94.

WATERS, E. and SROUFE, L. 1983: Social competence as a developmental construct. *Developmental Review, 3,* 79–97.

WATKINS, C. and MORTIMORE, P. 1999: Pedagogy: what do we know? In Mortimore, P. (ed.) *Understanding pedagogy and its impact on learning.* London: Paul Chapman.

WEBB, N. M., BAXTER, G. P. and THOMPSON, L. 1997: Teachers' grouping in fifth grade science classrooms. *Elementary School Journal, 98,* 2, 91–112.

WEINSTEIN, C. 1979: The physical environment of the school: a review of the research. *Review of Educational Research, 49,* 4, 557–610.

—— 1987: Seating patterns. In Dunkin, M. (ed.) *International encyclopaedia of teaching and teacher education.* London: Pergamon.

WEINSTEIN, R. 1976: Reading group membership in first grade: teacher behaviours and pupil experience over time, *Journal of Educational Psychology, 68,* 103–16.

—— 1985: Student mediation of classroom expectancy effects. In Dusek, J. B. (ed.) *Teacher expectancies* (pp. 329–50). London: Erlbaum.

—— 1991: The classroom as a social context for learning. *Annual Review of Psychology, 42,* 493–525.

—— 1998: Promoting positive expectations in schooling. In Lambert, N. M. and McCombs, B. L. (eds) *How students learn: reforming schools through learner-centred education.* Washington, DC: American Psychological Association.

WELLS, G. 1986: *The meaning makers: children learning language and using language to learn.* Portsmouth, USA: Hodder and Stoughton.

WERTSCH, J. 1979: From social interaction to higher psychological processes. A clarification and application of Vygotsky's theory. *Human Development, 22,* 1–22.

WHELDALL, K., MORRIS, M., VAUGHAN, P. and NG, Y. Y. 1981: Rows versus tables: an example of the use of behavioural ecology in two classes of eleven-year-old children. *Educational Psychology, 1,* 2, 171–84.

WHITE, B. and WATTS, J. (1973) *Experience and environment.* Englewood Cliffs, NJ: Prentice-Hall.

WHITING, B. and EDWARDS, C. (1973). A cross-cultural analysis of sex-differences in the behavior of children age three through 11. *Journal of Social Psychology, 91,* 171–88.

WILLES, M. J. 1983: *Children into pupils: a study of language in early schooling.* Boston: Routledge and Kegan Paul.

WILLIS, P. 1977: *Learning to labour.* Farnborough: Saxon House.

WINEBURG, S. S. 1987: The self fulfillment of the self-fulfilling prophecy. *Educational Researcher,* December.

WITKIN, H.A., DYK, R. B., FATERSON, H. F., GOODENOUGH, D. G. and KARP, S. A. 1962: *Psychological differentiation.* New York: Wiley.

WITTROCK, M. (ed.) 1986: *Handbook of research on teaching.* New York: Macmillan.

WOLF, D., DAVIDSON, L., DAVIS, M., WALTERS, J., HODGES, M. and SCRIPP, L. 1988: Beyond A B, and C: a broader and deeper view of literacy. In Pellegrini, A. (ed.) *Psychological bases of early education* (pp. 121–51). Chichester: Wiley.

WOODS, P. 1990: *The happiest days? How pupils cope with school.* London: Falmer Press.

WORD, E. R., JOHNSTON, J., BAIN, H. P. and FULTON, B. D. 1990: *The State of Tennessee's student/teacher achievement ratio (STAR) Project: Technical Report 1985–90.* Nashville: Tennessee State University.

WRIGHT, M. (1980). Measuring the social competence of preschool children. *Canadian Journal of Behavioral Science, 12,* 17–32.

YANDO, R., SEITZ, V. and ZIGLER, E. (1979). *Intellectual and personality characteristics of children.* Hillsdale, NJ: Erlbaum.

YOUNISS, J. 1980: *Parents and peers in social development: a Sullivan–Piaget perspective.* Chicago: University of Chicago Press.

ZAJAC, R. J and HARTUP, W. W. 1997: Friends as coworkers: research review and classroom implications. *The Elementary School Journal, 98,* 1, 3–13.

ZIGLER, E. and TRICKETT, P. (1978). I.Q., social competence, and evaluation of early childhood intervention programs. *American Psychologist, 33,* 789–98.

Index